Using Art as Research in Learning and Teaching

Using Art as Research in Learning and Teaching

Multidisciplinary Approaches Across the Arts

Edited by Ross W. Prior

intellect Bristol, UK / Chicago, USA

First published in the UK in 2018 by
Intellect, The Mill, Parnall Road, Fishponds, Bristol, BS16 3JG, UK

First published in the USA in 2018 by
Intellect, The University of Chicago Press, 1427 E. 60th Street,
Chicago, IL 60637, USA

A catalogue record for this book is available from the British Library.

Copy-editor: MPS Technologies
Cover designer: Aleksandra Szumlas
Cover image: The Iron Bridge, Ironbridge, Shropshire, England. Painting by Shaun McNiff, 2016
Production manager: Amy Rollason
Typesetting: Contentra Technologies

Print ISBN: 978-1-78320-892-0
ePDF ISBN: 978-1-78320-976-7
ePUB ISBN: 978-1-78320-975-0

This is a peer-reviewed publication.

This book is dedicated to Dan.

This book is dedicated to Dan.

I have come to believe that a great teacher is a great artist and that there are as few as there are any other great artists. Teaching might even be the greatest of the arts since the medium is the human mind and spirit.

– *John Steinbeck*

A picture is not thought out and settled beforehand. While it is being done it changes as one's thoughts change. And when it is finished, it still goes on changing, according to the state of mind of whoever is looking at it. A picture lives a life like a living creature, undergoing the changes imposed on us by our life from day to day. This is natural enough, as the picture lives only through the man who is looking at it.

– *Pablo Picasso*

Contents

Foreword

Shaun McNiff

Why do art-based research and for whom?

In my opening keynote address at the University of Wolverhampton conference on 31 August 2016 I asked – *If we advocate for art as a way of knowing that engages realms inaccessible to linear and logical thought, then why is it that we do not use it as a primary mode of inquiry when researching how the arts might enhance human experience?*

The general sense from the three days of presentations and discussions was that concerns about legitimacy were the chief deterrents to the use of art as research. Many spoke of how they feel compelled to provide research outcomes that will favourably impress 'decision makers' in government and institutional leadership, who almost universally assume that value is determined by what is considered scientific evidence. In response, I asked – *Why do we do research and for whom do we do it?*

I do research for my community of practice. I have explored methods of engaging others in artistic expression for five decades with a desire to perfect practice, to be as effective as possible in helping people express themselves with various forms of art, and to understand the ways in which these expressions impact personal and group experience. I have also examined the extent to which particular aspects of artistic expression are accessible to people everywhere, and the degree to which these practices have been present throughout history.

The common tendency since the beginning of applied arts research has been to examine art-related questions and issues through the methods, concepts and languages of psychology and social science, resulting in the general use of art as 'data' or raw material for a very different academic discipline. Many assume that this is what we are doing when we talk about art-based research. I define art-based research as the use of artistic expression by the researcher, either alone or with others, as a primary mode of inquiry. In the concluding session of the University of Wolverhampton conference, Megan Lawton, a College of Learning and Teaching staff member, may have defined it even better: 'It took some of us a while to see that it is not just about art as a subject of research, but art as a tool and process of research' (personal communication, 2 September 2016). I refer to *art*, like the German

Kunst, as including all of the arts and artists from every discipline of creative expression (McNiff 2013: x).

Since artistic outcomes emerge, often unexpectedly, from the process of inquiry and cannot be known at the start, this discipline is arguably the opposite of the scientific method with its planned procedures oriented towards documenting predictable and generalizable processes. Art is about the uniqueness of particular things and events, and is arguably more in sync with how life is experienced. The imperative to justify the use of art according to scientific evidence and objectives is thus incongruous, and it ensures continued marginalization in all levels of education and in research. I have never been concerned with 'proving' or 'measuring' artistic efficacy. I attempt to be more attentive to creative expressions. The same applies to what we do in helping others express themselves. I try to do the work as well as possible in the various settings of practice and let it speak for itself. At the conference, the presence of faculty members who are pursuing research in visual art, design, and performing arts settings helped to check the tendency within art-based research to become overly involved in the art vs. science polarization that happens within the arts in education and therapy domains. It was important to show that there are places where this dynamic does not exist.

The intricacies of human experience cannot be reduced to categorical and predictable principles and art is the timeless discipline for exploring, shaping and understanding these spontaneous realities. For example, in the visual arts painters talk about the importance of letting things happen with the application of paint, rather than the more controlled method of first drawing a composition and then applying the paint to it. Writers describe how the characters in a novel reveal the ensuing action and outcomes. And artists in every discipline consistently emphasize the importance of getting started, moving things around, playing with possibilities and sticking with the process of expression with a trust that the most significant things will emanate outside the scope of intended results (McNiff 2015). With artistic expression, very little of consequence and depth goes according to plan. Art operates within a different paradigm to science and ideally the two complement one another.

The hope of gaining legitimacy through something other than the main features of the creative process suggests a distrust of the very things we advocate. Rather than continue this impossible effort, why not concentrate on what art can do that science cannot? Can we focus on what art brings to human understanding, rather than persist in trying to prove ourselves through systems that marginalize artistic knowing?

Social scientists should do the same, according to Alasdair MacIntyre (2007). Due to its inability to establish law-like generalizations from the unpredictability of human actions, he believes that the attempts of social science to be like natural science are self-defeating. And to the extent to which the arts attach themselves exclusively to social science, we add to the negative chain reaction. MacIntyre feels that social science research will become more relevant by studying practical wisdom in relation to particular and dynamic life situations. He calls this *phronesis*, a term derived from Aristotle, who proposed different kinds of knowing; also including *epistémé* (theoretical knowing), *techné* (technical knowing) and *poiesis* (making or creating). This plural reality of intelligence is lost today in the pursuit of legitimacy through science alone.

I have always embraced artistic inquiry as a form of practitioner research. I have a pragmatic bias and resonate closely with an emphasis on *phronesis*, which supports questions like – *How might we explore challenges of professional practice, conflicts, and complex human experiences in ways that further competence and understanding? How can we be more effective in responding to the reliably unexpected and infinitely unique nature of human situations and interactions? And what can the arts offer in relation to these questions and issues that cannot be provided by other modes of action and inquiry? Can art further the well-being of persons, communities and the natural environments that sustain us?*

In assessing quality and relevance in art-based research I have consistently called for the standard of *usefulness*, with a special emphasis on generativity, and being helpful to others and to professional communities of practice. I have also encouraged the usefulness standard to counter the possibility of artistic inquiry becoming self-immersed, and the tendency to think that artistic inquiry is all about the person doing it, rather than the issues being explored through art.

But there is more to the arts than utility. I make the case for usefulness to not only serve my professional community, but perhaps also to keep the door open for decision makers and colleagues who have trouble seeing the relationship between art and research. However, if I step outside of the position of having to offer a practical rationale for art as research, I see that ultimately the determination of its quality, value and purpose corresponds completely to the same standards we apply innately to art. What inspires and arouses imagination; moves the emotions; influences our lives; helps us feel better; or deeply disturbs and thus invites change?

In his closing conference keynote dealing with art as a 'procedure of truth' Malcolm Ross described how the industry of research is driven by doubt: I say, *I saw it*, to which the response is – *So now you must prove it!* Ross's address enacted the experience of *agape*, an affirmation of artistic significance that happens naturally and loses its essential nature when we try to explain it. He crystallized the gap between the sensory, momentary and aesthetic nature of artistic expression, and the contradictory demands of what I call the corporate–academic research complex (see Chapter 2).

As much as this conflict seems unnecessary and distinctly repressive, it generates a creative tension that informs and fuels my lifework. The exclusion of artistic knowing from research motivates the effort to include it effectively. The tension between predictability and the unexpected, control and spontaneity, particular things and general laws, literalism and imagination, is archetypal and it is not going away. *So how can we put it to good use and make something from it?*

A place for wonder

Rather than persist in the quixotic effort to be something other than what they are, the arts might make their case by being true to themselves. In my own work I have begun to pair the standard of usefulness, which I still hold in the highest regard, with the distinctly aesthetic features of awe and wonder, which may be more useful than we realize.

I respond with wonder to the worldwide growth of art-based research. It is not something that I would have either predicted or imagined. My initial hope in writing *Art-Based Research* (1998) was to make a case within the arts in therapy and arts in education fields for establishing a more equal and logical partnership with psychology, in which art might sometimes take the lead as a mode of inquiry. At the Wolverhampton conference in 2016, I was surprised to hear Philip Taylor from New York University (NYU) describe how the majority of students in the Educational Theatre doctoral programme at the Steinhardt School were pursuing art-based research projects. This exponential increase in the number of students using art as research at NYU and elsewhere has generated a new imperative to support the work with a tradition of inquiry and inspirational precedents for those yet to come. Perhaps we are reaching a point with art-based research where we can focus less on arguing for its existence and concentrate on doing it well.

Throughout the conference our leader Ross W. Prior encouraged awareness of the natural environment and history of Shropshire. He spoke of the origins of the Industrial Revolution in Ironbridge Gorge on the River Severn, a river that eventually connects to the Irish Sea. It was not until I left the United Kingdom that I began to consider how the conference, the first international meeting concentrating completely on art as research, at the University of Wolverhampton's Telford 'Innovation Campus', near the Ironbridge Gorge UNESCO World Heritage Site, was inviting a new artistic revolution grounded in the transformative potential of artistic inquiry. It is not far-fetched to consider a synchronistic convergence of events past and present in this particular place.

The key to initiating something significantly transformative is a rekindling of a more generous presence of wonder in our all-too-often anaesthetized perceptions. Great artworks like the Iron Bridge over the River Severn (see my cover painting), built between 1777 and 1779, stand as evidence of what a community of people can create together. While the bridge presents a literal embodiment of the two features of usefulness and wonder, and gives a definite infusion of aesthetic and creative energy to anyone who gazes its way, it suggests what might be considered the grander dimension of a spectrum of artistic effects. The revolution of artistic inquiry must also happen in more mundane places accessible to all.

If art-based research is to continue to grow, it will be growth based upon the ability to appreciate wonder in small and subtle expressions of life – in the most ordinary things and moments. But perhaps the most challenging and necessary condition for the growth of art as research concerns the ability of the perceiver to relax pre-existing ideas and cultivate the ability to appreciate artistic evidence and be open to being influenced by it. Based on the surprises we have had to date with art-based research, it might be even possible for decision makers to develop this receptivity, and potentially be moved and changed by a sense of wonder.

References

MacIntyre, Alasdair (2007), *After Virtue: A Study in Moral Theory*, 3rd ed., Notre Dame, IN: University of Notre Dame Press.

McNiff, Shaun (1998), *Art-Based Research*, London: Jessica Kingsley Publishers.

——— (2013), *Art as Research: Opportunities and Challenges*, Bristol: Intellect.

——— (2015), *Imagination in Action: Secrets for Unleashing Creative Expression*, Boston: Shambhala Publications.

Preface

Ross W. Prior

> *Aesthetic beauty is the isomorphic correspondence between what is said and how it is said.*
>
> – Rudolf Arnheim[1]

The genesis of this book was the *Art as Research in Learning and Teaching Conference* hosted by the University of Wolverhampton from 31 August to 2 September 2016. As the convenor of the conference, I desired for delegates to share something of England's Victorian history. We therefore located the conference at the University's Telford 'Innovation Campus' in beautiful Shropshire (West Midlands). This venue brought us close to what has become known as the 'Birthplace of Industry' and our conference tour and dinner took us to the village of Ironbridge, where the world's first cast iron arch bridge was built; the project began construction in 1777, completed in 1779 and the bridge officially opened on New Year's Day 1781.

Set in a UNESCO World Heritage Site (which covers the wider wooded Ironbridge Gorge area), the cast iron bridge links the banks of the River Severn (Latin: *Sabrina*), the longest river in the United Kingdom (220 miles/354 km). Statistics aside, this area was an important metaphor for the world's first gathering of academics explicitly interested in art as research in learning and teaching. Professor Shaun McNiff refers to this as a place of 'wonder' in the Foreword to this book, a place where we were creating something of our own revolution in thinking: how art is actually used as research within higher education learning and teaching.

Whilst the Victorians laboured under harsh conditions, they worked with great purpose and as a community, continually solving the problems that beset them. They were forging ahead with new manufacturing technologies that completely altered the way things were done, both in the workplace and at home. Consequently, the Industrial Revolution marks a monumental turning point in world history. Similarly, our conference delegates stood observing the Iron Bridge and have since reflected upon the metaphor this provides us as academics committed to using art as a research methodology. The art as research 'bridge' builds a connection between the use of art on the one side and researched understanding on the other.

The cover of this book is a delightful and evocative painting of the world-famous Iron Bridge (from which the place of Ironbridge gets its name) captured by Shaun McNiff during his stay – I sincerely thank him for it. In his distinctive expressionistic style, Shaun has introduced colour and movement where heaven and earth are full of energy and dynamism. There is tremendous excitement captured in this picturesque vista. McNiff's personal commitment to art-based research is lived and breathed through all he does. This energy was present throughout the duration of the conference, and this book is testament to a collective vision for how we may shift artistic research and offer art(s) educationalists ways of honouring this in their educational practice.

By way of anticipating the distinct philosophy of this book, I would like to clarify the use of the term 'art-based research' (McNiff 1998). I have seen a recent trend in academic writing where the plural (and fragmentary) term 'arts based research' (e.g. Eisner and Barone 2012) is being freely used. One may ask: *Does this difference really matter?* The answer is: *Yes, it matters a great deal.* The oft-used plural form 'arts based research' presents an ongoing silo approach to our scholarship, when in reality we can usefully discuss the same common denominator, 'art'. The separations reinforce the current lack of integral vision, rather than strengthening the whole community, history and future potential of art and artistic understanding to reinforce a common purpose. Elliot Eisner and Tom Barone use the term 'arts based research' within a social sciences context and define it as: 'a process that uses the expressive qualities of form to convey meaning' (2012: xii). Essentially, these authors were interested in the role of artistry in projects of social inquiry – an important area, but artistic inquiry has much broader potential. Whilst Eisner and Barone have made a contribution, the earlier scholarship on art-based research, and indeed the subsequent scholarship, offers much in the way of understanding art as inquiry.

The term 'art-based research' (McNiff 1998) does not emphasize dividing the fields of 'art'; the principle of art-based research is *art as the methodology*. 'We use the term art-based research to affirm a community of art and artists including all of the arts' (McNiff 2013: 3). Regrettably the meaning of the term 'art-based research', exacerbated by the unfortunate plural term 'arts based research', represents much confusion within the field with many simply using the term 'art-based research' to instigate a discussion of *any* research involving the arts, including a departure to include social sciences! The two terms are becoming frequently confused by their interchangeable (mis)use. It is obvious that the misunderstanding is derived from a surprising lack of acquaintance with all that has been written thus far on art as the methodology pertaining to the specific use of the term 'art-based research' (McNiff 1998, 2009, 2012, 2013a, 2013b, etc). The integrality of 'art' is significant and this models the more comprehensive connectedness that we so desperately need today in the silos of education, 'subjects', thought and research methods. Unfortunately, the 'plural term' reinforces unhelpful separation. McNiff provides a particularly informative definition: 'Art-based research involves reflection on the interplay between these mental motivations and physical ones that appear through contact with the medium' (1998: 56).

I hope, in part, that this book may assist in furthering an acceptance of the term 'art-based research' and in seeing how it may be actively used within learning and teaching in higher education. Moreover, this book also explores art as research more broadly within the various multidisciplinary visual and performing art forms, as well as creative writing, as a way to provide a rich contribution and understanding of learning and teaching in further and higher education. It hears from some key figures in the field, providing the opportunity to share their art-based research and art-informed research, practice and philosophy. This book brings to life the arts within taught and learnt contexts across a variety of art forms and various levels of post-compulsory education – from the undergraduate to the doctoral candidate. In what is an invaluable collection, this book is of direct benefit to art(s) researchers and educators, addressing the key challenges and possibilities in a rapidly changing education environment.

I am tremendously grateful to the authors contained within this collection for their willingness in bringing together a range of experiences that point to how they are using art as research within their higher education practice. Like all of us who share a commitment to art as a research methodology, these authors are on a journey of discovery that never ends. They bring to this book a wealth of experience, personal commitment and enduring enthusiasm. Each with their own style and context, through them we gain a comprehensive understanding, not only about art-based research but how we can revolutionize the higher education curriculum to include our students in these research processes from the very beginning of their higher education journey. To exclude students from using art as research is to deny them a methodology that may well serve them the *most* value as *artists.*

Let's build bridges...

References

Arnheim, Rudolf ([1969] 1997), *Visual Thinking*, Berkeley: University of California Press.

Eisner, Elliot and Barone, Tom (2012), *Arts Based Research*, Los Angeles: Sage.

McNiff, Shaun (1998), *Art-Based Research*, London: Jessica Kingsley Publishers.

——— (2009), *Integrating the Arts in Therapy: History, Theory, and Practice*, Springfield: Charles C. Thomas.

——— (2012), 'Opportunities and challenges in art-based research', *Journal of Applied Arts & Health*, 3:1, pp. 5–12.

——— (2013a), 'Introduction: A critical focus on art-based research', *Journal of Applied Arts & Health*, 4:1, pp. 5–12.

McNiff, Shaun (ed.) (2013b), *Art as Research: Opportunities and Challenges*, Bristol: Intellect.

Note

1 From Arnheim's *Visual Thinking* ([1969] 1997: 255).

Chapter 1

Introduction: Artist-Educator-Researcher

Ross W. Prior

What I cannot create, I do not understand.

– Richard Feynman[1]

We may as well begin by defining what we mean by 'research', when discussed in this book. In some ways it may be easier to state what we are not considering, but even then we find disciplines such as science can inform some of our artistic research. However, in artistic research, science is not the *mode* of inquiry. Approaches to research depend on epistemologies, which vary considerably across disciplines and even within disciplines. However, as a tentative definition, we can begin by offering the following:

> Art as research involves a diverse range of human activities in creating visual, auditory or performed artworks, expressing the artist's imaginative and/or technical skill, intended to be appreciated for their beauty or emotional impact. Art as research uses systematic investigation into the study of process, materials and sources in order to understand art more completely and reach new conclusions. The primary components in using art as research are documentation, discovery and interpretation for the purpose of the advancement of artistic knowledge and furthering understanding of all of life and other disciplines too.

Shaun McNiff gives us a useful definition of the *specificity* of the use of the term 'art-based research', which neatly aligns to the process of art as research:

> Art-based research can be defined as the systematic use of the artistic process, the actual making of artistic expressions in all of the different forms of the arts, as a primary way of understanding and examining experience by both researchers and the people that they involve in their studies. These inquiries are distinguished from research activities where the arts may play a significant role but are essentially used as data for investigations that take place within academic disciplines that utilize more traditional scientific, verbal, and mathematic descriptions and analyses of phenomena.
>
> (McNiff 2008: 29)

McNiff's definition brings us close to the heart of the matter. Given that our research focus is similarly outlined in both of the above definitions, there are many ways in which we may use *art as methodology* and address evidence in research using the arts. McNiff (2009) directs us to the potential of the art form itself in responding to issues of research, rather than relying upon other methodologies. He recognizes that historically in the arts and in art therapy, these fields have been 'so thoroughly tied to traditional social science methods of research and the more general notions of scientism that we have not appreciated our own unique potential to further human understanding' (2009: 144).

The key here is *art for understanding*. Embracing all of the arts in the one act of epistemological communion, McNiff leads us to an appreciation of the natural processes found within art-making that can provide artists with the answers they seek within their own work. Faster to catch on in the United Kingdom and Europe than in the United States, using art as methodology is proving to be a highly relevant way of conducting artistic research, which allows artists to further understand what it is they do.

There are unhealthy divides within our higher education system that have created sizeable polemic divides; these include theory vs. practice, 'hard' vs. 'soft' research, qualitative vs. quantitative research, researcher vs. lecturer/teacher, practitioner vs. researcher and somewhat incredulously, research vs. learning activity. There is a simple basis for these divides, which frequently comes from the nature of the academy itself, where lecturers largely teach what they were taught and/or operate within research paradigms that they know best through their own postgraduate education experience. The unfortunate consequence of this conservatism is that, instead of furthering development, it can hinder and negate advancement. Henk Borgdorff usefully and tersely suggests:

> The debate often concerns issues of institutional or educational politics that are thought to be important for determining whether artistic research can be recognised as a type of academic or scientific research. Prominent issues are the standards needed to assess research by artists, the institutional rights to award third-cycle (doctoral) degrees in the arts, and the criteria to be applied by funding bodies in deciding whether to support research by artists.
>
> (Borgdorff 2013: 112)

Further difficulty arises within places of higher education when academic research excludes a most essential research type, which is research into learning and teaching. Key to advancing any discipline is found within both the philosophy and practice of its learning and teaching methods. Within these methods or approaches, a discipline can either experience great progress and awakening, or conversely, suffer a stultifying constraint adhering to an immoveable and arguably outmoded orthodoxy.

An academic colleague of mine once remarked that the great creative literary works have already been achieved and we will not see the likes of a William Shakespeare again. It may be true that we won't see another Shakespeare, but nor could we. Shakespeare was particular to his time and place. History has been punctuated with many individuals who have made outstanding achievements, making seismic shifts in thinking or creative contributions. Like all of us, artists are informed by those who have gone before and also by those currently around them. T. S. Elliot wrote that the poet 'must be quite aware of the obvious fact that art never improves, but that the material of art is never quite the same' ([1920] 1997: 42). We take inspiration in many ways from many people, and from our desire to do it our way, to do it differently. But how often in education do we find tutors wanting students to do it the instructor's way, even if this is an unconscious intention? I am reminded of McNiff's belief that 'the most valued and effective teachers are the ones who can help us assess our work more accurately' (2003: 149).

Equally, when students are encouraged to research they are frequently exposed to 'safe', unimaginative data gathering and presentation. Even when we believe we are being liberal as supervisors, as already mentioned above we frequently resort to research methods to which we have previously been exposed and/or used ourselves. We teach what we know; we limit others by what we don't know.

Whilst we obviously can't know all there is to know, our personal approach really must allow others to explore and we should support these journeys of inquiry. In this spirit, my firm belief is that art must stop trying to fit into methods and measures applied elsewhere. We have seen an arguably unhealthy clinical corporatization of the arts in order to find a 'respectability' and 'legitimacy' measured in financial terms. For example, this is found in the use of the term 'creative industries' or the preoccupation with trying to find clinical evidence within the applied arts and health field. This has frequently seen an over-reliance upon the use of models of social science research and procedural method. We have found ourselves asking less than useful questions and missing questions that art itself produces. We have tended to ignore the fact that *art can provide the topic of research, the process of research and indeed the outcome of research* (see Chapter 4). The artistic process allows for doing research to find questions, not only to find answers. Mitchell Kossak succinctly captures the essentially grounded nature of art as research:

> Art-based research, a natural outgrowth of art-based inquiry, utilizes creative intelligence through immersion in creative process and scholarly reflection. [...] In art-based research, the phenomenological experience is represented through the creative act itself. The artwork, no matter what the medium (sound, rhythm, movement, enactment, poetry, paintings), opens up a space in which both the world and our being in the world is brought to light as a single, but inexhaustibly rich totality.
>
> (Kossak 2012: 22)

So what can we do to have students develop their understanding of art as research much earlier in their learning journey? The answer seems to reside in the design of the curriculum and hence the tasks we wish students to undertake in order to assess them. Art-based research is more than examining the finished product hanging on a wall or witnessed on a stage – this is where art can encompass the topic, process and outcome of research. However, before specifically addressing art-based research within higher education, let us first consider some essential beliefs about education that underpin current thinking and ultimately shape our view of learning and teaching, and research more generally.

Education, knowledge and meaning

Philip H. Phenix defines a 'philosophy of education' as 'any reasonably coherent set of values and fundamental assumptions used as a basis for evaluating and guiding educational practice' (1963: 4). Various beliefs about educational practice and what matters most are evidenced in curriculum documents, learning processes and teaching methods. The language used in such documents or used to explain educational practices offers us clues as to the dominant spheres of influence at play. As a part of this, each fashion within education has produced its own buzzwords and implicit and explicit ideals, derived sometimes through purely political agendas and sometimes through trending academic research and scholarship. But how do we in higher education respond to these imperatives, which seek to pin us down further and further? How do we have the confidence to really know the most appropriate ways to educate?

We live in an era of uncertainty where everything has been opened up for scrutiny and question. On the one hand, this may be seen as healthy, but on the other hand, living with constant challenges and unknowns may be exhausting and stressful. Humankind has never had all the answers and we have always sought to know more. However, the more we learn, the more we realize how much we don't know – an essential tenant of education, of course. Throughout time, civilizations have risen and fallen in their quest for supremacy – be it military, wealth, land mass, technology or culture. Whilst we have understood this truth, we have not yet completely succeeded in safeguarding our own current existence on this planet.

Within this context we find that higher education is rapidly changing too. In its origins, those who possessed scrolls and books held the power within education. It was, after all, the Catholic Church that ensured the continuity of formal education after the Fall of Rome. Places of learning were revered and one's place within them was highly prized. To some, this may appear unhealthily elite. To others this may represent quality and gravitas. However, the main aim of higher education for our students, neatly summarized by Ronald Barnett (2007: 126), is one of eventual auto-didacticism where they become 'beings-for-themselves', *authentically* engaging with their educational experiences. This is described by Barnett as having 'their own will to learn and, being so energized, drive themselves forward of their own volition [...] determined to come into a relationship with their experiences that is *theirs*' (2007: 126, original emphasis).

The educational experience presents students with a range of curricula challenges designed to allow students to self-actualize, which is what education is most centrally about. Increasingly, places of higher education are being shoehorned into workplace training agendas. Businesses and politicians are applying pressure on universities to equip graduates for direct entry into the labour market. Whilst part of this thinking is economically laudable, these training agendas run the distinct risk of producing narrow-focused graduates who lack the ability to become 'beings-for-themselves' as Barnett puts it.

One thing that may be agreed is that the digital age has given widespread access to information – more information than can be humanly contemplated. Information is not the same as knowledge, yet they are frequently confused. Knowledge, like information, does not remain static. Both knowledge and information are only ever directly relevant if the receiver can purpose and repurpose what becomes known. However, information is of little use if we do not possess the knowledge to know what to do with it.

In my book *Teaching Actors: Knowledge Transfer in Actor Training*, in which I conduct an investigation of actor trainers' understandings of their own practice in an attempt to unravel educational philosophy, I point out that 'communicating knowledge is not necessarily easy or straightforward, especially when dealing with practices that are experiential and rely on inert or tacit understandings' (Prior 2012: 183). However, whilst there are multiple knowledge types and many categories of knowledge, the act of *knowing* broadly remains the same:

> *Knowing* is inherent in the growth and transformation of identities and it is located in relations among practitioners, their practice, the artefacts of that practice, and the social organisation and political economy of communities of practice.
>
> (Lave and Wenger 1991: 122, original emphasis)

'Artists call upon multiple ways of knowing, which are likely to become further enhanced through the experience of practice' (Prior 2013: 162). These complex understandings are entwined within the act of *doing* and *being*, and because they can be so embodied, the outsider may grossly underestimate all that is involved with being an artist. Therefore, within this complexity, it ought to be firmly acknowledged that 'knowledge is less a discovery than it is a construction' (Eisner 2002: 211). Knowledge acquisition is not linear but is gained more as a web of understanding over time.

As far as we are concerned here with art and artistry, knowledge is constructed *in* and *through* artistic practice. This contrasts with traditional scientific experimentation, although one could argue that in actuality science too shares a broader knowledge base that is constructed in and through practice. There has been an awakening of understanding leading to an acceptance of embodied knowledge, situated knowledge and enacted knowledge, which offer artist-researchers more useful insights than might be gained through scientific experimentation. Detachment, objectivity, controlled experimentation, random trials and rationality do not reach the heart of artistic inquiry. Artistic practice and experimentation tend to place the artist firmly in the middle, and every situation is entirely unique.

Elliot Eisner argues that *knowing* depends upon experience 'either the kind of experience that emanates from the sentient being's contrast with the qualities of the environment or from the experiences born of the imagination' (1996: 31). These types of experiential knowing for artists are derived through, for example, accident, playfulness, repetition, improvisation, intuition, inspiration, emotional response and experience itself.

An earlier figure to significantly influence educational thought was of course John Dewey. He wrote the highly distinguished book *Art as Experience* (1934) in which he expressed the idea that art functions *as experience*. Dewey places great value on the processes of inquiry: looking and finding meaning. He highly values the various components of artistry that involves hard to pin-down qualities such as intuition, impulse, invocation and spontaneity. He understood the entwined and embodied nature of meaning contained within art:

> As long as 'meaning' is a matter of association and suggestion, it falls apart from the qualities of the sensuous medium and form is disturbed. Sense qualities are the carriers of meanings, not as vehicles carry goods but as a mother carries a baby when the baby is part of her own organism. Works of art, like words, are literally pregnant with meaning.
>
> (Dewey [1934] 2005: 122–23)

Artistic research in higher education

Undoubtedly, much has changed for artistic researchers since the initial rise in the interest in this scholarship in the 1990s. By 2002, Elliot Eisner called for an 'agenda' for the field. He clarified this by stating:

> By agenda I mean not simply more unrelated studies, but, rather, research programs of related studies that ultimately will advance our understanding of some of the important issues and problems in the field. It is unlikely that single-shot studies will have the power needed to add significantly to what we come to understand about, say, the factors that advance various kinds of learning in the arts [...].
>
> (Eisner 2002: 209)

Where both Elliot Eisner and Shaun McNiff explore this terrain throughout their respective careers, the latter's 1998 *Art-Based Research* was the first book to name and consolidate the approach to research which has expanded significantly in the second decade of the twenty-first century, as academics have moved away from social science models of inquiry within the arts. Somewhat regrettably perhaps, many of the leading art education scholars prolific in the 1960s to 1980s never gained a Ph.D. as the system did not yet support or encourage methodologies that realized the focus of their art-centred studies. Even as we move through the twenty-first century we still find confusion about what research might mean to artists and art educators. White coats, controlled experiments and scientific laboratories remain dominant research paradigms extant in the human psyche. Whilst of course science has its essential place, it is not as much use to the artist. Like others in the field, Elliot Eisner was actively pushing for change:

> One of the most significant beliefs that has been challenged is that 'real' research requires quantification. For many, doing research in education required one to measure the phenomena investigated and then to apply statistical techniques to treat the quantified data [...] Young researchers, in particular, have recognized that form influences meaning and that much of what needs to be understood and conveyed needs a narrative more than it needs a number.
>
> (Eisner 2002: 210)

However, narrative, like numbers, can have limitations as it also provides a symbolic representation. The image, for example, can of course offer rich meaning, which adds yet another form of representation that should not be overlooked. According to Rudolf Arnheim ([1969] 1997: 274) art and science both share a need to interpret the world by constructing images to make concepts perceptible and understandable. Equally 'narratives, films, video, theatre, even poems and collages can be used to deepen one's understanding of aspects of educational practice and its consequences' (Eisner 2002: 210). It would be remiss of us in higher education if we did not broaden our full acceptance of the use of an array of approaches that should be encouraged at all levels.

Undoubtedly, one of the landmark moments in challenging the assumptions of the supremacy of the written word was indeed Arnheim's publication of *Visual Thinking* (1969), which builds upon his earlier work on the subject. Arnheim brings to bear an understanding of visual perception as a cognitive activity, describing this as: 'a reversal [...] of the historical development that led in the philosophy of the eighteen century from *aisthesis*[2] to aesthetics, from sensory experience in general to the arts in particular' ([1969] 1997: v, original emphasis).

By way of example, I have used with great success the reflective sketchbook as a method for students to capture their moment-by-moment processes, thoughts and reflections. These processes may be represented in multiple and eclectic ways. Typically, these books contain sketches, words, fragments of cloth, colour swatches, musical notation, references, photographs and so on. They can be created digitally using a device such as an iPad or tablet if preferred. However, I have seen greater engagement when students are enabled with the utmost immediacy and with the added dimension of tactile experiencing. In previously writing on the subject, I have suggested that:

> Too frequently research favours a single linguistic communication system as 'more effective' than other non-dominant communication systems such as, for example, the non-verbal, pictorial, idiomatic, symbolic and metaphoric. However, a reflective

> sketchbook becomes a type of living document that forms and informs the artistic process throughout.
>
> (Prior 2013: 165)

What the reflective sketchbook allows the artist-researcher to do is track their own processes and decision-making. It not only records inspiration, intuition and decision, but it also records indecision, creative blocks and departures. In a similar way, video recording of artistic processes allow for retrospection – reflection and careful study of empirical experience. Crucially for the artist, the sketchbook can be part of the process without adding non-related processes, enabling the artist to remain at all times focused and confident within their artistic medium.

Any form of research, be it experimental or not, must be sufficiently open to allow the indistinct to become apparent and sufficient space to facilitate the discovery of what is not yet known. Quite evidently 'this openness and room for not-knowing, or not-yet-knowing, cannot be imposed by stern methodological procedures' (Borgdorff 2013: 114). This is where art-based research offers learners, educators and art-researchers great latitude to engage. Undoubtedly, one of the strongest claims within art-based research is that the artistic experience is central to understanding and that written interpretations are not a higher form of knowing within the research process, although traditional doctoral theses very much privilege the written word. By way of illustration, Eisner provides the example that 'cars and parking lots are sensory before they are linguistic. In this sense, talk about those qualities is not the same as experience itself' (1996: 32).

Dewey neatly summarizes that the potential limits in aesthetics are determined experientially and by what the artists make of it in practice, by stating that 'the *medium* of expression is neither subjective nor objective, but is an experience in which they are integrated in a *new* object' ([1934] 2005: 299, original emphasis). To these ends, McNiff (2009: 164) reports that his graduate students often use more than one artistic mode to express their experiences, which underlines just how useful it is that we explore commonalities across the various art forms.

Conclusion

In part, the intention of this introductory chapter, and this book as a whole, is to give artist-researchers greater confidence in adopting an art-based methodology in various forms. The anticipated confidence will hopefully see artist-researchers using art-based research to understand and directly inform their own practices. Further, it is desired that artist-educator-researchers might renew the way they construct the curriculum in order to more closely align art-based research throughout the higher education experience, from undergraduate to doctoral candidature. There is no reason why students cannot be situated as enquirers or researchers of their own emerging practices, even as undergraduates. This does not imply a lack of needing to understand other artists' practices – on the contrary; comparing and contrasting the works and practices of others with one's own offers great learning potential.

The educational experience in all of the arts in higher education can be enriched with a greater understanding and active application of art as research. Artists interested in research – which significantly includes artists desiring to know more about their own practices – will come to recognize that the whole gamut of the artist's personal experience plays a part. In 1934, Dewey promoted the thought that:

> New ideas come leisurely yet promptly to consciousness only when work has previously been done in forming the right doors by which they may gain entrance. Subconscious maturation precedes creative production in every line of human endeavour. The direct effort of 'wit and will' of itself never gave birth to anything that is not mechanical; their function is necessary, but it is to let loose allies that exist outside their scope.
>
> (Dewey [1934] 2005: 76)

Dewey, like McNiff and others, understand and respect the artistic process that requires a helpful pre-condition to artistry: a 'letting go', a freedom from the constraints of formal analysis and over-thinking before one commences to make, do or become. Acknowledgement of this provides artist-researchers an immensely rich terrain in which to operate. It would be remiss of educators to deny this explicit exploration with students.

Seeing art as a process, in which understanding is constructed and co-constructed with others, is very much at the heart of using art as research. Whilst artistic research differs from science and the social sciences, it is simply a mode of inquiry that best suits the form, as it is the form that is of empirical interest alongside the artistic process. Once this is fully understood within higher education, we may begin to see the dissolution of those unhealthy divides pitting artist vs. researcher and practitioner vs. teacher. Using art as research provides a natural educational cadence for those of us who do not see necessary borders between artist, researcher and educator *in* and *through* the production of art. A convergence of roles allows for artist and academic to become one. Art as research seeks to reveal and understand that which is bound in aesthetic experience and is enacted and embodied both *in* and *through* artistic processes.

References

Arnheim, Rudolf ([1969] 1997), *Visual Thinking*, Berkeley: University of California Press.

Barnett, Ronald (2007), *A Will to Learn: Being a Student in an Age of Uncertainty*, Maidenhead: Open University Press.

Borgdorff, Henk (2013), 'Artistic practices and epistemic things', in M. Schwab (ed.), *Experimental Systems: Future Knowledge in Artistic Research*, Orpheus Institute Series, Leuven: Leuven University Press, pp. 112–20.

Dewey, John ([1934] 2005), *Art as Experience*, New York: Penguin.

Eisner, Elliot W. (1996), *Cognition and Curriculum Reconsidered*, 2nd ed., London: Paul Chapman Publishing.

——— (2002), *The Arts and the Creation of Mind*, New Haven: Yale University Press.

Elliot, T. S. ([1920] 1997), *The Sacred Wood: Essays on Poetry and Criticism*, London: Faber and Faber.

Kossak, Mitchell (2012), 'Art-based enquiry: It is what we do!', *Journal of Applied Arts and Health*, 3:1, pp. 21–29.

Lave, Jean and Wenger, Etienne (1991), *Situated Learning*, Cambridge: Cambridge University Press.

McNiff, Shaun (1998), *Art-Based Research*, London: Jessica Kingsley Publishers.

——— (2003), *Creating with Others: The Practice of Imagination in Life, Art and the Workplace*, Boston: Shambhala.

——— (2008), 'Art-based research', in J. G. Knowles and A. L. Cole (eds), *Handbook of the Arts in Qualitative Research: Perspectives, Methodologies, Examples, and Issues*, Los Angeles: Sage, pp. 29–40.

——— (2009), *Integrating the Arts in Therapy: History, Theory, and Practice*, Springfield: Charles C Thomas.

Phenix, Philip H. (ed.) (1963), *Philosophies of Education*, New York: John Wiley & Sons.

Prior, Ross W. (2012), *Teaching Actors: Knowledge Transfer in Actor Training*, Bristol: Intellect.

——— (2013), 'Knowing what is known', in S. McNiff (ed.), *Art as Research*, Bristol: Intellect, pp. 161–69.

Notes

1 Quote found written on the blackboard of Nobel-Prize winning physicist Richard Feynman when he died in 1988.

2 *Aisthēsis* comprises more than just visual perception; it stands for general perception with all the senses, as well as the impression that the perceived leaves on the body.

Part 1

Aesthetic Education and Ways of Knowing in Art

Chapter 2

Art as a Procedure of Truth

Malcolm Ross

One might connect the narrow instrumentalism of educational policies in Britain [...] with the lack of a developed understanding of 'aesthetic education'. Theorists from the tradition of a hermeneutics of suspicion are mostly silent about the politics and poetics of 'beauty'.

– Isobel Armstrong[1]

The banishing of beauty from the humanities in the last two decades has been carried out by a set of political complaints against it.

– Elaine Scarry[2]

I have had students at the Workshop tell me that until they came there they had never heard the word 'beautiful' applied to a literary text [...] If it is not recognized, the text is not understood.

– Marilynne Robinson[3]

The arts have long constituted a contested domain with its own defining tensions: between theory and practice, between saying and doing, between pure and applied, between teaching and making, between the sacred and the profane, between the market and the maker. Funding the arts in production, performance and the academy has now become the devil's supper – no spoon too long. We are being undone by an unholy alliance of higher education (the scramble for funding), the creative industries (the scramble for innovation) and the academic publishers (the scramble for copy). You may be sure of a warm welcome: they'll happily bend the rules every which way to accommodate you – and even sympathize with your latest take on what might just possibly count as 'research'. We are living in the research-or-bust world of a fully politicized academic system, and the strangehold upon the free spirit of the artist grows ever tighter. I guess the hope of the new 'universities of the arts' is that they will somehow manage to square the circle by polishing their research-based credentials.

Research, the engine driving not only higher education but industry, is the mad pursuit of innovation at any price – and the price has been very great. Once science had demonstrated the connection between research and profit, industry demanded it, academia was refashioned to provide it, and the publishers cashed in.

The following assessment by Torsten Kalvermark in *The Routledge Companion to Research in the Arts* (2010: 3) sums up the situation: 'The emergence of practice-based research in and through the arts is closely connected with politics in higher education' (2010: 3).

The arts inimical to research?

Of the writings I have sampled in preparing this essay, I have probably found Christopher Frayling's seminal 1993 paper, 'Research in art and design', the most level-headed and clear-minded – not that other more recent writers are not equally authoritative. But the debate seems to have heated up since his day, with infinitely more at stake now and with the arts constituency under siege. Frayling, then Director of the Royal College of Art, was addressing a community that felt itself, in 1993, also to be under threat. He wrote his piece to steady nerves and recover some sort of professional high ground. In an attempt to untangle some conceptual knots and get us thinking straight about 'the kinds of research which might suit, indeed grow out of what we actually do' (1993: 5), Frayling cites Herbert Read, who made the following distinctions:

- Research *into* art and design: e.g., artists and critics interrogating issues of meaning and relevance.
- Research *through* art and design: e.g., the therapeutic analysis of clients' art works as evidence of emotional and social problems.
- Research *for* art and design: e.g., Shakespeare's research into his historical sources; Constable's cloud studies.

(Frayling 1993: 5)

Where all three of Read's categories qualify as straightforward, *calculating* procedures of research as popularly understood, art as research, I would suggest, belongs to the procedures of *contemplation*. Aristotle's distinction, for me, is fundamental in considering the claims of art as research.

Frayling further cites what he sees as a powerful indictment of the idea of art as research by Picasso, '"In my opinion," said Picasso, "to search means nothing in painting. To find is the thing"' (1993: 2).

Should we therefore be following Picasso, and by implication Frayling and Read, and reject the claim of art as research? When he comes to spell out the position taken at that time by the RCA on the matter, Frayling seems to be saying we should:

> At the College we give Higher Doctorates or Honorary Doctorates to individuals with a distinguished body of exhibited and published work – but we do not at present offer research degrees entirely for work where the art is said to 'speak for itself'. Rightly

> or wrongly, we tend to feel the goal here is the art rather than the knowledge and understanding.
>
> (Frayling 1993: 5)

The painter Agnes Martin said:

> Everybody protests that artists are irresponsible, but artists are not concerned with the material world. I would advise them to turn away from this world and go on a picnic or something. Go into the forest and feel the difference [...]. Artists are intuitive. They wait for inspiration. That's what art is about, the intuitive, not the intellectual. Art about ideas stimulates ideas, but art that comes from inspiration stimulates feelings of happiness, innocence and beauty.
>
> (Martin 2009: 195)

Stimulating feelings of happiness, innocence and beauty seems to me both a sound and an exhaustive account of a proper aesthetic education. Feel the difference. If art-making is a procedure of truth, is a way of truth-finding, might it not also be a way of looking, of listening or 'hearkening after' truth? Does finding not actually imply searching? I believe it does. But there is perhaps a distinction to be made between having too clear an idea of what you're looking for and simply knowing you're hungry, or coming empty-handed to the feast. Where searching might be better understood as a *pursuit*, re-search, on the other hand, implies the superimposition of two orders of interrogation: of searching, and probing the initial search for its significance. Whereas this accounts for the 'interpretive' phase of scientific research, art eschews and rejects the force of *interpretation*. To make an impact, art does not await the second search that is interpretation, as Susan Sontag has argued in *Against Interpretation* (1966). The artist's pursuit or vocation, what 'calls' her, is her recognition of the Sirens' song that is a presentiment of the beautiful presence. It is her willing surrender to the temptation of the beautiful. To grasp the truth of art as research requires an act, not of interpretation, but of surrender. Facing the beautiful, suspicion is annihilated.

But our infinity is to be lived in air thick enough to breathe and in a world with substance to it. The 'insubstantial pageants' of art speak to an immortal truth: our aspirations of beauty.

Aesthetic truth is also moral truth: it is a judgement as to what is *contemplatively* right, not one of *calculation* as to what adds up. The sure touch, the true eye, absolute pitch, perfect timing, amazing grace. The call to beauty that is the artist's pursuit, her calling, is relentless: her work is never done; it is always in progress. How could it not be, since art lives within the realm of the eternal? We sing many songs, and we catch snatches of them here and there, now and again. We go in pursuit of each one, and recover, come to know it, just so far. We hum along awhile and then lose it. But every song is ours; the voice is always our own. 'Whatever we lose (like a you and a me) / It's always ourselves we find in the sea,' writes the poet e. e. cummings (1994: 5) in his poem, 'Maggie and Millie and Molly and May'. This is our infinity and it is our wholeness: the truth we clamour for. This is the moment of 'grace' that Simone Weil (2002) writes about: the alchemical transfiguration of mortal gravity in moments of *Serenissima.* Art is our eternal becoming. Art resists the 'right' of 'might' that would convert us all into objects. (Weil again.) Art resists the dicing and pricing of the academy. We may, in art, 'feel after and find' the truth that is beauty, in a brooding gesture of love: destination, the mythical city of Babylon.

> The poem finds the word that finds the feeling.
>
> (Winterson 2012: 187)

Art as a procedure of truth

I have recently been enjoying the French philosopher Alain Badiou's (2005) writings in praise of dance and love. For Badiou, the arts and love are two of four 'procedures of truth', the other two being science and politics. If, following Keats, we elide truth with beauty, Badiou might actually be identifying four distinctive procedures of the beautiful: the beauty of science and of politics, as well as of art and love. Why deny to the scientist and the politician the possibility of the beautiful? But what makes art special? I would say, art is a procedure for disclosing the truth latent in the human making of beauty: art is the lovely making of what Virginia Woolf (2008: 326) called 'rapture'. The creative conversation of the artist with the world is one of 'interinanimation' (John Donne, 'The Extasie', 1960: 7). Here is Elaine Scarry in *On Beauty and Being Just:*

> Beauty is, then, a compact, or contract between the beautiful being (a person or thing) and the perceiver. As the beautiful being confers on the perceiver the gift of life, so the perceiver confers on the beautiful being the gift of life. Each 'welcomes' the other: each – to return to the word's original meaning – 'comes in accordance with [the] other's will'.
>
> (Scarry 2000: 90)

The moment of beauty is a moment of serene aliveness. This is our deepest existential longing – and art holds the key. It is a longing born of our tragic destiny as separate, mortal beings. In play and then in art we recover our *Serenissima*, our wholeness, our integrity.

Scarry is writing about what Witkin and I (Witkin 1974; Ross 1978), in our research into the arts in schools in the 1970s, called *subject-reflexive action*, a reflexive conversation rather than an empirical inquiry, a conversation in which both parties are equally the cause and the effect, equally given to disclosure. It is a moment of perceptual transposition, a moment of enchantment. In my terms this means fading-in the intelligence of feeling and dimming-out the more pragmatic seeing that insists on the bare facts. The artist practises a kind of alchemy, her goal being what Yeats (1952: 217) wrote of in his poem, *Sailing to Byzantium*: to refashion human suffering as song – as the 'artifice of eternity'. Gathering the world into the artifice of song is what art *as* research is all about. May such a way of knowing be a procedure of truth? It may. May it happen *as* research? Yes, again:

> O sages standing in God's holy fire
> As in the gold mosaic of a wall,
> Come from the holy fire, perne in a gyre,
> And be the singing-masters of my soul.
> Consume my heart away; sick with desire
> And fastened to a dying animal
> It knows not what it is; and gather me
> Into the artifice of eternity.
>
> (Yeats 1952: 217)

How many miles to Babylon?

I have spent the best part of my working life modelling the creative process in arts education – trying to articulate a conceptual framework for my students that would underpin their understanding of the arts curriculum and the ways of the arts teachers. May these models (for my latest see Ross 2011), these frameworks, properly be called rubrics or 'procedures'? Do they qualify as tried and tested methodologies or reliable techniques? I think yes. However, my designs do not offer the certainty expected of universal processes or evidence-based strategies. So what are they? Techniques of creative improvisation, of the living interaction between feeling and form – *techne* and *poiesis*.

I have been thinking that perhaps they are more like those wonderful old medieval maps of the world, part fact, part conjecture, part fiction. More like charts for the uncharted, expressive rather of hope than certainty, promising adventure rather than prosperity, trials rather than safe havens. Of those regions beyond the known, the old map-makers simply warn, 'Here be dragons'. No matter how confident the artist in her art, there's no avoiding the dragons. Every art therapist's studio should have a notice to that effect hanging on the door: 'Danger: deep waters. Here be dragons'. I note how many of my cherished poets have described their own 'procedures' in terms of the perilous journey – what earlier we called the artist's pursuit or calling. Coleridge's 'Tale of the Ancient Mariner', Homer's 'Odyssey', Eliot's 'Journey of the Magi', Yeats's 'Sailing to Byzantium', Robert Frost's 'Stopping by Woods on a Snowy Evening'.

How many miles to Babylon?
Three score and ten.
Shall I get there by candle light?
Yes and back again.

(Anon.)

So, must the arts renounce their claims to research? At least any claim to research as conventionally understood: methodologies tried and tested against reliable evidence, offering certainty and credibility in the affairs of the world? Plutarch, in his *Lives: Theseus* would seem to think so:

> As geographers, Sosius, crowd into the edges of their maps parts of the world that they do not know about, adding notes in the margin to the effect that beyond this lies nothing but sandy deserts full of wild beasts, unapproachable bogs, Scythian ice or a frozen sea. So, in this work of mine, in which I have compared the lives of the greatest men with one another, after passing through those periods which probable reasoning can approach to and real history find a footing in, I might very well say of those that are farther off, beyond this there is nothing but prodigies and fictions, the only inhabitants are poets and the inventors of fables; there is no credit or certainty any farther.
>
> (Plutarch 2001: 1)

If 'proper research' means to remain within the bounds of 'probable reasoning' and 'real history', what hope, what 'footing', for the artist as researcher? Do our fable makers and poets deserve no credit, offer nothing certain, mere 'prodigies'? With due respect to Plutarch, I think they do better than that. Artists speak in their raptures and visions, of the heart's truth; they promise, as 'singing-masters of the soul', an answer to the heart's longing for what is worthy of its love. This is their calling, their vocation, the bearing witness to beauty. But we must understand them not as *asserting* themselves but as *effacing* themselves, in the name of the work. As conspiring to the annihilation of suspicion. Elaine Scarry (2000: 112–13) makes the crucial point that encountering the beautiful de-centres the self. This is what 'disinterested judgment' as a feature of aesthetic experience actually means. Scarry cites Iris Murdoch and her thesis on the 'sovereignty' of the good; 'Murdoch [...] specifies the single best and most obvious thing in our surroundings which is an occasion for *unselfing* and that is – "what is popularly called beauty"' (original emphasis).

Mapping the creative arts therapies

If we were to try to map the practice of a 'proper' arts therapy onto the beautiful world of the artist it might look something like my cyclical model (Ross 2011) of creativity in the arts (Figure 1).[4] Five distinctive forces make up the artist's creative work, and these same principles, I would argue, might provide a basic framework for the creative arts therapies.

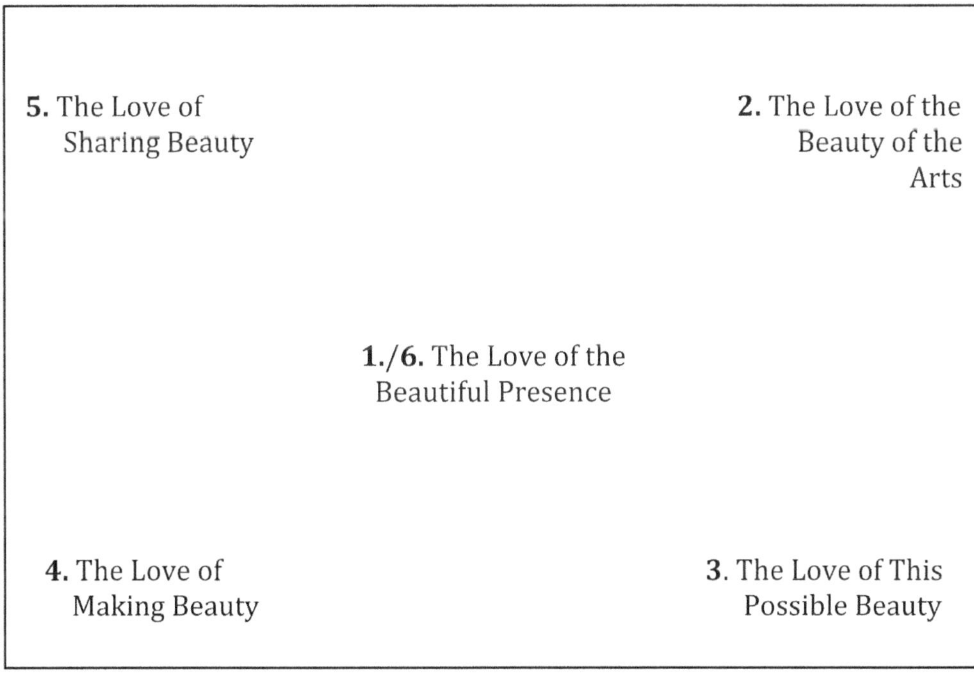

Figure 1: The five distinctive forces.

1. In the first place and at the centre of the cycle is Love. Love permeates and validates every aspect of the artist's work. Art cannot be done otherwise – whether in the studio, the concert hall or the classroom. This love is a passion for beauty, and for the truth to be found in loveliness: love as a procedure of truth. This is empathic love: *caritas*, *Agape* and *Eros*. This is the force at the hub of artistic creativity and revelation. It animates every other facet of the process.
2. This love is a passion first triggered in the child by the music she hears, the songs that are sung to her and the stories she is told. Also by the illustrations and pictures she looks at and the live performances she is taken to. By the hours she spends in solitary and shared playing. Slowly her own tastes in these things take shape and her preferences become the framework of her particular aesthetic sensibility. They become the first shoots of her own desire to refashion the world closer to her heart's desire. This she embarks on with frenzied devotion in the form of play. So, play marks the beginning of her technical/creative education: she wants to invent new worlds to wonder at and to wander in, and to do this she needs skills of handling. Her models as an artist are the repertoire of works and skills her parents and teachers introduce her to. Her impulse to learn is an impulse of imitation: *mimesis*. She has acquired a culture: she is a member of the wedding. She will acquire the skills and understandings (*techne*) to play her part.

3. The love of receiving art, nurtured by family, friends and teachers, is driven by an impulse of imitation, but gradually shifts into a project of independence and self-expression, fuelled by the aesthetic impulse to have her own say, to make her own mark in the world, to be recognized to count for something. Again, play is the site of the earliest manifestation of these tendencies. What she makes she becomes. She loves. Her inventions, constructions, pretences and fantasies all speak to her own desiring and of her own life. She brings her imitative impressions into the expressive domain of playing and if we are alive to them we shall recognize the personal transformations she is enacting upon the experiences that increasingly mark her independence as an emerging soul. She is working away at the love she has for the world she is, and for the world she inhabits, and to fulfil her wishes for them. The creative impulse of the maker is born.
4. A maker of that which she finds beautiful. Having tasted the joys of making worlds that come 'closer to her heart's desire', there is now no appeasing her passion for beauty except through creative making of her own, in which the feeling for beauty is not an incidental by-product but the driving impulse. We know this from the passion driving the making: angry, frenzied, obsessive, un-gainsay-able – a loving and a longing which brook no impediment. These are the treasures she makes, these lovely things, and she has in mind, more often than not, to whom she will dedicate them, offer them as a gift – or, at the very least, for kindly appraisal. Here technique becomes mystery: alchemy. The world becomes transcendent, immortal, *otherwise*. This what it is to love art-making. It is also passionate receiving, hoarding and capturing of the beautiful world, and, provided this impulse to beauty and truth, her truth, is encouraged and not discouraged, she will be safe in her love of loveliness all her life long.
5. With the fulfilment of the impulse to capture and lift the true and the beautiful into the eternal dimension of being, the work is then offered up, in a further act of love, to praise (appraisal). And as a personal gesture of life affirmation, of trust and truth, it must be so offered and so received. Every parent, every audience, knows this impulse to praise and to show gratitude in the face of the gift of the child, of the artist. This is a moment of intimacy: of what Daniel Stern (1985: 128) calls 'inter-subjectivity', corresponding affectively to the creative act of subject-reflexivity that governed the making of the work. In the act of presentation lies the impulse to be present and to be acknowledged in and by the world: in and by the world *otherwise*, the world *amorous*. Our appraisals must reinforce the other's impulse to art.
6. So finally the return to the love of the beautiful. Which is where we began: the 'good' at the hub of the artist's world, the passion for the beautiful, the truth that is beauty. Beauty is the truth that corresponds somehow to our deepest, most rapturous longings for the ineffable. Ineffability defines the mystery at the heart of the artist's world. There is no way but by mute clay and pigment, stone and wood, an approximation of language and a concatenation of sound. No other way but by the ecstatic body, the enraptured word. Taking the world into her hands and breathing love into it, handling not simply with care but love. I might be speaking of the therapist (or the teacher) here – and of course I

> am, since 'the therapist' properly so called is a studio artist rather than either a clinician or technician (see Moon 2002). *Serenissima* was the mother's first gift to her child: the oceanic feeling of total union with the beloved: feelings that with maturity come to be identified with love, authenticity, beauty. Rapture is indispensible. For Virginia Woolf as well as for Iris Murdoch the good is 'sovereign'. Woolf calls the marriage ceremony hollow. 'No I don't like the ceremony – oh I wanted some rapture – some precious stone to hold. None. None' (2008: 326). For Elaine Scarry 'the absence of beauty is a profound form of deprivation' (2000: 118). Subject-reflexive affect feeds every phase of the creative process in art. The disclosure of beauty is what the French psychoanalyst André Green calls, 'subjective epiphany': subject knowing as passionate revelation. The meaning of her epiphany for the subject is the recovery of lost affect – at the expense, Green argues, of its representation: 'When the affect is discovered in its manifestations – its subjective epiphany – its peculiarity is to recover, abolish, replace representation. Its most striking effect is negative hallucination' (1999: 226).

We might consider using Simone Weil's word 'grace' in conjunction with truth and beauty and goodness in the arts: grace as the gift of a 'subjective epiphany'.

Conclusion

The arrows of desire fly from our bows out into a world upon which we have designs of love. Eric Ravillious died as a World War II artist, but not before he had found and revealed in his love of life, the terrible beauty at the heart of war. Without such a vision how could any war be 'just', let alone fought?

Scarry again:

> When we speak about beauty, attention sometimes falls upon the beautiful object, at other times on the perceiver's cognitive act of beholding the beautiful thing, and at still other times on the creative act that is prompted by one's being in the presence of what is beautiful.
>
> (Scarry 2000: 95)

I want to say, 'prompted too by our presentiments of the possibility of beauty'. If art is to count as research then what the artist researches will be her presentiments of beauty, her intimations of immortality. Those who are called to join her in her moments of rapture, in her visions, her *Serenissima* – and we shall not all be so called – will recognize the truth they constantly long for, mirrored in hers. As Gadamer has argued, the symbols of art prompt *recognition* rather than interpretation. This is our holy ground. Here I am whole, holy.

And where does all this leave us? We must persuade the Academy to think again: if we must have 'a hermeneutics of suspicion' we also need a hermeneutics of good faith. We must speak up for 'the politics and poetics of beauty'. If not us, who? If we want to see changes in higher education, we must profess our vocation in the here and now of our schools, clinics and academies. *We* must perform the changes we want to see.

> What had Eden ever to say
> Of hope and faith and pity and love
> Until was buried all its day
> And memory found its treasure trove?
> Strange blessings never in Paradise
> Fall from these beclouded skies.
>
> (Muir 1956: 46)

If our strange moments of beauty ('subjective epiphany') speak to our infinity, they are only to be found beneath 'these clouded skies.' This is the promise of the arts. The 'treasure trove' of childhood is not lost but may be redeemed and upgraded to shape and empower our quest for adult truth in making and loving art – not for art's sake but for the sake of our human 'hope and faith and pity and love'.

References

Armstrong, Isobel (2000), *The Radical Aesthetic*, Oxford: Basil Blackwell.

Badiou, Alain (2005), *Handbook of Inaesthetics* (trans. A. Toscano), Stanford: Stanford University Press.

Badiou, Alain and Truong, Nicolas (2012), *In Praise of Love* (trans. P. Bush), London: Serpent's Tail.

cummings, e. e. (1994), *Selected Poems* (ed. R. S. Kennedy), London: W. W. Norton and Co., Ltd.

Deleuze, Gilles (1988), *Spinoza: Practical Philosophy* (trans. R. Hurley), San Francisco: City Lights Books.

Donne, John (1960), *Poetry and Prose* (ed. H. W. Garrod), Oxford: The Clarendon Press.

Frayling, Christopher (1993), 'Research in art and design', in *Royal College of Art Research Papers*, vol. 1, London: Royal College of Art.

Gadamer, Hans-Georg (1986), *The Relevance of the Beautiful and Other Essays*, Cambridge: Cambridge University Press.

Green, André (1999), *The Fabric of Affect in the Psychoanalytic Discourse* (trans. A. Sheridan), London: Routledge.

Kalvermark, Torsten (2010), 'University politics and practice-based research', in M. Biggs and H. Karlsson (ed.), *The Routledge Companion to Research in the Arts*, Abingdon: Routledge.

Martin, Agnes (2009), 'Interview with Irving Sadler, 1993', in D. Beech (ed.), *Beauty*, London: Whitechapel Gallery.

Moon, Catherine Hyland (2002), *Studio Art Therapy: Cultivating the Artist Identity in the Art Therapist*, London: Jessica Kingsley Publishers.

Muir, Edwin (1956), *One Foot in Eden*, London: Faber and Faber.
Plutarch (2001), *Plutarch's Lives* (trans. J. Dryden, ed. A. H. Clough), New York: Modern Library, Random House Inc.
Robinson, Marilynne (2015), *The Givenness of Things: Essays*, London: Virago Press.
Ross, Malcolm (1978), *The Creative Arts*, London: Heinemann Educational Books.
——— (2011), *Cultivating the Arts in Education and Therapy*, Abingdon: Routledge.
Scarry, Elaine (2000), *On Beauty and Being Just*, London: Gerald Duckworth.
Sontag, Susan (1966), *Against Interpretation*, New York: Farrar, Straus and Giroux.
Stern, Daniel N. (1985), *The Interpersonal World of the Infant*, London: Basic Books Inc.
Weil, Simone (2002), *Gravity and Grace*, Abingdon: Routledge.
Winterson, Jeanette (2012), *Why Be Happy When You Could Be Normal?*, London: Vintage Books.
Witkin, Robert W. (1974), *The Intelligence of Feeling*, London: Heinemann Educational Books.
Woolf, Virginia (2008), *Selected Diaries* (ed. Anne Olivia Bell), London: Vintage Books.
Yeats, William B. (1952), *Collected Poems of W. B. Yeats*, London: Macmillan and Co., Ltd.

Notes

1 Armstrong (2000: 2).
2 Scarry (2000: 57).
3 Robinson (2015: 26).
4 To avoid confusion the reader should note that I have re-positioned and re-named the different phases of the original model for the summary purposes of this essay, making what was originally number 5 (the hub) number 1; number 1 number 2 and so on. However, the phases themselves are unchanged in their import and their sequence in the cycle, which are fully elaborated in Ross (2011).

Chapter 3

'Not Sure': The Didactics of Elusive Knowledge

Peter Sinapius

In 1986, the Australian philosopher Frank Jackson wrote a treatise entitled 'Epiphenomenal qualia'. Its subject was the phenomena relating to our consciousness of the world that cannot be explained by the instruments of cognitive and neurosciences. The following thought experiment was at the centre of his treatise:

> Mary is a brilliant scientist who is, for whatever reason, forced to investigate the world from a black and white room via a black and white television monitor. She specializes in the neurophysiology of vision and acquires, let us suppose, all the physical information there is to obtain about what goes on when we see ripe tomatoes, or the sky, and use terms like 'red', 'blue', and so on. She discovers, for example, just which wavelength combinations from the sky stimulate the retina, and exactly how this produces via the central nervous system the contraction of the vocal chords and expulsion of air from the lungs that results in the uttering of the sentence 'The sky is blue'. [...] What will happen when Mary is released from her black and white room or is given a color television monitor? Will she learn anything or not?
>
> (Jackson 1982: 130)

Jackson's answer was rather unambiguous: 'It seems just obvious that she will learn something about the world and our visual experience of it. But then it is inescapable that her previous knowledge was incomplete' (1982: 130).

With this thought experiment Jackson contested physicalism per se, and the physicalist epistemological position in particular, which claims to deduct all knowledge from physical facts. We quite obviously don't acquire all our knowledge in that way. However, physical data has never been collected and processed to the degree that they are today – all fuelled by the hope to learn as much as possible about reality. These data are the basis from which theories, models and constructions about the world in which we live are developed. They are administered by way of huge encyclopaedias and databases that make our knowledge about reality accessible on demand. The availability of this knowledge appears virtually boundless.

The production of knowledge is often tied to our ideas about the standards that the knowledge that we access, has to comply with: it has to be correct to be seen to be valid, it has to be universal and therefore capable of being reproduced, and it needs to go beyond the individual case in order to be objective.

But what about the kind of knowledge that cannot readily be retrieved, as it is closely linked to our experience, that which is locked within our individual consciousness? What about the knowledge that Mary can only acquire once she is released from her science lab and experiences red tomatoes or a blue sky for the first time? Finally, what about the wealth of knowledge that can only be unlocked by way of our attention, participation and presence; knowledge that we can gain no certainty about as it is not easily reproducible or quantifiable, such as the beauty of a sound, the irresistibility of a situation, the gripping nature of a scene, or the intensity of a moment?

Scientific disciplines that are not confined to physically measurable facts, but also encompass subjective experiences that enable us to relate to the world, need to answer these questions. So, is there a didactic that allows access to the kind of knowledge that is *not* available as such – a didactics of elusive knowledge?

Each day, in my work as teacher, I attempt to access this kind of knowledge – but the step from action into the abstraction of language, in order to talk about it, is an enormous one. This touches exactly what this chapter is about: the transition between action and methodic availability, between implicit and explicit knowledge. The problem of the didactics of elusive knowledge not only concerns higher education degree courses in the applied arts; it fundamentally touches the core of artistic practice in the processes of development and change. These processes dwell more in the realm of the undefined and uncertain than that which can be spoken about with certainty.

Implicit and explicit knowledge

I would like to begin my approach to this issue by way of a metaphor and, from there, draw a possible outline for a didactic of elusive knowledge. What is to be understood by implicit and explicit knowledge in the context of artistic/art therapeutic teaching, and what kind of dichotomy does this imply?

The German scientist Hans Dieter Huber, who focuses on media theory and visual culture, differentiates both forms of knowledge by describing implicit knowledge as *knowing how* (or skill) and explicit knowledge as *knowing that* (or cognizance) (2015: 36). Huber uses cycling as an example to illustrate implicit knowledge: I cannot learn how to ride a bike by reading a book about it (*knowing that*); I have to try it out. I am learning by trial and error (*knowing how*). If I want to get to a certain destination on that bike however, trial and error won't get me very far. I need to have the way of getting to my destination explained to me or else use a map for assistance (*knowing that*).

Rather broad-brush, this hints at the subject to be investigated here: which roles do the learning targets in our curricula play (*knowing that*), and what kind of didactics are necessary for students to be able to proceed with their studies (*knowing how*)? If the metaphor of cycling were to apply to a particular destination, the greater part of the study course would cover cycling itself (*knowing how*). Accomplishment of the aim, however, would entail following a given path that leads to the given destination (*knowing that*). This notion corresponds to the classic understanding of learning and teaching as a mechanical way of respectively conveying and appropriating knowledge: both path and destination are largely predetermined, so students need only progress along a predetermined path in order to achieve a certain destination. Such an idea presupposes a deterministic view of human beings that defines 'development' as successfully attaining a predetermined destination. If this notion were true, teachers might just as well carry students to their destination and save them the effort of covering the distance on their own.

As an art therapist, I have learned that the course of an individual is not simply fashioned by moving directly towards a predetermined goal. That would only be possible by way of enforced conformity and incapacitation. The processes of individuation do not follow predetermined paths. We evolve because we want to know where the journey goes. A course of study is part of our individual development, geared towards a more or less determined professional future. This future, however, is no different from a journey to a location we've never been to: although we might have a destination, it is not yet known to us.

As a teacher, I have experienced that learning is not a process where the path is clearly marked out beforehand and one only has to follow a certain route. More precisely, learning happens individually and is especially effective wherever students venture into unknown territory accompanied by their teacher. From this perspective, riding a bicycle – the exploration of movement, the *knowing how* – is not just the means to an end but an opportunity to appropriate the world through an additional form of knowledge; one that does not fit between the covers of a book.

A didactic of elusive knowledge that understands learning as a process with an open outcome redefines the relation between path and destination: the map or the pursued route – the *knowing that* – that determines the frame of reference, is the precondition for development and learning. For a course of study dedicated to art therapy, such a didactic relies on references to visual culture and aesthetics. Further, it delves into phenomenological theories and that which is informed by the aesthetics of reception; it takes in the techniques of creative design and – according to the orientation of the course – explores therapeutic models and concepts. This framework provides the context of the learning process without being the actual content.

More so than other disciplines, artistic teaching leads us to the threshold between the appropriation of knowledge and individual experience: the colour yellow, a sound or a gesture are all fundamentally untransmittable as no curricular grammar applies to them. They only become accessible by way of individual aesthetic experience and are thus reflexively describable (Sinapius 2015). Accordingly, the traditional didactic that is still broadly practised in higher education is inverted: here, acquisition of knowledge does not happen by way of assimilation but as the transformation of subject matter.

This didactic principle is in the tradition of reform pedagogy, which defines learning not from the vantage point of an encyclopaedia of knowledge but from an understanding of its conditions and prerequisites. It proceeds from the premise that thought, cognition and understanding cannot exist without action or operations based on action (Piaget 2001). That is, reform pedagogy understands learning as an active process, and thought as a method of creative experience (Dewey 2009). The production of knowledge is understood as something based on physical experiences to be gained via objects or events.

In the following, I draw an outline of a 'didactic of elusive knowledge' derived from a study of my own practice of teaching art therapy and from a non-representative survey I conducted among students of the course Expressive Arts in Social Transformation at Medical School Hamburg (MSH).[1] Twenty-six out of a possible 60 students took part in the survey. The following perspectives are illustrated by means of quotes from the survey.

Learning requires the freedom of doing something for its own sake

> *Each day there are new personal experiences, we experience everything with our own bodies, try out everything by ourselves and have the option to direct our research according to our interests [...]*
>
> (Student 25)

Whenever I improvise with the students, we are not looking for right or wrong, good or bad. Rather, we relate to one another and notice: it works, a pattern emerges, it irritates or surprises us. With the word *it* I point out the so-called aesthetic Third, described in the literature on art therapy; though untransmittable, it can manifest among those who improvise (Sinapius and Niemann 2011). Improvisation is not unlike the dancing described by choreographer Forsythe: 'Dancing is like a living being. You cannot coerce it, you cannot get it. You have to make yourself cognizant and it comes to you' (as quoted in Odenthal 1994: 37).

This all seemingly has nothing to do with what goes on in a scientific course of studies: the aim of students writing a term paper and handing it in for assessment is primarily about them demonstrating what they have learned. They then receive a mark in order to measure their success in learning. This process has a significant effect on the understanding of learning and teaching and is often deeply rooted in our own biographic experience. This type of learning is part of a system of reward and punishment that is all about marks and attainment and therefore categories of right and wrong, good and bad. Its aim is a number, which can raise the student's self-esteem or strike at its very heart. This system could possibly produce (or is based on) fear: the fear of failure or that of not living up to the expectations of others.

I consider this system to be absurd. It is based on a learning culture that regards knowledge not as something that arises from a situation but as something in existence just waiting to be picked up and reproduced. But learning is something else; when students are interested in a theme, they want to find out about it for themselves. Their writing of an assignment starts with a burning question about how to access a certain topic. Then they start collecting material, which they can question. They try to understand, make observations and establish connections. This is an open-ended process, often onerous, sometimes exhilarating, during which the students need the support of their teacher. In principle, this process is no different from musical improvisation; the writing of a term paper requires the same openness and focus on the subject.

John Dewey (1993: 218) mentions five characteristics to describe the conditions that instigate a type of learning dedicated to an object for its own sake:

- The student is faced with a 'real situation befitting the acquisition of experience', which 'interests him for its own sake'.
- From this situation a real question has to arise that stimulates thinking.
- The student has to possess the 'necessary knowledge' and to undertake the 'necessary observations' in order to deal with the situation.
- The student ought to come up with possible answers.
- He or she should have the opportunity to test them in practice to 'explain their meaning and to discover their value independently'.

Learning is intrinsically motivated. According to journalist and filmmaker Reinhard Kahl, learning requires the freedom to do something for its own sake (Kahl 2014). To back up his point he quotes the sociologist, Richard Sennett: a '[...] basic human impulse (is) the desire to do a job well for its own sake' (2008: 9).

Learning requires an object that kindles it and which it relates to

> *A clear task that serves me as a good frame of reference allows me to steer everything in that direction. The time I spend with my task by myself is therefore one of intensive learning.*
>
> (Student 21)

Sometimes I invite students to paint sounds or noises. What does a 'hum' look like in contrast to a 'squeak' or a 'beep'? Surprised by the unusual task, the students start experimenting with colours. What does a lemon yellow sound like in contrast to an orange or blue? What do two colours whose surfaces meet sound like? The task leads the students into a dialogue with that which comes into being under their hands. Afterwards we all sit down in a circle and look at the pictures that have come about and try to 'listen' to what they convey. The students thereby learn to differentiate their perceptions and to study the quality of the colours closely. This type of learning is not a repetitive but an active process, which has an object it relates to.

This is not a matter of course. In many universities we find learning environments that follow a very different idea of learning: the student is not confronted with an object, a situation or a theme, but with a teacher faced by rows of chairs. The teacher is supposed to be in possession of the knowledge that the students are to absorb. The learning thus follows the notion that the objective is a transmission of content rather than an interaction with it.

The training in art therapy can hardly be described as a mere collection of content ready for effective dissemination. The core of such training rather consists of learning situations that open up a range where content is not disseminated but (aesthetically) worked with and where meaning is developed. The duality of content and dissemination is replaced by an approach to learning through transformation of the subject matter. In this case, didactics as a method of dissemination can no longer be separated from the content that is its object (Sinapius 2008).

Learning processes require room for discovery

> *To evolve artistically and to express myself, I found it very helpful to learn to pay attention to myself and to become intensely conscious of my surroundings. In this I was also aided by the fact that there was always the freedom to try myself out and experiment.*
>
> (Student 5)

> *Those click-moments keep astounding me. That is, most of the time I am not conscious of learning but it happens to me by the way: when I come home and am asked what I've done, I always notice how much of it has stuck with me.*
>
> (Student 8)

From 1933 onward, as head of painting at Black Mountain College and later from 1950 as head of the Department of Design at Yale University, Josef Albers developed a didactic of seeing and put it into writing in his book *Interaction of Color* (Albers 1963). For his teaching he devised a setting that was as simple as it was clever. I use it as a vantage point when dealing with the theme 'relativity of colour'. An array of different coloured cardboard, scissors and glue provide the basis for the students to produce distinct arrangements investigate the different ways that the colours interact with one another. How does a red look on a blue background and how does the same red look on a yellow background? In turn, how do distinct colours appear on the same background? The students work in groups of three and are asked to develop hypotheses that describe observable, recurring phenomena. As a stimulus, I send them on their way with two possible experimental arrangements: try to make two distinct colours appear as one or try to make one colour look like two. For this I give them 45 minutes. Then the whole group comes together to compile the results.

No group comes out of this setting without any surprising or stunning discoveries, and after their first observations, they come up with the ambition to track down the reasons for the observed colour phenomena. What is so special about this learning situation? The topic of the lesson does not describe the content to be conveyed, but determines the setting, the frame of reference and the range outlined by the organization of time and space. In this setting, the students can make numerous distinct discoveries and come up with hypotheses about the effect of colours. The subsequent presentation of Albers' discussion on 'the relativity of colour' finally allows the students to recognize their own experiences in his words.

The arrangement of a lesson resembles a stage play. The teacher resembles the director of the learning process, rather than a knowledge broker. He or she has to be capable to kindle the interest in a theme and to provide the necessary instruments that the students need to access a certain topic. The teacher also has to be able to come up with the conditions under which discoveries can be made. His or her task is not to produce knowledge but to open up the space in which it can be tapped.

When everything is clear, there is no more to be discovered. When everything has been said already, nothing more needs to be said. When the curricula of our university courses are misunderstood as a content summary of what needs to be covered and studied later, then there are grave consequences for learning, which becomes merely a passive appropriation of knowledge. However, when the curricula provide the frame of reference for individual learning processes, the students can use existing spaces to individually experience resonance. Learning thus ceases to be an appropriation and becomes the construction of knowledge (Reich 2012).

Teaching and learning are all about uncertainty; negative capability

> *[...] the affirmation that it is ok to try out everything and that everything is possible; the recognition that even seemingly unimportant byways can provide an impulse for something new; that you don't have to have something prefabricated in your head [...]*
>
> (Student 18)

When I give an assignment to my students, I prefer to put aside preconceived ideas and assumptions. I'd rather like to be surprised by what the students make out of the task at hand. For example, when a student apologized to me for the dog-ears and coffee stains on her drawings, I suggested she might have her breakfast on her drawings for the coming two weeks and use the markings produced in this way as an incentive to engage with the coincidental traces of everyday life and so take them as an invitation to deal with uncertainties.

Irritations or disturbances can be rather productive for the artistic process. They are often vantage points for new insights. I use them in art therapy as I do in workshops to promote awareness (Sinapius 2014). If agreed upon beforehand, the intervention in someone else's painting can lead to surprising results just as much as the mutual observation of a picture viewed from a different angle, such as when we turn it on its head. The act of seeing is no less productive than the painting of a picture.

Just like the later occupational routine of an art therapist, learning doesn't consist of a succession of predictable events. What are predictable and calculable are the conditions that allow us to get a perspective on individual aspects of the reality that surrounds us. Students are quick to learn that their creative products don't just follow inner ideas or images but that what comes into being depends on how they look at it. Just like in a conversation, they are constantly oscillating between the production and the reception of images. They learn how to deal with the unpredictable, with disturbances or irritations; to incorporate them as productive elements into their creative process.

I am convinced that intensive research and learning begins at the point where we question seeming self-evident facts and venture into unknown territory. The English poet John Keats calls this 'negative capability' – not 'inability', mind you. 'Negative capability', he writes, 'that is when man is capable of being in uncertainties, mysteries, doubts without any irritable reaching after fact and reason [...]' (1899: 277). This capability to deal with uncertainties and 'perhaps even feel a certain pleasure to have lost oneself temporarily' (Weymann 2014) is seen by music therapist, Eckhard Weymann, as a resource that can bring about creative solutions. Without a certain measure of uncertainty, the process of learning and teaching remains an unproductive matter, only capable of reproducing a system that itself is no longer capable of adapting.

Learning requires an environment of benevolence

> *Finally, I managed to have been disabused, something that never happened to me at school. On the one hand, this has to do with me studying something I'm interested in and that I enjoy. More importantly, however, my teachers give me the feeling that I am capable and good. Good in the sense of: I believe in you, you are important.*
>
> (Student 26)

> *An open, trusting learning atmosphere – concretely: teachers revealing themselves by conveying their own thoughts and experiences, familiarity at the workplace [...] meeting at eye-level, no more chalk-and-talk teaching, instead a sharing of thoughts and experiences.*
>
> (Student 22)

Conclusion

It would appear that the relation between students and teachers in higher education is traditionally defined by study and exam regulations. They sketch out the limits within which students and teachers meet. They lay down educational objectives and define the instruments with which the teachers can check whether the students have reached the learning goals. In the end, grades provide the standard that decides whether they have achieved this or not.

Such an understanding presupposes a hierarchical gap between teachers and students and leads to an output-orientated learning and teaching behaviour, and a performance-orientated learning atmosphere. From that perspective, learning is determined by what is required to be known in the end; detours and bottlenecks relating to the acquisition of this knowledge are seen to represent failure, and success regarding learning and knowledge can be quantitatively measured according to the subject matter that the curriculum stipulates.

Such a hierarchical organization of teaching is not suited to foment learning processes or to facilitate a learning experience that:

- is intrinsically motivated;
- relates to an object, through which experiences can be made;
- contains space for discovery; and
- is backed up by uncertainty and the readiness for failure, which are significant catalysts for learning.

The handling of study and examination regulations may sometimes turn out a balancing act. However, study and examination regulations can be understood as merely providing a thematic frame of reference for learning processes. There are no didactic guidelines for lessons. Learning is not a hierarchical event where knowledge is power and ignorance is paralysis. It is the task of the teacher to accompany the learning process and to provide the space and the necessary instruments for the students to trace their questions and find answers to them.

More than anything, it is with regard to artistic or social problems that learning reveals itself as a process closely tied to individual experience, which requires a space in which to take place. For this, the philosopher Hartmut Rosa uses the term 'resonance', which links a successful appropriation of the world with subjective experiences of resonance:

> Successful relations to the world are those, in which the world appears to the acting subjects as a responsive, breathing, and supportive resonance system, which at times can even be benevolent, accommodating, and benign.
>
> (Rosa 2012: 10)

That such a system must necessarily be distinct from one that categorizes knowledge as right or wrong, and that rates subjective performance as good or bad, is blatantly obvious.

Learning requires a protected setting and an atmosphere of benevolence. That is, we need to view learning processes not from the angle of study and examination regulations but from the perspective of the students. Or, to say it in the words of the educational researcher John Hattie, 'If the teacher's lens can be changed to seeing learning through the eyes of students, this would be an excellent beginning' (2009: 252).

References

Albers, Josef (1963), *Interaction of Color*, New Haven: Yale University Press.

Dewey, John (2009), *Democracy and Education*, Radford, VA: Wilder Publications.

Hattie, John A. C. (2009), *Visible Learning: A Synthesis of Over 800 Meta-Analyses Relating to Achievement*, London and New York: Routledge.

Huber, Hans Dieter (2015), 'Das Wissen der Sinne', in G. Schmid and P. Sinapius (eds), *Artistic Research in Applied Arts*, Wissenschaftliche Grundlagen der Künstlerischen Therapien, Band 5, Hamburg, Potsdam and Berlin: HPB University Press, pp. 33–47.

Jackson, Frank (1982), 'Epiphenomenal qualia', *Philosophical Quarterly*, 32, pp. 127–36.

——— (1986), 'What Mary didn't know', *Journal of Philosophy*, 83, pp. 291–95.

Kahl, Reinhard (2014), 'Wie Musiker die Bildung verändern', *WDR 3 Kultur am Sonntag*, http://www.wdr3.de/programm/sendungen/wdr3kulturamsonntag/index.html. Accessed 1 August 2014.

Keats, John (1899), *The Complete Poetical Works and Letters of John Keats, Cambridge Edition*, Cambridge: Houghton Mifflin and Co. and The Riverside Press.

Kolb, David A. (1984), *Experiential Learning: Experience as the Source of Learning and Development*, Englewood Cliffs: Prentice Hall.

Lave, Jean and Wenger, Etienne (1991), *Situated Learning: Legitimate Peripheral Participation*, New York: Cambridge University Press.

Odenthal, Johannes (1994), 'Der Raum vor seiner Zeit. Ein Gespräch mit William Forsythe über Ästhetik, Trance und Ballett', *Ballett International/Tanz Aktuell*, 1:2, p. 37.

Piaget, Jean (2001), *The Psychology of Intelligence*, London: Routledge.

Reich, Kersten (2012), 'Konstruktivistische Didaktik', *Das Lehr - und Studienbuch mit Online-Methodenpool*, Weinheim: Beltz.

Rosa, Hartmut (2012), *Weltbeziehungen im Zeitalter der Beschleunigung - Umrisse einer neuen Gesellschaftskritik*, Berlin: Suhrkamp.

——— (2013), *New Directions in Critical Theory - Social Acceleration: A New Theory of Modernity*, New York: Columbia University Press.

Sennett, Richard (2008), *The Craftsman*, New Haven: Yale University Press.

Sinapius, Peter (2008), 'Über das, Eingießen, von Kunst und andere didaktische Methoden in der kunsttherapeutischen Ausbildung', *Kunst und Therapie, Zeitschrift für bildnerische Therapien*, 1, pp. 25–34.

——— (2013), 'What didn't exist, happened - About the third', *Lecture at European Graduate School (EGS)*, https://www.academia.edu/9680571/_What_did_not_exist_happened. Accessed 6 April 2016.

——— (2014), '…man lernt, den Ton des Anderen wahrzunehmen… Burnout-Prävention mit künstlerischen Mitteln', *Kunst und Therapie, Zeitschrift für bildnerische Therapien*, 2, pp. 71–81.

——— (2015), 'Wissen und ästhetische Erfahrung', in G. Schmid and P. Sinapius (eds), *Artistic Research in Applied Arts*, Hamburg, Potsdam and Berlin: HPB University Press, pp. 69–89.

Sinapius, Peter and Niemann, Annika (2011), 'Das Dritte in Kunst und Therapie', in P. Sinapius, M. Wendlandt-Baumeister and H. Gruber (eds), *Wissenschaftliche Grundlagen der Kunsttherapie*, Band 4, Frankfurt am Main: Verlag Peter Lang.

Terhart, Ewald (2009), *Didaktik – Eine Einführung*, Stuttgart: Reclam.

Weymann, Eckhard (2014), 'Dynamische Spielverfassung als Voraussetzung für den Umgang mit Nicht-Wissen', *Musiktherapeutische Umschau*, 3, pp. 228–36.

Note

1 The survey was conducted through open questions answered online and in writing between 8 January and 20 January 2015.

Chapter 4

Art as the Topic, Process and Outcome of Research within Higher Education

Ross W. Prior

It is by logic that we prove, but by intuition that we discover. To know how to criticize is good, to know how to create is better.

– Henri Poincaré[1]

Art has tended to suffer great misunderstanding when it comes to how we might research within it and this is in part to do with the way we have perceived art over the centuries. For example, *l'art pour l'art* (or in English, 'art for art's sake') was a philosophy of the late nineteenth century that promoted the idea of the intrinsic value of art, and the thought that only 'true' art is divorced from any didactic, moral or utilitarian function. In a rebellion against Victorian moralism, 'art for art's sake' was the motto of bohemian artists who rejected the notion that art need be for any other purpose than the art itself. On this point, Shaun McNiff comments on the marginalizing of artistic experience in our culture: 'Art for art's sake may have significance for an elite few, but it is not in step with our more pragmatic society' (2003: 25). The sequestering of meaning generated from art is of course nonsense as all art evokes meaning, even if it is not intended to have a didactic purpose. Art will mean whatever the artist intends it to mean and whatever meaning is generated by the receivers of art through the ideas and feelings it creates for them. Art is a particular act of expressing feelings, thoughts and observations. Therefore, the learning potential in art is 'powerful as it leads us to the deepest places of human feeling, provides enlightenment and raises the human spirit' (Prior 2017: 266).

Indeed, we must never lose sight that '*the making of art consists of the selection of appropriate life realities* to create a new canvas, to make a new living, breathing statement' (Hagen 1991: 90, original emphasis). Even if the artistic statement is one of pure beauty there is an interpretive function and process that the artist must go through in the creation of the artefact – ephemeral or otherwise. All creative acts essentially involve the formation of meaning, which is continually changed and nuanced throughout the process of creation and then, of course, forever remain open to receptive interpretation.

In art-based research and in the teaching leading to it, art is both the object of investigation and the method of inquiry – an equally exciting and challenging proposition at the same time. Art-based research has been defined as involving 'reflection on the interplay between these mental motivations and physical ones that appear through contact with the medium' (McNiff

1998: 56). To these ends, the growing appreciation of using art as research within higher education is gaining momentum but has been somewhat slow to become widely appreciated and used with confidence. There are several reasons for this, but the most significant reason is that, more broadly, only a small percentage of arts lecturers in higher education, who are also likely to be practitioners, tend to be active researchers themselves – 'active researchers' in the sense of a more formal definition of university research, with doctoral qualifications. This has probably occurred through the Academy's separation of practice and research and a lack in clear understanding of the intersection between art and pedagogy/andragogy – in general the lack of universally explicit promotion of *art as research* when it might have been of most relevance to them as artist-educators.

Further, there has been an incoherent understanding of how to move from pedagogically based instruction, more suited to teaching children, to instruction that actively develops an andragogical model appropriate for more mature learners with the aim of developing auto-didacticism. Consequently, the curriculum has been slow to evolve in order to comprehensively include the use of art as research with the focus on the individual as researcher throughout their higher education. After all, the learning and teaching processes within higher education (i.e. adult learning) should consistently involve inquiry and research.

This is a puzzling situation within the arts, as artists are well positioned to be inquirers of their own complex processes extant in their specific arts practice(s). Artists have long understood that there is a blended approach to research within their practice but they have

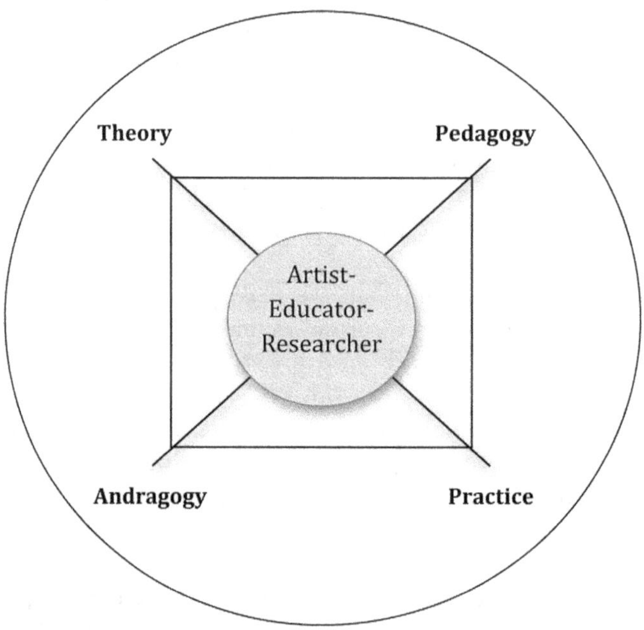

Figure 1: Intersection of imperatives for the artist-educator-researcher.

traditionally failed to identify this *as research* since *intentionality* is key to justifying their creative act – seen by many outside of art-making as just too *practical* and *subjective* to hold the tenants of 'valid' research. This chapter proposes that at the centre of art as research, the artist-educator-researcher (Figure 1) brings together the tensions evident in higher education to successfully make what I term later in this chapter the 'threefold primacy of art in research, learning and teaching' – art as the topic, process and outcome of research.

The creative process of art within learning and teaching

The Ancient Greek aphorism called for us to 'know thyself', which is surely a principal tenant of education no matter what the discipline or level. Here within our interest in using art as research, we witness the natural intersection of pedagogy/andragogy and artistic practices offering rich opportunities for investigation. As we use artistic processes in the creation of artefacts, ephemeral or permanent, collaboratively or alone, we engage in a complex act that is informed by the known and the unknown. We draw upon both conscious and tacit knowledge. Further, through the process of creation we generate new knowledge and the increased discovery of one's self and one's relationship to art. The completed artwork then becomes its own source for understanding, both for the artist and for the 'recipient'.

This process of creativity offers a richness of process that may not be witnessed in quite the same way elsewhere in the curriculum. In his exploration of creativity and its broader applicability, McNiff usefully captures the dynamism of the process this way:

> Creative energy flows through every environment as blood courses through our bodies and sap rises in the trunks of trees. When the circulation of creative energy is blocked and diminished, the environment loses life-sustaining nourishment. When negative and harmful forces arrest the free movement of energy, the same thing happens within our bodies, relationships, families, and organizations.
>
> (McNiff 2003: 233)

Processes, if studied, reveal a great depth of knowledge. Art-based inquiry, therefore, 'includes multiple ways of knowing, including affective, sensory, creative, observational and intuitional, as well as the use of experimentation, risk taking, discovery and meaning making through art-making' (Kossak 2013: 20). There is tremendous richness and endless possibilities for a researcher in these types of investigations, and therefore the potential for learning and teaching is immense.

A serious current concern for many who work in higher education is how we develop the necessary craft-based skills within our students given the minimal contact hours timetabled. Those of a certain age will remember the emphasis upon craft and technique in art education, recalling the long hours afforded in the studio honing our skills. This studio culture in the arts was unquestioned as being necessary in the development of skilled artists within their craft. One model of teaching frequently used was demonstration, where the tutor would commence the class by demonstrating a particular technique himself or herself; throwing a vase on a potter's wheel or playing a particular piece of music on the oboe, for example. This act of demonstration had a bifocal effect of bringing the group to attention in focusing the day's work for the class; it also signalled very clearly to the students that someone who could do it was in fact teaching them (not always a given in universities today). The progressive teacher would not use this to merely 'show-off', retain the power within the learning environment, or to merely cultivate imitation, but would use it to place themselves within this community of practice and at one with the art. The current concerns within higher education arts faculties include the limited amount of time made available to students in order to develop skills within the studio; how we might preserve the sometimes manual nature of those skills; and pertinent to our discussion here, how what we do within art aligns with politically and academically enforced research agendas extant within our respective countries and their systems.

In addition to developing an essential skill-base in higher education, there is a need to assist students to more comprehensively develop their understanding of the importance of the artistic process, in order to develop deeper understanding of creative inquiry. It is essential that we demand that *intellectuality* informs understandings of the intuitive, sensory and emotional as we go about our art-making and the coexisting process of artistic inquiry. The act of developing students' essential craft skills aligning to the particular art form in use is undoubtedly part of the higher education remit. However, there must also be a clear emphasis upon the *artistic research process* if we are to create an embedded culture of inquiry. Authentic learning will only arise when students make discoveries for themselves. The creative process of art-making should allow students to pose their own questions and reframe these questions continually over time in order to seek out those essential discoveries.

The current discourse surrounding adult learning, which frames learning as inquiry and transformation, is not unlike the earlier initial progressive education movement for children that took root from the 1880s to 1940s. John Dewey was one of the leaders of the early movement that helped promote notions of the benefits of group work, learning by doing, integration of entrepreneurship into education, personalized learning, problem-solving, critical thinking and so on. These tenants of education have become widely accepted and applied within education at all levels. It would seem perfectly in line with this thinking to also progress our accepted understanding of research too, and to use art to promote in-depth, student-centred knowledge.

How we make art is very much a part of an area of artistic inquiry that begins many years before reaching university. Therefore it is essential to ask: *What models of art-making and inquiry are secondary school students being presented with in their various arts classes? Is the art-making founded on creative inquiry at all?* Chances are that students are not being presented with processes that develop depth and, therefore, very quickly come to view the art they are doing as incidental and even 'a waste of time. This cycle of misunderstanding will not be completely broken until the higher education experience is renewed to entwine *art as the methodology for inquiry throughout the entire art-making process.* This approach would helpfully be made explicit to our students, and the arts curriculum must take full advantage of an art-based approach if anything is to change. Graduates might in turn emerge from their university experience much more confident as artist-researchers and be able to articulate what it means to engage in art-based research – only then will we see a significant change in education. Using art as research very much provides for us clear synergy with current educational thinking by using processes to gain knowledge and understanding.

Empirical critical inquiry in art

Art research is of no less importance to knowledge construction than science or social science research is to those questions where the methodologies suit their particular questions. Whilst science is interested in classification, 'general laws and theories, connected with observable particulars by way of prediction and verification' (Phenix 1964: 141), artistic inquiry is interested in the *particular* where generalizability is not the primary quest. The purpose of scientific inquiry and the purpose of artistic inquiry are quite different and serve different ends. The debate over their respective merit or hierarchy of standing is redundant – each has its place and art is particular.

Traditional fine art criticism, music criticism, literary criticism and performance criticism along with their respective study have tended to place art as the *topic of research*. Important to this criticism, scholarship and research, includes understanding the questions raised in the artwork, understanding the science or technique of the artwork and the historical and social context of the artwork. By 'artwork' I of course include reference to all of the arts. In many instances the biographic information of the artist comes into play, which frequently provides the background story – the motivation – in search of an understanding of the work.

It is true that everyone can make aesthetic judgements and create aesthetic meaning; it is something we possibly do many times each day without being overtly conscious of it. The practised artist, however, may have highly developed skills, aesthetic awareness and consciousness that the non-artist might not possess. Nonetheless, art has an openness to be examined, interpreted, accepted or rejected according to personal taste, and can be experienced with deep or superficial appreciation. Art, and again I do include all art forms, is a result of an individual or collaborative process, and the finished artefact, ephemeral or enduring, can of course be researched and reviewed in multiple ways.

The perception of what one senses from art is deeply personal to both the creator and the interpreter but it can be empirically examined. In this way there is some marginal commonality with scientific approaches – empirical evidence being information acquired by observation or experimentation. However, unlike science, artistic expressions cannot be reduced to mere 'data' as such. Artistic expressions are alive and would be limited by being called 'data' and by the very idea of 'data analysis'. Additionally, secondary sources in art describe, discuss, interpret, comment upon, evaluate, summarize and process art as the primary source. Secondary source materials in art are, of course, typically found as research articles and reviews that discuss or evaluate someone else's original art.

Using technology to capture process

David Hockney's 2017 retrospective is recorded in *The Guardian* newspaper as the fastest selling exhibition in the Tate Britain (Brown 2017: n.pag.). The show, which covers six decades of Hockney's work, opened in London before travelling to the Centre Pompidou in Paris and then the Metropolitan Museum of Art in New York. His use of an iPad to create art is displayed amongst the exhibition.

What is clear with Hockney, as an artist, is that he understands the value of investigating process. His curiosity has extended from a growing understanding that some early painters used basic optical devices to improve and expand their technique. One such device was the *camera lucida*, patented in 1807, which was a small prism mounted at the end of a metal arm that enabled an artist to refract an image onto their canvas. The use of this device allowed the artist to duplicate key points of the scene on the canvas, thus enabling the most accurate rendering of perspective. This discovery, amongst others, became the subject of Hockney's book *Secret Knowledge: Rediscovering the Lost Techniques of the Old Masters* ([2001] 2006). Hockney, himself, has now embraced an array of technology ranging from video cameras to iPads, and has integrated them into his art. These new technologies allow for a full investigation of the process of art-making.

Hockney has collected fascinating videos by using the playback feature of the Brushes app, for example, showing him actually creating the drawings. This is exciting for Hockney and this energy is reflected in the enormous collection of work he has made using these new technologies. This departure from the expected orthodoxy has therefore received much media attention. Martin Gayford from *The Telegraph* writes:

> One discovery that came with the iPad was that the process of drawing could be re-run at the tap of a finger. The screen goes blank again, then lines and washes reappear one after another, apparently of their own accord. The result is, in effect, a performing drawing [...]
>
> Hockney is tickled by the experience of watching himself at work. 'Until I saw my drawings replayed on the iPad, I'd never seen myself draw. Someone watching me would be concentrating on the exact moment, but I'd always be thinking a little bit ahead. That's especially so in a drawing where you are limiting yourself, a line drawing for example. When you are doing them you are very tense, because you have to reduce everything to such simple terms'.
>
> (Gayford 2010: n.pag.)

The key here is not so much the medium in itself but the potential that new media allows for fascinating art-based research. Even for such an established artist as Hockney, this was the first time he had viewed himself making art while being able to watch the moment-by-moment additions to the artwork itself. Hockney and others can now see a work of art unfold before them. Witnessing the placement of lines, shading, colour choices and even hesitations or rapid instinctual decisions become areas of interest to the art-based researcher.

Technology offers the art-based researcher many possibilities to investigate, understand and document outcomes and has for some time been advocated by Shaun McNiff who, for several decades, has proposed that 'through videotape we have the opportunity to see and hear people reflect first-hand on their experiences and motivations' (1998: 193). In line with Hockney's use of the iPad, many of us recognize the rich possibilities of new media, yet are frustrated by the lack of progress within academia to develop this as legitimate artistic research, still continuing to largely privilege the written word or reliance upon other methodologies that are not so pertinent to artistic practice.

An innovation such as the Doodlecast Pro iPad app allows for the use of multimedia and provides a playback function, giving the artist multiple options when investigating their work more closely. There is also a growing range of Android drawing and illustration apps such as ArtFlow Studio, LayerPaint HD, Art Rage, Sketchbook (multi-platform) and Painter. Dance and movement-based practices can also benefit from the use of motion capture devices. All of these and other technologies offer artists new possibilities to research their moment-by-moment practices and they can further consider new questions in the light of these evolving technologies. Never before have the possibilities been so diverse and interesting for the artist-researcher.

Criticism and feedback as a research process

Malcolm S. Knowles (1970), the father of andragogy, provided us a clear distinction between the preferable andragogical approaches, more appropriate in adult education, and pedagogy that he believed was more suitable for child education. In adult education the educator is positioned as a *facilitator* within the learning environment, which is an important distinction from that of a 'teacher' or 'instructor'. Knowles et al. further propose that 'effective facilitation means that learners will be challenged to examine their previously held values, beliefs and behaviours and will be confronted with ones that they may not want to consider' (1998: 106). In making these challenges, this poses the question: *How do we best carry out criticism and feedback within the higher education environment?*

T. S. Eliot in one of his famous essays 'The perfect critic' makes the closing point that 'it is to be expected that the critic and the creative artist should frequently be the same person' ([1920] 1997: 13). This advanced proposition brings both together and yet allows for distance. In line with this, western higher education fundamentally holds as a primary aim that 'students come to a state of self-criticality' (Barnett 2007: 126). An essential outcome of art-making is criticism that, at its best, is enabled by creating both close aesthetic engagement (artist) and also clear aesthetic distance (critic). Of course, what makes art so enormously powerful is the ability to evoke emotion and enliven our senses by drawing us closely in. However, when critically viewing art, we empirically report what we see and understand of the process, underlying its creation.

Within the learning environment, McNiff picks up on this point by suggesting – 'If you are in a position to evaluate another person's work, you might ask: What works well? Is there something that needs to be altered? Are you achieving the desired outcome?' (2003: 147). These are pertinent questions that focus on particular phenomena rather than forcefully presenting our personal opinions, judgements or critiques. By working this way, McNiff, again, believes that this 'helps to prevent the recipient of criticism from feeling attacked and to defuse any defensive reactions' (2003: 147).

Criticality is developed and matured through a combination of looking at other people's work in addition to one's own, but this must be done carefully and the process clearly articulated. McNiff goes on to propose that:

> Effective criticism is characterized by an ability to separate from the object of reflection, whether it is personal behaviour or something we make. Both the critic and the person being criticized need to maintain this aesthetic distance.
>
> (McNiff 2003: 147)

Of course, within the performing arts such as dance and acting, for example, the integration of the mind and body of the artist is so heavily entwined with the work that this distancing becomes particularly challenging but also rather exciting. The notion of experientially acquired embodied knowledge (Gallese 2005; Kemp 2012; Prior 2012) has become the academic topic in current fashion and offers new investigations for researchers across the various art forms. 'Being' and 'doing' are concepts that offer a rich platform to carry out a range of research studies that might explore critical processes and aesthetic distancing. *Criticality* in higher education is developed within the essential context of research. This point, even to many academics, may remain slightly unclear. Ronald Barnett helps to clarify this precise aspect:

> This is not a point about universities as institutions themselves engaging in research, but is rather a point about the pedagogical ethos. Whether the research is conducted by the student's tutors or other staff in the department, or by other universities, or by non-university organizations, *or by the students themselves*, the student's enquiries and pedagogical acts are proffered in the context of research. Such a spirit – the spirit of research – supplies a tentativeness not just to the student's enquiries, but also to her profferings, her claims and her actions.
>
> (Barnett 2007: 126–27, original emphasis)

So according to Barnett it is the 'tentativeness' in the research environment that offers benefit. However, there has been much emphasis in recent times, particularly in the United Kingdom, on dividing academic staff on the basis of those who are substantially research-active and those who are not, in order to maximize the Research Assessment Exercise (REF) metrics. Previous to this, the emphasis was on higher education lecturers/tutors being *active researchers* and teaching being informed by that research. Whilst partly laudable, this imperative marginally misses the more important point of *research-informed* learning and teaching – that learning occurs within the context of critical engagement where absolutes are not simply accepted or rejected and that *criticality* frames all that is read, written and made. Although this criticality should surround the work in higher education, it does not mean that criticality should be destructive, harsh, disempowering or non-affirming.

Helpfully, McNiff describes the way he works with students to engender a productive and constructive criticality:

> In my studio groups, we work at describing what we see in a purely structural and physical way and what we feel in response to an image or performance. We make a real effort to reinforce that all these responses are based upon the perceptions of the person offering the feedback. Sensitive attempts to help the creators see their work in a more comprehensive way are clearly distinguished from responses that only express the judgement of another person. These methods developed in group art studios can be applied to the work-place.
> (McNiff 2003: 148)

The above example demonstrates the epistemological attending to the 'being' of the expression – its nature – as distinct from attaching a particular meaning to it. Similarly, Uta Hagen, the noted actor trainer, always asked the actors who had just played out a rehearsal scene to say how *they felt* about their work before offering any other feedback. This strategy is the 'golden key' to allowing the actor to retain the knowledge generated within the artistic process of 'being' and keep the acting process internal, rather than an external display of mere 'doing'. McNiff and Hagen both understand the importance of beginning with the participants' feelings as an essential part of the critical process to avoid mere external judgement and damage to the artist's ability to create.

By taking a well thought-through approach to how criticism and feedback can supportively assist the research process, a productive process is integrated into teaching approaches and reinforced through andragogical opportunities. Some current television programmes such as the fashion designer US reality show *Project Runway* (2004–present) take us through the creative process within the context of a competition. We see into the design and sewing workshops of competing fashion designers who respond to various design and construction challenges (or 'assessments' as we term them in higher education). We hear first-hand the criticism of the judges who critique the work of the designers. Although the judges are industry professionals, they may not necessarily possess the understanding that we would expect from professional educators. However, they are provided with an on-air mentor, Tim

Gunn, who is skilled at eliciting a positive but critical conversation with the contestants. Gunn frequently begins by asking each designer what he or she *feels* about what they are creating and this is followed by a series of questions. In describing his teaching style on *Project Runway* and in the classroom, Gunn is quoted as saying:

> I always say I have a Socratic approach to most things that I do. I pummel people with questions, because I need to know what they're thinking, what they're trying to achieve, what they believe the final outcome is going to be. And then I try to examine their work with them, and articulate as well as I can how well they are actually achieving those goals, or whether they are in fact delusional.
>
> (Viderfeb 2013: n.pag.)

Not so incidentally, Gunn served for many years on the faculty and was Chair of Fashion Design at Parsons School of Design, The New School. He has a well-honed understanding of what is required to productively help the creators see their work more comprehensively and critically. This approach is precisely what adult learning theory (Knowles 1970) and associated educational methods would support as a way to use questioning to do more than ask about meaning.

The feedback offered by tutors and others also provides a potentially rich area for research within one's own artistic practice. This might involve looking critically at how one's own artistic vision changes as a result of feedback or a dialogical understanding of the many influences at play in the envisioning and re-envisioning towards the finished artwork. The observation of physical and environmental conditions too may play a part in influencing the artistic process and the eventual artwork itself. Exploring self-assessments of how we feel during and/or after different types of artistic activity can also provide a major focus for art-based research (McNiff 1998: 204). None of these aspects of criticism and feedback should be dismissed as incidental in terms of the student's research of creative processes.

Art as a process of co-participation

Higher education is changing over time in how the learning experience is constructed. Learning is now seen as a way of being *in* the social world, not simply as a way of coming to know about it (Lave and Wenger 1991). 'A challenging notion to emerge in more recent years relates to the changing relationship between professional and student' (Prior 2012: 208). The notion of *co-participation* in learning, with students learning alongside practitioners and other students, acknowledges the collaborative and ongoing nature of learning and of knowledge construction itself:

> This thinking seems to have come about through a growing mistrust of absolute professional authority, the acknowledgment that co-participation may result in more

> being known than one line of thinking alone, and that individuals must learn for themselves. Indeed the ownership of knowledge is nurtured organically rather than merely being imparted from an external 'authority'.
>
> (Prior 2012: 208)

It is true that traditionally artists of all types learnt from the 'acknowledged masters', which undoubtedly consisted of some imitation and direct instruction alongside the apprentice's own essential experimentation of the form. Knowledge was/is generated through the tireless practising of one's craft. Some areas of academia may find the direct skill-based training approach confronting, seeing it as not 'academic' enough. More traditional past academic approaches perpetuate the model that authority is largely derived from the possession of declarative knowledge with the belief that it is turned into procedural knowledge. However, subsequent artistic research has successfully demonstrated that there is much to be learnt *in* and *through* the artistic process itself – to the artist, this is generally self-evident.

Even between various art forms we see a considerable collaborative working to achieve the art itself. Music and the performing arts such as drama and dance know full well the primacy of working together to produce a unified effect. Whilst individuals play their own part, there is a collective will that governs the artistic process. But how might we see a range of art forms co-participating, not only amongst themselves, but working with communities more generally? Jean Rumbold et al. put forward the view that 'using collaborative and cooperative forms of art-based inquiry can translate what may start as very personal quests into projects with practical social relevance' (2013: 66). Rather than assuming that collaborative learning waters down the experience, there is rich interconnectivity at work that enhances the learning experience and can have positive social implications. McNiff in his work also addresses the potential of collaboration:

> Everything is shaped from something else and in cooperation with agencies other than ourselves. Life is always created from interplay among different participants who make contact, influence one another, exchange their essential natures, merge, and generate new forms.
>
> (McNiff 2003: 2)

It is self-evident that within the collaborative act there is tremendous potential for art-based research to be undertaken, moving away from the idea of the lone researcher or lone artist. This type of research offers great benefit to developing understandings of processes when two or more artists come together and further engage within the community. McNiff additionally suggests that 'if creative expression is to enlarge its place in our communities, there has to be a clear value attached to it [...] and benefits of creativity in group[s]' (2003: 25). This is where the idea of art is moved into the realm of communal or collective working, promoting benefits for community as well as new ways to research the collective impulse.

It is always the case that the purpose of the research should be kept firmly in mind, which is particularly true when working with co-participation, for example a group of students working with an external organization. The researchers must be clear about the method of inquiry and how they are to go about the problem, which includes being open to diversion should the creative process move the work in different directions. In the work we proposed with the Ironbridge Gorge Museum Trust, located in Shropshire, UK, students from the University of Wolverhampton will contribute to the use of various art forms to enhance the visitor experience at several of the museum's key sites. In leading this overarching project, it is our intention that not only will students collaborate in the art creation, but that they respond to a defined problem and use the art as the method of inquiry. For example, students may be asked to consider how a soundscape might be constructed to enhance the aesthetic experience of those entering a technology museum. In order to create the orchestration of sounds, the students might spend time listening to the existing sounds generated by the machines and gadgets in the museum and listen to the silences when there was less activity. The brief might be to add an audio response to those existing live sounds to enhance the sense of energy, and curiosity, and for the overall space to feel bigger and busier than it is.

The process might begin with artistic experimentation of sounds that engendered the theme of the exhibition. At first, the students might work on their own to establish an individual sense of the problem and initial possibilities in the project. Following this, the students could begin to involve others, both to expand the range of the experimental process and to develop skills in working together in developing a more comprehensive soundscape. Sound improvisation and improvised performance would be used to establish empathy with the expressions of movements within the exhibition. The soundscape would evolve in various iterations, variously tested in situ and assessed through the observation of how the public respond in the environment. As a research project, video would be used to record the creation process, the moments of reflection and the overall process of working together. This could result in individual videos, edited into their own artistic representations and accompanied by in-depth written reflections of the entire creative process.

Art as the outcome of research

Like many things in life, the answer to a problem is often more obvious than not. The outcome of art *is art* – art as the topic, process and also the outcome of research, which I see as the final (not necessarily end) part of the 'threefold primacy of art in research, learning and teaching' (Figure 2). Artefacts are forms of artist knowledge that are open to investigation, developing critical insights into the multiplicity of influences, actions, histories, practices and processes, and thus providing rich sites for legitimate ongoing reflexive inquiry.

The interplay between the object and the creative expression provides an area of investigation between artist and artwork. In other words, in art-based research we can

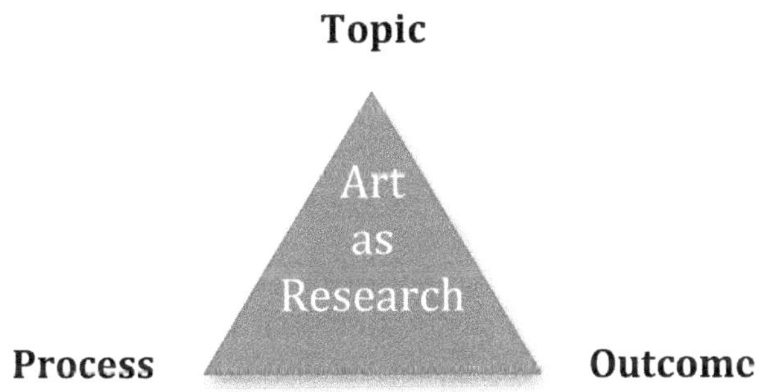

Figure 2: The threefold primacy of art in research, learning and teaching: art as the topic, process and outcome of research.

ask what the object or creative expression *reveals about itself* and *what role the artist plays*. Rather than providing an accompanying narrative by the artist giving a self-referential, one-sided emoted account of what the artist experienced or intended, art-based research offers a more complete research approach that 'recognizes objects as full participants' (McNiff 1998: 55). In further clarifying the dynamics at play within art as research, Kathryn Church (2008: 433) makes a case for the artefact and the active interplay between the artwork, process and the artist as researcher:

> [...] taking objects seriously, encountering them directly, proceeding object by object to unfold a study, tracking back and forth in the dialogic space between objects and their makers/users, and working reflexively with our limitations, confusions, and discoveries. (Church 2008: 433)

In art-based research, it is highly acceptable to respond to artworks that one creates (or are created by others) through the use of other artistic media such as poetry, dance, performance, drawing and so on. These various media offer the researcher expressive interpretations that move beyond the limits of written narratives of analysis, which have traditionally been the modus operandi of research inquiry. As McNiff states, 'If [...] words are incapable of revealing the unique qualities and spirits of art [...], why do we persist in using them as exclusive modes of research?' (1998: 193). However he would also agree that in order to more widely communicate findings, it will most likely be inevitable in a research study that these will be written-up or verbally communicated.

Through systematic inquiry, art-based research seeks to find answers to artistic phenomena. Essentially, this type of research must connect to practices within the discipline if it is to be of use to others. The true value may reside in the depth of observation and value one may give to an object or performance. The development of a creative relationship with an artwork offers students the opportunity of learning something new from both their process and their own artwork. The outcome of artistic inquiry leads to unpredictability because meaning is created in and through the expressive process. This unpredictably should be uniquely celebrated and not marginalized by the language of the sciences.

Conclusion

In this chapter I have made a case for the multiple meanings in art to be fully acknowledged and that the various meanings generated inform our knowledge *in* and *through* practice. Using art as research brings together the known and the unknown, the planned and the unplanned, the seen and unseen, the incidental and accidental, all in the creation of new knowledge, both for the artist and the field more generally. In particular, this offers exciting potential for learning possibilities within higher education. To these ends, Church asks:

> Will we value the 'accidental' quality of the journey that they open up for us? Can we lose control over how we come into knowing? Or will we turn creative inquiry into familiar order: a step-wise and predictable set of practices, planned and tidy, learned as part of a formal curriculum?
>
> (Church 2008: 433)

Clearly, aesthetic education must reject the predictable – the potentially *anti-creative*. It would seem essential, therefore, that art as research is seen to acknowledge and actively engage in repositioning our understanding of knowledge construction to accommodate a range of knowledge sources and types. This chapter has sought to underline the point that art as research is of no less importance to knowledge construction than science or social science research is to those questions suited to these methodologies – where these methods are useful to collecting particular data. Within all art forms the threefold primacy of art in research, learning and teaching – art as the topic, process and outcome of research – is essential to the artist-researcher's quest for knowing. One of the most exciting challenges to face us today is how we can embed these research processes into the higher education student experience, allowing for authentic artistic knowledge construction through artistic practice.

References

Barnett, Ronald (2007), *A Will to Learn: Being a Student in an Age of Uncertainty*, Maidenhead: Open University Press and McGraw Hill.

Brown, Mark (2017), 'David Hockney retrospective becomes Tate Britain's most popular show', *The Guardian*, 31 May, https://thegaurdian.com/artanddesign/2017/may/31/david-hockney-retrospective-becomes-tate-britain-most-popular-show. Accessed 16 March 2017.

Church, Kathryn (2008), 'Exhibiting as inquiry: Travels of an accidental curator', in J. G. Knowles and A. L. Cole (eds), *Handbook of the Arts in Qualitative Research: Perspectives, Methodologies, Examples, and Issues*, Los Angeles: Sage, pp. 421–34.

Eliot, T. S. ([1920] 1997), *The Sacred Wood: Essays on Poetry and Criticism*, London: Faber and Faber.

Gallese, Vittorio (2005), 'Embodied situation: From neurons to phenomenal experience', *Phenomenology and Cognitive Science*, 4:1, pp. 23–48.

Gayford, Martin (2010), 'David Hockney's iPad Art', *The Telegraph*, 20 October, http://www.telegraph.co.uk/culture/art/art-features/8066839/David-Hockneys-iPad-art.html. Accessed 16 March 2017.

Hagen, Uta (1991), *A Challenge for the Actor*, New York: Scribners and Macmillan.

Hockney, David ([2001] 2006), *Secret Knowledge: Rediscovering the Lost Techniques of the Old Masters*, New York: Penguin.

Kemp, Rick (2012), *Embodied Acting: What Neuroscience Tells Us About Performance*, London and New York: Routledge.

Knowles, Malcolm S. (1970), *The Modern Practice of Adult Education: Andragogy versus Pedagogy*, New York: Associated Press.

Knowles, Malcolm S., Holton III, Elwood F. and Swanson, Richard A. (1998), *The Adult Learner*, 5th ed., Houston: Gulf Publishing Company.

Kossak, Mitchell (2014), 'Art-based enquiry: It is what we do!', in S. McNiff (ed.), *Art as Research: Opportunities and Challenges*, Bristol: Intellect, pp. 19–27.

Lave, Jean and Wenger, Etienne (1991), *Situated Learning*, Cambridge: Cambridge University Press.

McNiff, Shaun (1998), *Art-Based Research*, London: Jessica Kingsley Publishers.

——— (2003), *Creating with Others: The Practices of Imagination in Life, Art, and the Workplace*, Boston: Shambhala.

——— (ed.) (2014), *Art as Research: Opportunities and Challenges*, Bristol: Intellect.

Phenix, Philip H. (1964), *Realms of Meaning*, New York: McGraw-Hill.

Poincaré, Henri ([1914] 2003), *Science and Method* (trans. Francis Maitland), Mineola: Dover.

Prior, Ross W. (2012), *Teaching Actors: Knowledge Transfer in Actor Training*, Bristol: Intellect.

——— (2017), 'Afterword: Confidence in art as evidence', in M. Reason and N. Rowe (eds), *Applied Practice: Evidence and Impact in Theatre, Music and Art*, London: Bloomsbury Methuen Drama, pp. 262–327.

Project Runway (2004–present, USA: Miramax).

Prosser, John and Burke, Catherine (2008), 'Image-based educational research: Childlike perspectives', in J. G. Knowles and A. L. Cole (eds), *Handbook of the Arts in Qualitative Research: Perspectives, Methodologies, Examples, and Issues*, Los Angeles: Sage.

Rumbold, Jean, Fenner, Patricia and Brophy-Dixon, Janine (2013), 'The risks of representation: Dilemmas and opportunities in art based research', *Journal of Applied Arts and Health*, 3:1, pp. 67–78.

Viderfeb, Stephen (2013), 'You, too, can make it work', *New York Times*, 1, http://www.nytimes.com/2013/02/03/education/edlife/teaching-tips-from-tim-gunn-mentor-on-project-runway.html. Accessed 17 April 2017.

Note

1 Poincaré ([1914] 2003: 129).

Chapter 5

A Different Way of Knowing: Assessment and Feedback in Art-Based Research

Mitchell Kossak

This chapter will outline some of the overarching opportunities and challenges toward assessment and giving feedback to those who are engaged in art-based research. In understanding how to assess and give feedback in art-based research it must first be understood what this method entails and how best to think about all factors involved. Art-based research can be challenging because of the process of having to have both the language of the art(s) and scholarly academic language speak equally, each as clearly and concisely as possible, and in the end explain what the research question is attempting to answer. If this dual aspect is achieved, art-based research has the potential to deepen and broaden understanding, comprehension and overall knowledge of the subject being studied in ways that more traditional methods of research cannot. Conversely, if this dual aspect is not achieved, then the research will be unclear, misunderstood and perhaps even disadvantageous to the field it is trying to address.

Challenges to assessment and feedback

My primary focus for the past 35 years has been in the use of art in psychotherapy, as a therapist and as a professor teaching in a programme that prepares students to enter into the world of applying the arts in therapy. In addition, I have spent the better part of my academic career overseeing master's theses and doctoral dissertations. It has been my experience over these years that when art is used in therapy, it is typical to have to educate, re-educate or deprogramme someone from their ideas about what art is supposed to look or sound like or a strong belief that they cannot engage in art. Perhaps this belief manifests because very early on in the educational system (or in direct comments from friends or family members) emphasis is placed on qualitative aesthetic measures regarding what is good or bad art. This strong emphasis lends itself to someone either believing that he or she can or cannot engage in art-making. (I am mostly talking here about those who are above the age of about 7–10 years old, since young children for the most part have not been indoctrinated into the value judgements given to art and dive into playing with all kinds of materials without thought of being critiqued.) In most school systems there is a weeding-out process that occurs systematically as one goes through the grades, so that by the time of middle or high school there are clearly demarcated 'artists' and 'non-artists'. Certainly by the time one attends college or university there are even fewer individuals involved formally or informally in serious art-making. This aesthetic value placed on utilizing the arts is geared toward art as product. As art therapist and art-based researcher Michael Franklin wrote, '[A]rt is considered an intimidating result created by a talented "other" hanging on a museum or gallery wall. It exists over there rather than as an embodied, viable pathway to cognitive, emotional and cultural knowing' (2013: 86). I find this deep-seated feeling and belief in the graduate and doctoral students I teach. Students often come into higher education with very strong value judgements about being 'good' in some art form and 'not good' or even 'bad' in others.

The point here is that if the general public and even those trained in the arts harbour a strong negative belief about their abilities and connection to art-making, then it follows that this would lead to an acceptance of the marginalization of the arts in general, and certainly a misunderstanding of how the arts can be utilized to enliven and illuminate the human condition. Given the pervasive belief that art is only to be experienced by the so-called talented and the subsequent value judgements placed on art-making, it stands to reason that the art-based researcher is not only up against this very large bias of who can and cannot be an artist (or even engage in artistic explorations), also a general non-acceptance and misunderstanding of the efficacy of the arts to express, illuminate or bring greater insight, meaning and new knowledge to a research study.

Tawnya Smith has written clearly about the doubts that a student might have in thinking about doing an art-based dissertation. Smith completed her dissertation at the University of Illinois, a fairly large traditional research university. As a musician she was very interested in art-based research and even went out of her way to study with some of the leaders in the field outside of her university. She wanted to study the inner felt experience and conscious awareness of musicians who are learning to improvise. However, questions came up for her such as, 'Can I really do an art-based study for my dissertation? Will that really count? Will anyone take me seriously as a researcher when I look for a position? How can I make my art-based inquiry fit into a recognizable form that my committee members and colleagues will accept as legitimate research?' (Smith 2013: 191). These are typical and legitimate questions often asked by students in a doctoral programme contemplating using an art-based method. However, as Smith also points out:

> While there were certainly some scholars not open at all to art-based methodologies, I failed to understand that many of the scholars with whom I most resonated would be supportive of my quest to entertain a topic as I adapted and continually explored an art-based approach.
>
> (Smith 2013: 192)

Art has its own unique language

While it is possible, as Smith points out, to find supportive committee members, it might also be the case that not all on the committee or in academia or in the larger field of study will understand fully the language of the arts and its importance in research. As already stated, art has its own unique communicative language, which is the language of the unconscious and symbolic meaning making. As scientist and philosopher Michael Polanyi ([1966] 1983) said, not all meanings can be made explicit through articulated language. That is, some knowledge can and does come in many forms and this understanding must be taken into account when assessing or giving feedback for a research study that utilizes the arts.

In art-based research there is a blending between primary and secondary process communications. In primary process communications such as dreams and art, a non-linear process is at play. The tricky and yet essential part of art-based research is, then, to take the primary processing and translate it into secondary understanding. If the researcher can clearly and elegantly blend the two worlds of primary and secondary process, then the research itself can have a great impact on the field, and perhaps related interdisciplinary fields. However, conversely, if the researcher cannot find a way to address both the language of the arts and the language of the conscious rational mind, then the research can be assessed as failing or not meeting the overall goals, which are to communicate clearly what the research was and how it is contributing new knowledge – this is not an easy task. For one thing, as already stated, aesthetics are rife with socially and culturally constructed judgements, which many academics and reviewers might harbour consciously or unconsciously. Therefore, the researcher's job is to translate the notes and observations from the art-making process into cognizant and sensible renderings; especially for those who might not fully understand artistic language.

For example, music, even if it is just listened to can be deemed good or bad. It is often a matter of taste or exposure. In graduate classes I often take the time to have students listen to a wide range of music and give feedback. As can be expected, the music that is popular or familiar in the culture is said to be pleasant and to have meaning. When I play music from a foreign culture or even music in the culture that is unfamiliar or might utilize very different harmonics and scales, most often the response is negative and the music is considered unpleasant and dissonant. Similarly, in an art-based research study, if the art form is unknown or less known to the reader or experiencer (as in performative arts), then there very likely will be an instinctual bias to reject or not clearly understand what the art is communicating.

As a doctoral committee chair or committee member or just from reading many art-based research studies, I have found that the best studies communicate the art and the discourse about the process of being engaged in the art clearly, concisely, coherently and with a depth of knowledge that in turn allows me as the reader/experiencer to feel and understand something new. When this combination of variables occurs it leaves me with more insight into the subject that was studied, broadens my way of thinking and changes my perceptions of how I work as an artist, therapist and educator. In my doctoral classes I ask students to evaluate and critique art-based studies. The most positive feedback I regularly receive relates to how the artwork and the writing came together in an emotional and heartfelt way and opened up new ways of thinking. Conversely, I have received critiques implying that the art itself was not very sophisticated, the process or method of involving the art was unclear and/or the explanation and discussion of the results were written poorly, i.e. there was no cogent argument made for how the results connect back to the art, research question, literature reviewed or the overall intent of the research itself.

I also receive negative feedback from students when the writing itself is just bad, in the sense that there are two or three thoughts rambling along in one paragraph and then a thought jumps to another disconnected thought in the next paragraph. The inability to write in a coherent way that builds a sound argument clearly distracts from the art itself, which in some cases can be extremely clear and even brilliant. When there is a disconnect between the primary and secondary processing modes of communication, it creates an overall detachment that affects the overall assessment and efficacy of the study.

As an example, researchers at Drexel University conducted an art-based research project acknowledging the difficulties in translating artistic language into discursive language:

> In our artistic inquiry, the challenge of translation was identified as occurring in two particular phases: (1) the emergence from the artistic process and the translation of the immediate experience into written and oral language; and (2) the retrospective reflective translation of cumulative artistic, written and oral data about the overall phenomena.
>
> (Gerber et al. 2012: 46)

It is also important to keep in mind how the aesthetic qualities in the study will be published. In my own art-based study on embodied transcendent experience explored through sound and rhythmic improvisation (Kossak 2008), I engaged with professional musicians and expressive arts therapists, both in groups and in individual 1:1 improvisation sessions. After watching the videotaped sessions many times, I responded to the improvisational experiments with poetry and paintings as a way to broaden the aesthetic knowledge. What I did not realize is that when the dissertation was published the images were printed in black and white and were blurry, which in my mind did not accurately represent the intent of the reflective paintings. Many students in my classes, when critiquing art-based studies, have made reference to the art not being presented in the most aesthetically positive way. Again, in my experience this will take away from the overall clarity and importance of the study and what the study might contribute to the larger community.

In addition, in my own study I had created a short compilation video that I felt captured the essence of the study; felt that this artistic rendering was essential and could have a strong impact on the overall findings. However, at the time there were not easy ways to embed a digital link within the text for others to access the video. Therefore, the video was never part of the published dissertation. Today I see that my students are finding many creative ways to embed links to video, audio or performance in their text, and these performative artistic expressions enliven the research study in ways that previously could not be imagined. Technology is really enriching and enhancing how art-based studies are being presented and published, and I assume that these digital technologies will only increase the availability and efficacy regarding this kind of methodology. In my doctoral class critiques I often get feedback that watching video files and re-reading the corresponding text in the paper is what finally solidified understanding of the project.

The art in art-based research

While art itself has its own language, each art form has its own unique communicative language that artists take years to understand: in music – sound, rhythm and harmony; in visual art – colour, texture and shape and the various media that can be employed; in dance/movement and dramatic enactment – embodied shaping of space and in drama and poetry the shaping of words. Artists will spend years mastering how these materials communicate in a way that is viscerally and emotionally moving or what can be thought of as utilizing an embodied creative intelligence (Kossak 2015).

The exploration of art material, whatever the form, may be more similar to a scientist exploring in a laboratory where the essence of the material is examined for what it is expressing or how it reacts with other materials. Visual artists do this all the time with colour and with various media such as watercolour or oil, as do ceramicists where very specific calculations regarding the firing process have to be employed in order for the clay to harden properly, not to mention the properties of the glaze that goes on to the clay to create the colour, texture, design and to make the clay hard enough to hold liquids.

Artists in their practice also, like scientists, repeat experiments over and over in order to clarify and further their understanding. For example, Michael Franklin in his art-based study reflecting on his personal journey through prostate cancer worked with clay to make pots and kept repeating the same technique, each time observing the process and results while taking meticulous notes in relation to the experiment he was conducting. After six years and 80 pots, something new eventually emerged, which was a replication of the x-ray images of his diseased prostate (2010: 89). Other examples of artists experimenting with material might be visual artists repeating an image over and over again, examining light at different times of day or other conditions; adding other colours or media such as washes. Musicians, dancers or actors might repeat a line, gesture or sound over and over again until something new emerges. When art is used in therapeutic or educational settings this technique of repeating an artistic expression until clarity emerges is used all of the time. The difference between the therapeutic process and art in research is that perhaps these artistic expressions are not notated or documented in a way that would occur in a formal research study. Regarding taking meticulous notes similar to what a scientist might do in the laboratory, Yvonna Lincoln and Egon Guba (1985) suggest the researcher can benefit from keeping a field journal in order to minimize bias. Similarly, Ross Prior introduces the idea of keeping a 'reflective sketch book' for actors and his doctoral students as a way to provide reflective distance to 'being in the process' and as a way to begin to create explicit knowledge (2013: 165).

Exploring unknown territory

Another consideration in steering art-based research toward appropriate assessment and feedback is the understanding that art-making itself can be messy and there can and will be moments of exploring in unknown terrain. In my own study, in which I engaged in experimental and free improvisational sound and rhythm experiences, I reflected on the process by looking back at the video tapes and listening to the co-created sound and rhythmic dynamics. One of the major observations was that creating together as a group or with individuals results in moments of disorder; or what I came to understand as misattunement (Kossak 2008). It was then useful for me to look at the literature of misattunement in developmental psychology, where mistuned moments are regarded as essential toward positive growth. From this discovery another area explored was chaos theory, which points to how unpredictable states found in nature tend to fall apart before coming back to a unified state (Prigogine 1980). This theoretical literature was all extremely useful in furthering my understanding of what occurs in improvisational sound-making experiences and how important staying with uncertainty is, not only in the specifics of improvisation but also within the art-based research process itself.

Art-making in all forms inhabits messy or unpredictable states, which like in chaos theory result in unpredictable outcomes and unforeseen perspectives. I remember several art-based dissertations and theses on which I served as a committee member or chair where the researcher was confused and unclear as to what was happening in the study or with the information being collected. In these cases, it has always been important to encourage and give feedback to the researcher to stay with the uncertainty and go back into the art form, encouraging them to paint, make music, dance etc. Franklin in his own art-based research study stated clearly the need to see the art and process as collaborative partners. He writes, 'Images, as symbolic others, kept arriving as unexpected emissaries bringing information that was ripe for research' (2010: 89). Additionally, researcher and art therapist Laury Rappaport, explaining her art-based research on the felt sense, wrote about the importance of reflecting 'on the art itself and the unfolding moment-to-moment direct experience of the process' (2013: 100). One additional example of a doctoral research study, on which I served, was an exemplary dissertation written by Tammy Einstein (2012) who, while immersed in her study, felt confused and stuck. Her doctoral committee chair Michele Forinash reflected on this moment in an article jointly written with Einstein, stating:

> [I]n those moments of not knowing it was important that these thoughts and images percolated inside her. By this point in her research journey I had witnessed her ability to dive deep in the art and return with a pearl of knowledge from the experience. The art-making informed her thinking and knowing. Trusting it led her to where she needed to go.
>
> (Einstein and Forinash 2013: 188)

It is important to remember that art-making in all forms inhabits messy or unpredictable states, and if we can give the feedback to go back to the art-making there is a strong possibility that the art itself will begin to reveal new insights and knowledge.

Improvisational nature of art-based research

Following the theme of unpredictability, art-based research can be compared to improvisatory arts where diving into unknown territory is central. Improvisatory arts as a presentational form are only impactful if the artist engaging in the presentation has done their homework and honed their artistic skills. The homework here includes reading the relevant literature in the field and understanding the nature of what is being studied from as many perspectives as possible. The researchers must immerse themselves in the material being studied until there is saturation, in the sense that one is fully absorbed and has left no stone unturned. Like in a jazz improvisation, the art-based research study needs to find the right notes in the right key and begin to play with them in a way that eventually not only makes sense to the researcher but to the audience to which the research is presented. This might also include allowing the research design to take shape or emerge, and unfold, rather than pre-determining the way it should be.

Similar to the jazz musician who takes the form of the composition and then creates an improvised solo based on a deconstruction of the chordal and melodic structures, an art-based research project is also one of deconstruction. In an art-based research study one must de-construct, re-construct and re-present material. For example, an ethnographic study might start by talking to individuals about a certain subject that will then be deconstructed into a narrative to be performed and enacted with possible feedback from an audience in order to make sense and make visible the co-constructed amalgamation of ideas, impressions and voices from the community.

Like the jazz improviser, the art-based researcher can get lost within the spontaneous flow of notes, and can feel uncertain as to where the solo is heading. Toward this uncertainty and specifically addressing not only the research process but also the presentation, researcher Donal O'Donoghue asks, 'What degree of ambiguity can arts-based researchers employ in presenting their work without running the risk of their work losing its communicative value?' (2009: 359). There is always potential ambiguity in the art process and in the presentation of the art. This aspect of the arts as improvisational sources of knowledge that can bring with it uncertainty and ambiguity as the process unfolds and in the presentation of the art itself needs to be kept in mind when giving feedback and when assessing any study.

Co-constructed knowledge

Similar to a jazz ensemble composition, art-based research can share the intent to co-construct knowledge. What is created by the researcher and/or participants needs to be articulated, described and depicted in the way it unfolds and in the way the phenomenon is experienced by those involved in the research. In qualitative research this shared constructed knowledge is called a 'dialogical triad' (Bauer and Gaskell 1999; Giorgi 1985; Patton 2002; Salner 1986; Smeijsters 1997), which includes the researcher, respondent and object (in this case the artwork) in an attempt to discover universal themes and connections. The same premise of co-constructed knowledge holds true for art-based research.

Looking again at my own research (Kossak 2008), the shared co-constructed knowledge came from playing improvisationally together in small groups and 1:1 sessions and then talking about the experience immediately afterwards in order to arrive at a grounded definition of attunement. The discussions with all group members and individuals as well as the improvised sound experiences were then used to create poems and reflective paintings for each session. In this way I was hoping to capture the core knowledge that each participant had contributed toward understanding the phenomenon and essence of attunement. Taking this creative process one step further, after completing the poems and imagery, I then immersed myself back into the captured video and created a 30 minute (and subsequently a seventeen minute) summative video, with the intent of capturing the co-constructed meaning or co-constructed knowledge base.

The collaborative process that takes into account a co-constructed knowledge base is at the core of art-based research and must be understood in order to appropriately access and give feedback. If as an educator and art-based researcher, James Rolling proposes that art-based research is a naturalistic form of inquiry or a post-positivist response to 'the inadequacy of positivism', then this method must embrace a participatory co-constructed way of 'knowing and understanding the world we live in' (Kossak 2013: 23–24).

The importance of clarity in the method

As emphasized throughout this discussion on assessment and feedback, a large and essential part of the art-based researcher's job is to explain, elucidate and rationalize as clearly as possible the argument for using this method, as well as writing in as clear a manner as possible as to what happened in the research and how the results offer greater insight, awareness and understanding into the subject at hand in a way that other methods would not. The method in any study becomes the guidelines or roadmap that gets the researcher as well as the reader from point A to point B, or from the experiment used to the results and conclusions. If the method is unclear, then there is clear potential to get lost along the way.

In art-based research, perhaps because of the many misunderstandings that can lead to conscious or unconscious bias from the larger community, the depiction of the method used needs to be simple and clear from the beginning. Some specific critiques I have heard from my doctoral students who have reviewed art-based studies had to do with the lack of clarity regarding how the information gathered was going to be analysed, sorted or explained. However, more encouraging critiques noted how important it was when the overall appropriateness of the design was well supported with organized literature reviews and sound methodological reasoning.

It is also important and essential to keep in mind that the artwork must reflect what the research question is asking. The research question in any study must be clear and must be the central seed that guides the process. Many researchers I have worked with and studies I have read lose the essence of the research question itself. My doctoral students consistently give the feedback that either the research question in a study was unclear, or the research question was not answered with the method used. Another critique is that there were too many questions and when reading the study there is the sense of feeling lost, confused and unclear as to what exactly the researcher was getting at. I always encourage those I supervise to ask one essential question. As one committee member on my doctoral research warned me quite correctly, one question will begin to mushroom out into many facets, ideas and information. As with most research, simplicity will always lead to complexity. The clarity of the research question is very important to keep in mind when doing any kind of research, but perhaps in art-based research it is essential to keep things clear and simple.

Issues of clarity can also be attributed to the art-based researcher trying to fit in other methods because as previously mentioned they feel that the academy or the so-called 'authority' might not really understand art-based methodology. Researchers who are attempting to utilize an art-based approach often feel the need to make it more 'legitimate' by adding a quantitative measure. Others try to locate their method in a qualitative design, which does not necessarily correlate to art. Many of the art-based research studies are coming out of therapy-based or educational-based programmes that are positioned in social science paradigms. The methods of social science are very useful; however, mixing the two methods can diffuse the multi-layered knowledge that the art is communicating. As Shaun McNiff reminds us, art cannot always be reduced to social science analysis and codes. McNiff states that art itself does not lend itself to themes and data but rather needs to be described through observation of 'characteristics, features, aspects, principles, ideas, patterns, structures, designs, compositions and similarities and differences' (McNiff 2015: 30). Feedback I have received from students reviewing art-based studies indicates that by skirting the lines between trying to please too many constituencies the study often begins to lack any coherent focus.

By not fully embracing the art in the art-based study one runs the risk of diluting the results or confusing the reader. By trying to do too much, art-based studies can often become overcomplicated and unclear in the end. If the research question is too broad the information gathered from the study will be too diffuse, and asking too many questions can lead to unclear results. As Ardra Coles and Gary Knowles remind us, 'A rigorous arts-informed "text" is imbued with an internal consistency and coherence that represents a strong and seamless relationship between purpose and method (process and form)' (2008: 66–67).

Final thoughts

Assessment and feedback in art-based research depends first and foremost on understanding the nature of the method. As outlined above, this method is often misunderstood and bias is brought to the process of assessment because of preconceived ideas regarding art itself as a valued process toward gaining new knowledge in a unique language that goes beyond linear thought processes and toward a more holistic and embodied creative intelligence. Art-based studies have distinct qualities and must be evaluated and assessed through this uniqueness. Inherent bias influences how any art-based research study will be assessed and any feedback given. Towards this end and despite these challenges, it is the responsibility of the art-based researcher to inform their audience as concisely as possible of the research question, the method, the literature in the associative fields of study and to represent the artwork in a clear and convincing way.

As an evaluator given the responsibility to assess and give feedback, it is my job to understand, perceive, observe, take in and make sense of what the researcher is attempting to examine. Some additional questions to consider when assessing art-based research might include:

- How is the ephemeral documented?
- What is the aesthetic element and what is important about the aesthetic?
- Is the aesthetic communicating and/or illuminating something important that words alone could not (as in interviews)?
- Does the art extrapolate, and as Maurice Merleau-Ponty (1962) poignantly said, make the invisible visible?
- Does the research reliably document, elucidate, clarify and communicate the importance of the art process and the meaning making that is presented?
- Does the research influence the researcher and participant(s) and/or the broader social contexts in new ways?
- Is the research transformative?
- Does the aural, poetic and visual language presented help to enlighten, explain, communicate and expand the overall knowledge base of what is being studied?
- Is the method clear?

And lastly and perhaps most important,

- Does the research illicit more questions than when the research started?

By creating a framework that stimulates thought, raises important questions and furthers inquiry, hopefully the *art* in art-based research will be recognized for its importance as a vital method unto itself in advancing the knowledge in the field.

References

Bauer, Martin and Gaskell, George (1999), 'Towards a paradigm for research on social representations', *Journal for the Theory of Social Behaviour*, 29:2, pp. 163–86.

Cole, Ardra and Knowles, J. Gary (2008), 'Arts informed research', in A. Cole and J. Gary Knowles (eds), *Handbook of the Arts in Qualitative Research: Perspectives, Methodologies, Examples, and Issues*, Thousand Oaks, CA: Sage, pp. 55–70.

Einstein, Tamar R. (2012), 'Sew it seams: Wearing the symbols of distant neighbors', *ProQuest Dissertations and Theses Global,* Lesley University, 289, http://ezproxyles.flo.org/login?url=https://search-proquest-com.ezproxyles.flo.org/docview/1251734559?accountid=12060. Accessed 8 March 2018.

Einstein, Tamar R. and Forinash, Michele (2013), 'Art as mother tongue: Staying true to an innate language of knowing', in S. McNiff (ed.), *Art as Research: Opportunities and Challenges*, Bristol: Intellect, pp. 181–90.

Franklin, Michael A. (2010), 'Aesthetic mind – meditative mind: Reflections on art as yoga and contemplative practice', *ProQuest Dissertations and Theses Global*, Lesley University, http://ezproxyles.flo.org/login?url=https://search-proquest-com.ezproxyles.flo.org/docview/762771865?accountid=12060. Accessed 8 March 2018.

——— (2013), 'Know thyself: Awakening self-referential awareness through art-based research', in S. McNiff (ed.), *Art as Research: Opportunities and Challenges*, Bristol: Intellect, pp. 85–94.

Gerber, Nancy, Templeton, Elizabeth, Chilton, Gioia, Cohen-Liebman, Marcia S., Manders, Elizabeth, Shim, Minjung (2012), 'Art based research as a pedagogical approach to studying intersubjectivity in the creative arts therapies', *Journal of Applied Arts & Health,* 3:1, pp. 39–48.

Giorgi, Amedeo (1985), *Phenomenology and Psychological Research*, Pittsburgh: Duquesne University Press.

Kossak, Mitchell S. (2008), 'Attunement: Embodied transcendent experience explored through sound and rhythmic improvisation', *ProQuest Dissertations and Theses Global*, Union Institute and University, http://ezproxyles.flo.org/login?url=https://search-proquest-com.ezproxyles.flo.org/docview/304833022?accountid=12060. Accessed 8 March 2018.

——— (2013), 'Arts based enquiry: It is what we do!', in S. McNiff (ed.), *Art as Research: Opportunities and Challenges*, Bristol: Intellect, pp. 19–28.

——— (2015), *Attunement in Expressive Arts Therapy: Toward an Understanding of Embodied Empathy*, Springfield, IL: Charles Thomas.

Lincoln, Yvonna and Guba, Egon (1985), *Naturalistic Inquiry*, Thousand Oaks: Sage.

McNiff, Shaun (2015), 'Philosophical and practical foundations of artistic inquiry: Creating paradigms, methods, and presentations based in art', in P. Leavy (ed.), *Handbook of Arts-Based Research*, New York: Guilford Press, pp. 22–36.

Merleau-Ponty, Maurice (1962), *Phenomenology of Perception* (trans. C. Smith), London: Routledge and Keegan Paul.

O'Donoghue, Donal (2009), 'Are we asking the wrong questions in arts-based research?', *Studies in Art Education: A Journal of Issues and Research*, 50:4, pp. 352–68.

Patton, Michael Q. (2002), *Qualitative Research and Evaluation Methods*, Thousand Oaks: Sage.
Polanyi, Michael ([1966] 1983), *The Tacit Dimension*, Gloucester: Peter Smith.
Prigogine, Ilya (1980), *From Being to Becoming: Time and Complexity in the Physical Sciences*, San Francisco: W. H. Freeman.
Prior, Ross W. (2013), 'Knowing what is known: Accessing craft-based meanings in research by artists', in S. McNiff (ed.), *Art as Research: Opportunities and Challenges*, Bristol: Intellect, pp. 161–69.
Rappaport, Laury (2013), 'Trusting the felt sense in art-based research', in S. McNiff (ed.), *Art as Research: Opportunities and Challenges*, Bristol: Intellect, pp. 201–8.
Rolling, James (2013), *Arts Based Research Primer,* New York: Lang Publishing.
Salner, Marcia (1986), 'Validity in human science research', *Saybrook Review*, 6:1, pp. 107–31.
Smeijsters, Henk (1997), *Multiple Perspectives: A Guide to Qualitative Research in Music Therapy,* Guilford: Barcelona Press.
Smith, Tammy (2013), 'Shall I hide an art-based study within a recognized qualitative framework? Negotiating the spaces between research traditions at a research university', in S. McNiff (ed.), *Art as Research: Opportunities and Challenges*, Bristol: Intellect, pp. 191–200.

Part 2

Developing Our Practice in Postgraduate Education

Chapter 6

Doing Art-Based Research: An Advising Scenario

Shaun McNiff

Artistic inquiry is a transdisciplinary process that can be applied to the full spectrum of life experience. Where the formal practice of art based research has generally emerged within the arts in education and therapy, these initiatives are in my view models for broader application. After publishing the first book on art-based research in 1998 and using the arts in therapy as a focal point, I was surprised and pleased to see how there was an immediate response and adaptation of the ideas and principles to many areas beyond therapy and education – fine arts, design, architecture, communications, psychology, politics, history, literature and other domains of inquiry. Support for this breadth of application is intended in everything stated here.

Within my field, which integrates the arts and psychology, there is a rich history of artistic inquiry by researchers, with C. G. Jung's early twentieth-century *Red Book (Liber Novus)* (2009) being one of the best examples, demonstrating how all of his fundamental methods of practice grew from this work. And today, the use of artistic expression to reflect upon and understand issues encountered in professional practice has become increasingly common in training, supervision and doctoral dissertations. In addition to using artistic expression as a primary mode of inquiry, doctoral researchers have engaged it to reflect upon and interpret research experiences and contents: forms to identify and articulate significant contents in interviews; body movement, painting, vocal improvisation and performance to establish empathy with the expressions and life conditions of others; video to hold and show the active process of creation; and various other modes of artistic reflection.

Since I cannot present a single model for doing art-based research due to the infinite variability of the creative process, I will create a hypothetical advising scenario to give a concrete sense of how I supervise others in formulating research questions and methods that will be the basis of a dissertation research proposal. I have learned that the crafting of a proposal is as important as the ensuing study, in that it informs everything that is done. Although fictional, the scenario integrates features of many research projects. In the interest of simplicity and clarity, I will try and create a straightforward and empirical example.

Infinite possibilities vs. standard procedures

In the Foreword to this book I define art-based research as the use of artistic expression by the researcher, either alone or with others, as a primary mode of inquiry. As I have repeatedly stated, I prefer to simply talk about all forms of systematic inquiry as 'research' (1998) rather than add to the increasingly long list of research types existent today in social science. The term 'art-based research' has emerged as a practical necessity to distinguish this approach from others and to make the case for artistic inquiry as a respected approach to research within academic settings.

Research begins with a question, and ideally methods are individually developed to explore it in the best possible way. However, there is a general assumption in academic communities that research will be conducted according to pre-established and approved methods. In contrast, art-based inquiry corresponds to the variability of the creative process in the arts with different media. Where science is based upon the determination of consistent and predictable outcomes within a logically controlled and exactly replicable process of inquiry, art does the opposite. Nothing is ever exactly the same, and artistic expression encourages uniqueness and infinite variation as in nature. The flexibility of artistic inquiry and especially its ability to hold complexity, subtle elements, emotions, and contradictions account for its capacity to access and explore often illogical human conditions, but these factors also present considerable difficulties for those seeking predictability and control.

Yet it is possible to write concretely about issues and features that permeate the range of possibilities. There are also in my experience, fairly consistent structural principles that include the formation of a research question and method of inquiry; the doing of the artistic experimentation alone and/or with others and the documentation of it; the artistic reflection on the experimental process; and the presentation of the research outcomes and artistic evidence in a format that captures the research process.

The research question and determining what will be done to explore it

The practical doing of artistic inquiry begins with the articulation of an essential question. The word 'question' is pervasive today in relation to research methods. I use the term here for the sake of consistency. However, the work does not necessarily have to begin with an interrogative structure. Research also explores issues, problems, situations, decisions and the perfection of methods of practice. When beginning a research project, I encourage the often-challenging task of creating a terse and clear starting point for the inquiry. The research question serves as the anchor for the complete process of experimentation, the documentation of it, and the presentation of outcomes. It is the organizing principle of the study and the basis to which the process should always refer and check itself for relevance.

After developing a preliminary sense of a foundational question that may have accompanying questions or sub-questions, I ask researchers to think about *what they will do* to explore it. *How will you research the question?* I discourage reference to the multitudinous and aforementioned typologies of social science research, which tend to complicate the process and take us away from empirical actions. As per my more general focus on the relationship between depth and simplicity, I encourage concise descriptions of methods at the start, with the assumption that we are trying to get a sense of how the research might be conducted and why this is a viable way of addressing the research question. I say 'might' because an artistic inquiry and art itself involve the emergence of significant discoveries and forms from the process of the work.

There have been situations in my experience where the research method changed significantly as a result of things that presented themselves during the inquiry that were not previously known. However, the preliminary sense of questions and methods stays largely intact for most people throughout the course of a study, although it is common to modify and adjust approaches based upon experimentation. Thus, researchers planning to work with other people often benefit by conducting the inquiry first on their own, as a solo experiment, to clarify and perfect methods.

In my work we give considerable time to identifying the research question and then establishing the research design or methods. I encourage empirically oriented research preferably focused on improving practice. Abstract concepts are minimized, and I support speaking in the first person in simple, clear, organic and natural language free of academic jargon, which can sometimes hold manifold biases and assumptions about the research process.

With doctoral dissertations, I emphasize how the creation of a clear method of inquiry is the scaffold for the total work. In generating a method statement, we focus on who, what, when and where questions. *What are you going to do? With whom? How many times? For how long? In what place or places? How will the work be documented? How will you reflect on what happened? How will you present the evidence and the outcomes? And why are you going to do it this way?* I do everything possible to encourage an organizational structure that does not become overly complex and unwieldy.

In keeping with what I myself emphasize about the spontaneous emanation of significant things through elemental movements (McNiff 2015), it might be asked: *Why not start to identify a research question by creating freely in a medium of choice without a specific direction and see what emerges?* In response, I encourage this open-ended exploration, but from a practical vantage point we do it earlier in the process of inquiry as a way of determining a research focus or perhaps during the study when feeling stuck or unsure (Forinash 2016). Even when people have a longstanding sense of what they would like to investigate, I encourage relaxing specific plans, which can be challenging for those who tend to quickly lock onto a concept. Invariably this helps to test the sense of direction. The original purpose may be reinforced, refined or altered.

The structures that I am describing are inherent and guiding forms of artistic action that allow new things to emerge. They are distinguished from the predetermination of content. For example, an artistic structure might be the development of a painting with certain colours, making a drawing by repeating particular marks and gestures or dancing with repeated movements. Structure supports and holds unplanned expressions distilled via the whole complex of the artist's history, thoughts, feelings, imagination, craft and aspirations in the present moment. Within a flexible and creative context, structure and spontaneity are reciprocal partners.

Designing a research proposal

A consistent concern in the work that I do as a practitioner-researcher is the creation of reliable and even fail-proof methods for helping all people, regardless of past experiences, express themselves authentically and successfully. Within the studio sessions that I lead, I invite participants to begin drawing or painting through repeated gestures. I ask them to simply move in the most elemental and sustained way, to let the body lead and thoughts follow. I say, if you can move, you can paint. We focus on the quality of the movement and not on the representation of something in the mind. The same applies to other art forms.

Let us imagine that my fictional advisee, Lee, an artist and arts therapist who is doing a doctoral dissertation, is interested in researching this process and we can use it to create a hypothetical art-based research proposal.

In practice any vital and valuable research direction will spin off endless possibilities from itself, and thus it becomes necessary to limit what question or questions will be explored in a particular study. A fertile research interest contains a lifetime of potential inquiry. With the people I supervise, I do the best I can to help them take a particular step in this direction, realizing that they cannot do it all in one study. As mentioned above, an empirically based question, as free as possible from conceptual abstraction, is the key to clear organization and purpose. Research methods are apt to follow organically from it. In our hypothetical advising situation, we discuss my exploration of how the East Asian idea of *ch'i* (material or vital force of creative energy) closely corresponds to the movement basis of expression (McNiff 2016). But we decide that it will be better to limit the inquiry and concentrate on physical actions in relation to both the process of expression and the resulting compositions, since more theoretical questions will generate a whole spectrum of issues.

We craft a research question and sub-question: *How does simple, movement/gesture-based drawing repetition influence expression? Does it further authenticity?* Although the primary question could be sufficient, there is a desire to focus on the issue of authenticity as a characteristic of what is experienced as satisfying. The emphasis on repetition is not about mechanical exactitude. It encourages variation and change but within the overall constancy of a rhythmic structure like breath or a sustained beat in music.

I believe the exploration of repeated gestures as the basis for expression can be applied to any artistic medium. For example, with voice and performance, a simple word, phrase or sentence can become the focus for exploring vocal range and intonation involving the whole body. Sustained movements can generate a dance and within the visual arts they can be used to sculpt with malleable wire or other materials. The issue of authenticity might also be explored with other modes of expression. And rather than focus on the sense of authenticity, studies might ask whether sustained gestures further empathy, change or a sense of the sacred. The research questions and directions emerging from this one example of sustained gestures are potentially vast. Our purpose here is to select a particular possibility as an illustration of how a method committed to researching a question can be designed.

In selecting a medium, we discuss the importance of discerning and documenting the physical gestures of the drawing process. We decide to use black markers of different sizes on large sheets of Bristol board paper with a minimum size of 18x24 inches. Charcoal could be an equally effective possibility, with greater ability to blend, but it is decided that limiting media will further continuity in this study. Although we typically make simple percussive sounds to support expression in studio sessions, this would add another element to the study and so sound will be restricted to the process of drawing.

Although a valuable and detailed research design can be created with the researcher working alone, there is a desire to involve others, both to expand the range of the experimental process and because Lee wants to develop experience and skills in working with other people. In keeping with past studies of a similar nature, we conclude that two to four people in addition to the primary researcher will potentially generate considerable content for the study.

Working alone

Before engaging others as participants and co-researchers, we feel that it will be helpful for Lee to personally experiment with a process that will hopefully serve as the basis for what will be done with others. Three sessions of approximately an hour of free drawing will happen on a weekly basis. Materials will be limited to black markers, with the ability to make lines ranging from fine to bold. The images will be movement-based, with the goal of building a composition through repeated and sustained line gestures. Every effort will be made to sustain whatever elemental gesture is first made (straight, curved, circular, jagged, etc.) and build a composition from it through ongoing marks, but, as mentioned above, variation is a natural extension of rhythmic expression. The artist will be encouraged to stay with the same image for a sustained time, possibly for the full hour. However, multiple images may also be made and in subsequent pictures the same gesture may be repeated or changed. It is felt that the primary emphasis on repetition is needed to prevent excessive self-consciousness, inhibiting judgements and distracting thoughts while keeping the expression grounded in natural movement.

A journal will be kept and used between the three sessions to record thoughts about the process in whatever medium seems appropriate, including free writing and visual imagery. After each session, journal entries will reflect on how the artistic experimentation informs the research questions.

I describe how contemporary art-based research tends to universally use video to record the process of the work, both with one or more cameras mounted on tripods and adjusted to focus on the image and gestures, and the artist wearing a device on the forehead to capture the hands and arms at work. We discuss how this documentation is crucial to giving a sense of the artistic process, the acts of creating, and the progressive emergence of the visual images.

As we continue to contemplate methods, we confront what I said previously about the extensive contents that are generated by the simplest research designs, especially when the questions concentrate on empirical acts recorded on video. We consider how to reflect on the sequence of three sessions, document what happened, and identify outcomes and discoveries.

In addition to describing and presenting the work in a written form, Lee is interested in not only carefully examining the video footage for insights into the research process but also creating an edited video to present evidence and outcomes. It is felt that creative expression is to inform the final presentation of the work as well as the process of inquiry.

Photographs will be taken of the final drawings. The images will show both the full compositions as well as details. As we continue to discuss the research methods, it becomes clear how this 'preliminary' exploration conducted alone can become a multifaceted inquiry in itself. In addition to the drawings and photographs of them and the journal, there is also considerable video footage. We discuss how important it is to view the entirety of the raw footage a number of times just as with the review of the journal. This can be likened to multiple reviews of recorded interviews in addition to studying transcriptions. A goal of the video review will be to establish a sense of empathy and responsiveness to the various qualities of bodily movement, pauses, heightened action, and other features that happen outside the scope of spoken language. We want to develop an aesthetic and felt-sense of the emergence and total impact of the drawing process. The footage also offers a wealth of possibilities for still images of the art-making process that can be used in the written text of the study as well as in the edited video presentation, both of which I recommend organizing in a way that most effectively addresses the research questions that anchor the study.

The examination of video footage in art-based research happens in the same ways that a filmmaker works during the editing process. We live with it for a period of time repeatedly viewing the contents. Whenever I watch video footage, I take notes on significance and poignant moments and mark their place in the timeframe. We have learned how a terse and carefully constructed video presentation tends to have a greater impact than a long one, and it is decided that a video of no more than seven minutes will interpret the three drawing sessions. The editing process will occur after completing the three sessions. All of the modes of inquiry will work together to generate a culminating form of artistic interpretation and integration. The editing process becomes a significant mode of artistic reflection, in that decisions need to be made as to what is presented, the sequence of content, and so forth.

I encourage art-based researchers to approach the video or filmmaking as a thoroughly artistic activity rather than feel the need to follow a linear narrative corresponding to the temporal sequence of the sessions. Arguably, the aesthetic impact of the video will significantly determine its influence on others and the assessment of the overall quality of the work. Artistic devices such as presenting multiple frames simultaneously, perhaps showing different versions of the same essential activity, can further both concision and breadth.

A written reflection on the artistic evidence and the study outcomes will respond to the video and all other aspects of the study. Words and text have an essential place in this study, but they are not exclusive modes of understanding and presentation.

Engaging others

After completing this process of inquiry alone, Lee concludes that the structure was effective in addressing the research questions and now prepares to engage other participants. It is determined that the essential methods will stay in place, but there will be the added element of Lee's presence together with the participants in four individual sessions. The original thought was to engage as many as four participants, resulting in a cumulative total of sixteen sessions with all of the resulting art and video footage – a total of nineteen when including the preliminary solo experimentation. I suggest that conducting these individual sessions with two other people, resulting in a total of eight sessions, will generate considerable research content, and we leave this question open at this point in the process of designing methods.

It is not yet clear as to whether or not it will be preferable to engage a mix of experienced art-makers and beginners or whether it might be more effective to involve just beginners. I express support for either approach, describing how both have their respective areas of interest and unique features. This again reinforces how a doctoral dissertation can be just the beginning of a career-long experimentation with the same essential questions.

In this next dimension of the experimentation, the research questions and core methods stay the same. The primary new issue that we address is Lee's presence as a guide and witness who coordinates the sessions, introduces the various research activities, and is available to answer any questions. It is decided that a minimum of spoken communication will happen while the co-researchers are making art. They will wear a camera on their foreheads and Lee will also record the art-making process with a small camera. A fixed camera will be placed on a tripod and will be focused on the drawing surface to act as a back-up, assuring full coverage of the drawing process. A separate audio device will be used during conversation to record the best possible sound quality for use in the edited video.

Most of the experimental process will be consistent with the earlier solo sessions. Major differences will include the presence of two people, one drawing and the other supporting the process, and discussion with both people, who reflect on the drawing process after it has been completed. This conversation will focus on the research questions and any other areas of interest or concern that may emerge organically. It will take place for ten to twenty minutes, resulting in a total session of approximately 90 minutes. The conversation will be transcribed. These procedures will be repeated in the three sessions. The research project with co-researchers will also differ from the preliminary study, in that there will be a fourth and final meeting with the co-researchers reflecting upon all of the drawings they made and viewing an edited five to seven-minute video made from footage of the previous three sessions. The audio-recorded discussion will explore how the experimentation addressed the research questions.

The experimental work will be documented and reviewed in much the same way as in the preceding solo experimentation. The transcribed conversations including responses to the shared viewing of the video will provide new elements. Lee will continue to keep a personal journal in response to each session. In addition, time will be taken after each session to respond artistically through the drawing process, making one or more pieces with the same materials in response to what was made by the co-researchers and the process of creating it. The process of Lee making drawings after each session will add a further dimension of artistic interpretation and reflection. These artistic responses could be video recorded, but it is decided that that this would add yet another dimension of content that could overload the study, demonstrating again how each phase of the experimentation can be a major work in itself. It is possible, however, that photos of Lee's artistic responses will be included in the edited videos in order to give the co-researchers a sense of this aspect of the reciprocal process.

As we finalize these procedures, it is increasingly clear that the scope of research contents and artistic expressions generated from everyone involved will be considerable, and Lee now appreciates the possible value of limiting the study to two or three additional co-researchers rather than four or perhaps conducting two drawing sessions rather than three.[1]

In addition to the experimental use of artistic expression to address the research questions, the methods described in both the solo sessions and those with co-researchers make significant use of art as a primary mode of reflection on the whole spectrum of research activities. Various forms of artistic inquiry identify and show the outcomes and discoveries of the research. But in our hypothetical situation we can imagine a colleague unfamiliar with these review methods asking from a social science perspective: How will you do the data analysis? What tools are you going to use to code the text and identify themes?

As the advisor, I reply that artistic reflection and interpretation will be the primary mode of understanding and discovery both when responding to artworks and in the making of them. We immerse ourselves in them as artists do in every medium, viewing the images repeatedly as both whole compositions and details, reading and re-reading the transcriptions of conversations and identifying what we feel are significant and poignant passages, patterns and aesthetic forms. Themes might be part of this but they are not the whole and they tend to introduce a narrative bias that again is an element but not the totality; thus, we speak about identifying patterns, qualities and essential elements, terms that reflect the breadth of artistic expressions. The process includes analysis as an aspect but not as a complete orientation since insights are also gained outside the frame of linear logic and the counting and coding of repeated words through a computer programme. Referring to all of the contents of the study as data tends to approach them as quantifiable substances and raw materials informing an analytic process. In our art-based research, the artistic expressions are more accurately described as ways of knowing and inquiry rather than data. They are dynamic and animated entities that continuously act upon us. And ultimately, they are presented as the evidence of the study.

The editing of the video perhaps exemplifies how artistic interpretation can be a selective shaping process informed by aesthetic factors that build, highlight and express themselves. So, if we have to give a one-word answer to how we will interpret, organize, and present our research, I would say *artistically*.

Consideration of the final form and mode of presentation

We discuss how the final form of the study will probably show all of the drawings created and possibly details from them, still images from the various sessions showing progressive moments in the making of the drawings, and a single new composite edited video presenting the outcomes and discoveries of the study. In condensing the extensive footage into a single concise presentation, it is felt that the objective of showing outcomes will guide the selection process. There will be a written description of the entire process, but it is anticipated that the photographs and still images of the drawings together with the video will be the primary and most convincing evidence supported by the written text. A gallery exhibit of the work might also be considered. All phases of documentation, presentation, and conclusions will consistently respond to the research questions – *How does simple, movement/gesture-based drawing repetition influence expression? Does it further authenticity?*

Summary

This sequence of questions and methods is a fiction, but it is a composite based on the actual things I do as a supervisor of research. Hopefully, it demonstrates how a research project involves making choices as to how to formulate specific and uncomplicated questions and then develop methods of inquiry to explore them. Perhaps it also shows how a good question is always connected to others and the need to make decisions about going in a particular direction that may sacrifice other areas of interest to be explored at another time. This illustration does not address processes for participant selection, Institutional Review Board ethical procedures within academic and professional settings, dealing with required IMRaD formats (Introduction, Methods, Results and Discussion), literature reviews and many other issues involved with the doing of research within higher education. Also, space does not allow discussion of important facets of art-based research that I have explored in other writings. These include letting art speak for itself as evidence (McNiff 2014a), presenting the work in ways that correspond to it (McNiff 2014b), the extent to which artistic skills are needed by researchers, and most essentially the paradigmatic distinctions between artistic and scientific inquiry (McNiff 2018).

Conclusion: A reality check

Within an artistic paradigm, research is composed of many vital things, all of which are interdependent and constantly influencing one another. Thomas Berry might have called this a creative communion within a spontaneous and expressive world 'shared by every being, not a world of objects' (2009: 88). In this respect we are in communion with not just other people but also with artistic expressions, materials and processes. Even when creating alone, the work is thoroughly interactive. Thus, I have repeatedly insisted that although art-based research has what is today called a 'heuristic' or completely personal dimension (1998), this is an aspect of the work and not the whole. A successful study generally concentrates on empirical and practical things as I have tried to show here and avoids any suggestion of self-absorption that blocks attentiveness to the interactions with others upon which all experience is based.

Kurt Lewin (1946) introduced the notion of research involving active participation in mutual relationships and dialogue with other people. This position is more aligned with reality than the assumption that other human beings can be researched as subjects by researchers operating from a vantage point of transcendent objectivity. Building on Lewin, Peter Reason (2003) and others have emphasized the mutual creation of experience between researchers and the people they engage in 'cooperative inquiry'. Contributing further to this perspective and adding the dimension of artistic inquiry, Warren Lett and his colleagues in Melbourne, Australia, have coined the even more intimate term 'companioning' (2016) for the relationship between a researcher and other people participating in a study. This usage underscores not only the co-creation of human understanding but also the reality of inquiry as an undertaking that is inseparable from the ongoing process of life created with others.

To assume that any study dealing with human experience inside or outside the realm of artistic inquiry can completely remove the personal dimension arguably contradicts the nature of reality since the personal is the ground and perspective from which each of us operates. In the human realm we create knowledge and inevitably this is done together with others both present and past.

References

Berry, Thomas (2009), *The Sacred Universe*, New York: Columbia University Press.

Forinash, Michele (2016), 'On supervising arts-based research', *Music Therapy Perspectives*, 34:1, pp. 41–45.

Jung, Carl Gustav (2009), *The Red Book* (trans. M. Kyburz, S. Shamdasani and J. Peck), New York: W. W. Norton & Company.

Lett, Warren (2016), *Creative Arts Companioning in Coconstruction of Meanings*, Melbourne: MIECAT Institute.

Lewin, Kurt (1946), 'Action research and minority problems', *Journal of Social Issues*, 2:4, pp. 34–46.
McNiff, Shaun (1998), *Art-Based Research*, London: Jessica Kingsley Publishers.
——— (2013), *Art as Research: Opportunities and Challenges*, Bristol: Intellect.
——— (2014a), 'Art speaking for itself: Evidence that inspires and convinces', *Journal of Applied Arts and Health*, 5:2, pp. 255–62.
——— (2014b), 'Presentations that look and feel like the arts in therapy: Keeping creative tension with psychology', *Australian and New Zealand Journal of Arts Therapy*, 9:1, pp. 89–94.
——— (2015), *Imagination in Action: Secrets for Unleashing Creative Expression*, Boston: Shambhala Publications.
——— (2016), '*Ch'i* and artistic expression: An East Asian worldview that fits the creative process everywhere', *Creative Arts Education and Therapy: Frontiers in China – An International Academic Journal for Research and Practice*, 2:2, pp. 12–20.
——— (2018), 'Philosophical and practical foundations of artistic inquiry: Creating paradigms, methods, and presentations based in art', in P. Leavy (ed.), *Handbook of Arts-Based Research*, New York: The Guilford Press, pp. 22–36.
Reason, Peter (2003), 'Doing co-operative inquiry', in J. Smith (ed.), *Qualitative Psychology: A Practical Guide to Methods*, London: Sage, pp. 205–31.

Note

1 Other art-based researchers have completed a protocol similar to what co-researchers do rather than experimenting alone at the start. A colleague might be invited to be a witness in much the same way as Lee acted with the co-researchers in this model. Thus, recorded conversations between Lee and the witness would take place after each of the artistic experimentation sessions. But there would also be inconsistencies, such as the somewhat peripheral role of the invited witness. Each approach has its relative strengths and here it was felt that it would be helpful to experiment alone and become more familiar with the process before engaging others.

Chapter 7

Research-Practice-Pedagogy: Establishing New Topologies of Doctoral Research in the Arts

Jacqueline Taylor

There are an increasing number of artists and practitioners entering the academe and undertaking doctoral research that incorporates practice. This increase has meant that the parameters of what research may mean and the forms it may take have been expanded as doctoral students in the arts work towards building new research paradigms that articulate its complexities, particularities and peculiarities. At the same time, there is an increasingly explicit agenda in the UK higher education doctoral landscape in which Universities are required to embed research training to support the development of their doctoral researchers. This discourse of Researcher Development primarily focuses on skills and research methods training and is often administered centrally by Graduate Schools (or equivalent) alongside localized subject specialist communities of practice. However, for doctoral students in the arts, there is a very real risk that such provision does not sufficiently acknowledge the specificity, slipperiness or complexities of artistic research and its relation to practice. Despite their tension with one another, this chapter purposefully and critically brings together the two discourses of art-based research and Researcher Development to support doctoral researchers engaging in artistic practice.

I draw on two ongoing and interrelated bodies of research: the first, research about doctoral research in the arts started nearly a decade ago as prompted by my own fine art Ph.D., and the second, research in relation to my pedagogic practice where I coordinate and develop Arts, Design and Media doctoral education in my institution. Rather than simply developing a programme of provision 'on the ground' to support those negotiating art as research, I argue that it is crucial to develop a conceptual framework that underpins how this provision is approached to create a meaningful dialogue between art-based doctoral research and Researcher Development discourses. In doing so, I hope to open up spaces of possibility and establish new topologies of doctoral research in the arts at the intersection of research–practice–pedagogy.

Typologies of doctoral research in the arts

Over the past twenty years, there has been an unprecedented increase in artists and practitioners undertaking Ph.D.s that incorporate practice, resulting in a rich and distinct discourse. Such work has expanded the very parameters of what research itself may mean, the forms it may take and has begun to establish new research paradigms that more fully articulate the complexities of research incorporating artistic practice. This complexity is encapsulated in the emergence of a wide variety of terms, or what Andris Teikmanis calls 'typologies' (2013: 163), such as practice-led research, practice-based research, art-based research, art practice as research, artistic research, research 'into', 'through' and 'for' practice, research-led practice and research by design, to name just a few.[1] These terms vary globally, by institution and discipline (even within the same institution). In addition, different terms are often used interchangeably and there are also a great many contradictions amongst the same terms. For example, Linda Candy defines practice-based research as comprising the creative artefact as the basis of a contribution to knowledge, by the means and outcomes of that practice, demonstrated in a doctoral thesis through creative outcomes (such as designs, performances, exhibitions) and textually with direct reference to those outcomes (2006: 3). By comparison, she identifies practice-led research as research that leads primarily to new understandings about practice that include 'practice as an integral part of its method' (Candy 2006: 3). Sarah Rubidge, on the other hand, notes that practice-based research is an umbrella term for academic research that incorporates artistic practice as a research methodology (2004). The UK Arts & Humanities Research Council (AHRC), the largest funder of doctoral research in the arts, in turn, defines practice-led research as 'research in which the professional and/or creative practices of art, design or architecture play an instrumental part in an inquiry' (Mottram et al. 2007: 11).

There is therefore no one definition of practice in relation to art as research, and those definitions that do exist have been subject to critique; for example, as being 'too loose a term to be useful' (Emlyn Jones 2006: 228). Indeed, in my own doctoral research that explored writing/painting and theory/practice relations, I used the term 'art practice research' to problematize hierarchical and dualistic relations between practice and research in practice-based and practice-led research. Instead, the concept of 'art practice research' was theorized as having an entangled relation between art practice and research in which the two functioned on the same epistemological level. Whilst there has been a drive to define such research in its various forms in order to legitimize it within the institution (Nelson 2013; Elkins 2013), there is concern that attempts to confine it to a set of descriptors does not recognize the many fields of practice it might encompass (Wilson 2008: 2) or may 'usher in a new orthodoxy as preferred interests and methods function to normalize practices' (Sullivan 2005). In recent years, 'practice as research in the arts' (PaRa) has also emerged as an all-encompassing term used across a variety of disciplinary and global contexts, yet there is a danger that such a broad term homogenizes the richness and complexity of artistic research. In the context of this book and throughout this chapter, I use the term 'art-based research' (McNiff 1998) to acknowledge the multiplicity of related terms or typologies in which the meaning attached to them is fluid. Rather than getting caught up striving towards a singular definition, or the specificity of particular terminology, I would like to propose that art-based research can instead be defined precisely by its resistance to be defined; as a heterogeneous, multi-layered, highly nuanced and fluid concept that comprises various complexities, particularities, peculiarities and possibilities, and qualities such as reflexivity, interdisciplinarity, emergence and performativity. In the context of the 'arts', this research might relate to a breadth of disciplines such as visual art, performance, dance, creative writing and design.

Taking into consideration the fluid and multifaceted nature of such research outlined above, it is both difficult and problematic to generalize on the position of practice in the context of the Ph.D. in the arts because of its highly individualized nature. Indeed, practice may refer to one's own artistic practice as a process of inquiry and a site of praxis. In some Ph.D. projects, practice *is* research and therefore cannot be easily disaggregated from the wider research project. Practice can equally *lead* to research, and 'scholarly' research to creative work. One's own practice may also result in 'outputs' such as object or performance-based works that are a crucial part of the research inquiry that may but do not always form part of the doctoral thesis. The art-based research Ph.D. may also manifest in ways more akin to the traditional Ph.D. thesis, but be directly informed by one's own artistic and/or professional practice activities or through imbricating oneself with another individual's practice (for example, artists, designers, curators, performers) primarily through 'theoretical' or 'historical' frameworks. Practice may also function *as* method. To add to this complexity, there is no one established method or approach to undertake such research. Indeed, those engaged in research in the arts have traditionally drawn from other disciplines and work within and against more traditional and entrenched paradigms such as the Social Sciences. The practitioner-researcher is often likened to a bricoleur, using a multi-method or polyvalent approach to overlap, intersect and interweave different fields and disciplines, and may, as Robyn Stewart notes, appropriate available methods, strategies and materials, or invent or piece together new tools as necessary (2007: 12). Art-based research requires a great degree of reflexivity as the methods it involves are 'necessarily emergent and subject to repeated adjustment, rather than remaining fixed throughout the process of enquiry' (Barrett 2007: 6). This resonates with the performative potential of such research, in which the practitioner-researcher tends to dive in and commence practising to see what emerges (Haseman 2006: 101–2). In all these cases, practice and theory adopt – or indeed enact – their own particular relation, but are more often than not complexly intertwined with one another in recognition that they form a non-hierarchal and dialogical relationship. Indeed, in my own doctoral research I developed a 'writing//painting' methodology that facilitated slippages and collisions between the two. Navigating this interrelation through mechanisms such as 'textstallations' (see Figure 1) that performatively mapped out and connected ideas amidst writing and painting, functioned as method – practising and thinking through – as well as writing and art practice.

The epistemological ambiguities of art-based research remain a contentious issue within the academe; often perceived as either elusive or incomprehensible as such research is not easily reconciled with more traditional notions of academic research (Nelson 2013: 4). In the context of the Ph.D., this is largely because one of the qualities of 'doctorateness' is that it is a contribution to knowledge and there is an expectation that such knowledge(s)

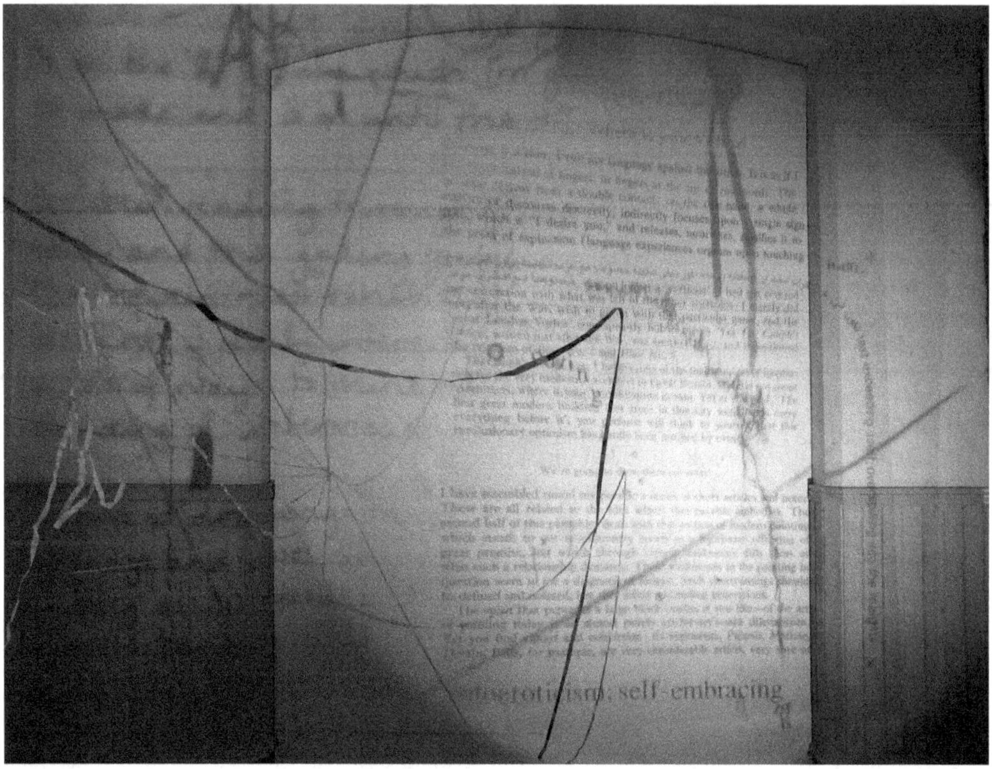

Figure 1: Jacqueline Taylor, detail of textstallation *Blisses of Materiality* (2011).

must be clearly communicable. However, in a similar vein to the performative paradigm Brad Haseman elucidates, a core aspect of what drives the creative process is that artists often 'begin something without knowing how it will turn out' (Fisher and Fortnum 2013: 7). Artistic practice instead produces knowledges that, as Kim Vincs suggests, happen in a 'unique material and specific way' that cannot generically be mapped onto other fields or works of art (Vincs 2007: 11). Rather, it can be perceived to be a form of 'material thinking' or 'praxical knowledge' that arises through the material handling in practice (Bolt 2007: 29). However, difficulties arise in articulating research where this tacit and slippery knowledge is embodied in process and visual, material and performative art forms, eluding normative signifying structures and communicative language.

In response to the predominance of text and theory in established research paradigms, those undertaking art as research have been increasingly invested in reconceptualizing the doctoral thesis itself to encompass material, visual, sound or performance-based elements and articulate the knowledge bound up with practice. Katy Macleod and Lin Holdridge's notion of the art practice Ph.D. comprising 'related objects of thought' is pertinent here, in that the doctoral thesis does not necessarily reside in the written text alone but is made up of 'multi-parts' and their relations that are a panoply of ways to deliver thought (Holdridge and Macleod 2005: 144). Writing may also function *as* method and/or practice and take different forms in the thesis; indeed, there are multiple examples of theses that develop alternative textual economies and illuminate the poetic, performative or experimental potential of language to more appropriately articulate art as research.[2] The delineation between practice, research, theory, method, output and dissemination is thus inherently intertwined, manifesting uniquely to its context. It seems that art-based research is underpinned by a tension between producing research that is robust, rigorous and valid, and yet at the same time retains its very qualities as a site of possibility. Rather than coming towards answers, this discourse, in fact, prompts more questions; it is instead what a colleague calls 'gloriously messy'. This presents a huge pedagogic challenge in how we may best support Ph.D. researchers in the arts dealing with these complexities, which I hope to address in this chapter.

Researcher training and development

The terrain of doctoral research in the arts – albeit a perhaps wild and unruly one – has emerged alongside an increasingly explicit agenda in UK higher education to support doctoral researchers by embedding research training. This was prompted by Gareth Roberts' government report 'SET for Success' in which he subsequently stated:

> The product that the PhD researcher creates is not the thesis – vital though that is to their subject area through the creation of original knowledge – no, the product of their study is the development of themselves.
>
> (Universities UK 2009: 17)

The resulting 'Roberts Agenda' highlighted a need to enhance training and development opportunities for research students. Whilst Ph.D. students do still very much work in isolation, this agenda promoted cohorts of researchers as doctoral learners, prompting a shift from the traditional doctoral experience as an almost exclusively solitary activity, with minimal supervisory meetings, over a long period of study and with high attrition rates. Supported by the UK Government and the Research Council UK (RCUK), funding was allocated to institutions to support this vision, informing numerous policies and research bodies to support doctoral researchers through what has emerged to become the discourse of Researcher Development.[3] The more recent third cycle of the Bologna Process (2009) has also been a key driver in advocating research training to increase the employability and human capital of Ph.D. researchers in the job marketplace through enhancing disciplinary expertise, transferrable skills and competences, as well as the application of knowledge.

As a government requirement, Researcher Development provision takes place in all UK universities. Whilst taking different forms it most often encompasses a core Researcher Development Programme usually administered centrally by Graduate Schools (or equivalent) alongside local subject specialist communities of practice. These programmes are informed – either explicitly or implicitly – by Vitae's Researcher Development Framework (RDF) (see Figure 2), a national framework that identifies the knowledge, behaviours and attributes needed to be a 'successful researcher' (Vitae 2010: 1). The RDF is structured into four

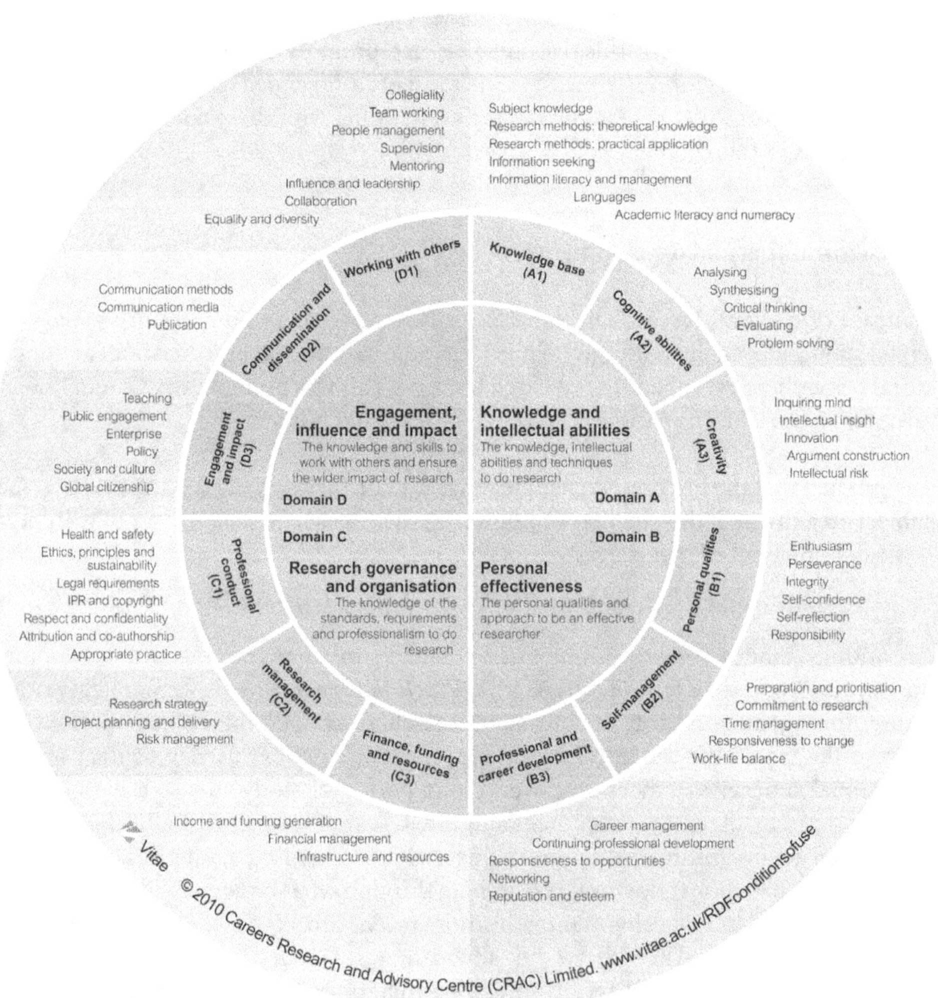

Figure 2: Vitae's Research Development Framework (2010).

domains: (1) Knowledge and Intellectual Abilities, (2) Personal Effectiveness, (3) Research Governance and Organization, (4) Engagement, Influence and Impact. These domains are then broken down into twelve sub-domains, across 63 descriptors, each with three to five phases representing different stages of development or performance, totalling 254 stages of development in the framework. Underpinned by these competencies, Researcher Development provision for Ph.D. students typically consists of skills training to enhance the 'productivity and capabilities of researchers' (Vitae 2013: 6), research methods training, employability and careers support as well as other areas of personal and professional development such as writing, ethics and funding. There is also a more recent focus on 'doctoral well-being' and developing cohorts of Ph.D. researchers to address the isolation experienced as part of the doctoral process. These areas have the potential to strategically contribute towards enhancing the university research environment by retaining Ph.D. researchers after completion and in the longer-term increasing the quality and quantity of research outputs. In turn, these inform both the UK's Research Excellence Framework and Postgraduate Researcher Experience Survey as indicators of success. Notably, the impetus on research *training* means that pedagogically, many Researcher Development Programmes tend to adopt a 'how to' approach, for example, training researchers *how to* manage information literacy, create an effective CV, build resilience and even be a part-time researcher.

I would argue that the ethos underpinning Researcher Development is indeed valuable and has great potential to enhance the doctoral experience and the development of Ph.D. researchers, including those undertaking art as research. From my own experience of working with doctoral researchers in a Faculty of Arts, Design and Media, many doctoral students in the arts do not enter the Ph.D. from a traditional academic background. Whilst they may come with a wide array of professional, creative and transferrable skills, other skills need to be learnt as part of the Ph.D. itself, such as critical thinking and reflexivity in negotiating art-based research itself. Many Ph.D. students in the arts also grapple with the entwining of multiple and sometimes conflicting roles (for example, professional, academic, practitioner and creative) all too easily encapsulated in the thorny hyphen of the identities artist-researcher, composer-researcher, designer-researcher and so on. In addition, many students undertake an art-based Ph.D. to enhance their own professional and career trajectory, and aspire to be what my colleague and I have called a 'para-academic', working both within and outside the academe on their own terms (Taylor and Vaughan 2016). Researcher Development thus has the potential to support doctoral students in the arts and equip them with the necessary means to address these challenges. However, as Paul Spencer and Neil Willey assert:

> Even for those supervisors and doctoral candidates who welcome developmental activities, these activities can still be perceived and experienced as separate to their research. Overall, there can frequently be barriers […] to the integration of the development and research activities that doctoral candidates undertake.
>
> (Spencer and Willey 2013: 12)

For doctoral researchers in the arts in particular, there is a very real risk that such provision does not sufficiently acknowledge the specificity, slipperiness, messiness or complexity of art-based research. Indeed, the recent AHRC Student Survey (2015) noted that generic and professional research skills training is perceived to be neither useful nor appropriate for Arts and Humanities researchers. Moreover, much research training is based on an assumption that researchers aspire to be academics and that certain tropes must be performed to successfully assume the identity 'academic'. For example, Rowena Murray and Evcrarda Cunningham (2011: 831–33) note that 'writing for publication is a feature of academic life' as researchers are expected to publish in journals and therefore developing these skills are crucial 'if academics are to make the transition to active researcher'. In this instance, an awareness of the potential that different modalities of writing, articulation and dissemination can offer *as well as* academic writing skills are needed to best support those engaged in undertaking art as research. It is therefore highly problematic to develop Ph.D. students to be 'successful researchers' when the definition of both 'successful' and 'researcher' are highly unfixed concepts that cannot be reduced to a set of descriptors.

New topologies of doctoral education in the arts

There is now a substantial body of literature on art-based research in its various forms. This has focused almost exclusively on examining what such research is, practice/theory relations, its methods and philosophical grounding. Literature also includes a multiplicity of Ph.D. case studies across a number of disciplines such as creative writing, dance, performance and visual art that explicate and articulate how the different aspects of art as research are played out. In more recent years, doctoral research in the arts has begun to be discussed pedagogically; however, this remains limited and has tended to focus on supervision and research methodology (Wilson and Schelte 2013; Nelson 2013; Ings 2014). Despite increasing critical discussion of Researcher Development, this tends to take place through practice-sharing in sector events and literature, but not on a philosophical, theoretical or conceptual level. Furthermore, whilst doctoral pedagogy more broadly has been discussed in the context of Ph.D. supervision and the Professional Doctorate (of which a marginal proportion are in the Arts and Design disciplines), there is limited discussion in relation to Researcher Development. Not only do the discourses of art as research and Researcher Development therefore have limited engagement with pedagogy, but I would argue that there is also a tension between the two and a resistance for them to be brought together. I would like to propose that in order to fully support doctoral researchers in the arts negotiating practice in its many forms, it is crucial that art-based research and Researcher Development paradigms are in mutual dialogue with one another.

My discussion here will be underpinned by ongoing research undertaken at my own institution in the Faculty of Arts, Design and Media (ADM). Prompted by the formation of ADM in 2014 from the merger of two smaller Faculties, this research includes a number of pilot projects and the development of ADM doctoral education more broadly for Ph.D. students working in and across its nine disciplinary schools of Acting, Architecture and Design, Art, English, Fashion and Textiles, Media, Music (the Birmingham Conservatoire), Jewellery and Visual Communication. Here, art-based research Ph.D. students do not exist in discrete and coherently formed groups easily discernable from those who do not negotiate practice. Rather, they are an abundantly heterogeneous group that embody the multifaceted, nuanced and fluid nature of art as research itself. Moreover, whilst such research has specifically emerged out of the artistic disciplines (most notably in fine art, dance, performance), there are also a large number of Ph.D. students engaging in practice in the areas of architecture, design, jewellery, fashion and media more commonly aligned with professional practice research paradigms. Such research places emphasis on practice as action inquiry in relation to professional contexts and is distinct from the more nuanced, complex and peculiar terrain of art as research as I have previously discussed, yet ADM Ph.D. students in these disciplines purposefully appropriate aspects of art-based research to further open up possibilities for incorporating practice.

To account for the diverse spectrum of research practice and proclivity to transcend disciplinary boundaries, provision for those engaged with practice research is purposefully enfolded within the wider doctoral education context at ADM. Rather than simply developing a Researcher Development Programme for these doctoral students 'on the ground', I have developed a conceptual framework that underpins how ADM doctoral education provision is approached. This conceptual framework is theorized as a multidimensional, heterogeneous, plural and fluid space that acknowledges that art-based research happens in a 'unique and particular way', to refer back to Vincs, and where students engage with a spectrum of practice also intertwined with praxis – that is, the lived experienced of engaging with practice. Conceiving of this conceptual framework as a topology enables it to be understood as comprising various components and interrelations that remain unaffected by flux amongst its parts. Here, particular aspects or values of Researcher Development have been adopted and woven into the very fabric of this topology. In doing so, I presuppose a shift from supporting those engaging with practice with research training per se to doctoral pedagogy that instead facilitates spaces of teaching *and* learning within this topology. This takes the form of a multiplicity of pedagogic activity that is performative, reflexive, fluid and emergent – underpinned by the very characteristics and possibilities of art-based research itself.

Alongside Ph.D. supervision and communities of research practice embedded in and across various schools, doctoral education at ADM incorporates a Postgraduate Certificate in Research Practice (Pg.Cert.) and what is conceived as 'The PGR Studio'. The Pg.Cert. is a ten-week course undertaken by all new Ph.D. students at the university. Whilst the Pg.Cert. is administered centrally within the university's Doctoral Research College, its content and delivery is entirely devolved to each of the university's four Faculties. Structurally, this is crucial as it affords the Pg.Cert. to be developed specifically for ADM Ph.D. students in ways both aligned with and functioning as part of the topology I have established and thus acknowledging art-based research and its nuances within the course. I am the lead for the ADM Pg.Cert., which I coordinate with two colleagues from different disciplines, together representing a range of – sometimes conflicting – perspectives that are vital in challenging any singular approach. The course is guided by a series of provocations that address various foundations and principles of research and practice, and simultaneously facilitate the continual (and sometimes uncomfortable) questioning of the nature of knowledge, and the articulation of the to-ing and fro-ing of knowing and unknowing embodied in negotiating practice/theory relations. Rather than attempts to teach researchers 'how to do' art-based research, which I would contend is a paradoxical task, given its very resistance to definition, there is an emphasis on facilitating students to come towards their own critically grounded ways of working.

The course is structured into three interrelated arenas of praxis comprising 'Principles of Research' and 'Principles in Practice', which take place over the first half of the course, followed by 'Methods in Practice' in the latter. The course then concludes with presentations by students that articulate and enact their own research practice. The first session of the Pg.Cert., 'How Do We Find Things Out?', facilitated by the Associate Dean for Research at ADM very much encapsulates the ethos of the course. Rather than a presentation about how we find things out, this session performs the complexities and possibilities of doing a Ph.D. through an uneasy series of questions that engenders understanding precisely through the co-constructed experience of getting lost and dealing with unknowing and uncertainly. It simultaneously brings to the fore complex issues, such as challenging assumptions, knowledge, truth, asking questions and what research is, as vital concepts to undertaking a Ph.D. It could be seen to enable students to learn about learning through learning to understand the Ph.D. and relate it to their own contexts. Crucial to this is that it also raises questions about authority, rules and power structures that implicitly play out in the session; these constructs are unravelled in a way that both students and staff emerge as being reframed as peers within a rich ADM research community. This particular session is then followed by my own session called 'Practice and Research' that enacts the aforementioned 'Principles in Practice'. Here, I problematize any singular and rigid definition of art-based research, and facilitate critical discussion of its complexities, possibilities and challenges as outlined at the beginning of this chapter through my own and others' work, in the wider context of ADM disciplines.

As there is no one established method or approach to undertake research in the arts, it is therefore problematic – if not impossible – to 'teach' research methods in this context. In the first instance, there is no one singular 'thing' to be taught or learnt, but arguably a key aspect of art-based research itself is in developing critically grounded methods and approaches to account for the specificities of practice and of unveiling, articulating and making sense of embodied knowledges in the individual Ph.D. project. Instead, 'Methods in Practice' sessions facilitate an 'exposure' to multiplicities of research practices, positions, approaches and paradigms. As Mick Wilson and Schelte von Ruiten note, in the context of art-based research there is huge value in:

> [t]he discussion of concrete examples of doctoral work and artistic practice that have an explicit engagement with ideas of research, knowledge and enquiry (e.g. What does this art practice do in this particular case? What knowledge is happening in this situation within art? What kind of knowledge work does this particular artwork or performance 'do'?).
>
> (Wilson and von Ruiten 2013: iv)

These sessions are delivered by a range of speakers, from fellow Ph.D. students to professors, which represent diverse ways of undertaking research in the context of ADM. These include more traditional approaches such as ethnography and interviews deliberately set alongside approaches that disrupt and expand conventions. For example, talks have included a performance-lecture enunciating writing as method, a cabaret enacting performative inquiry and the discussion of reflexivity when using 'glittery methods'. In this last example, an early career researcher discussed their recent art-based research Ph.D. that explored non-figurative queer art practice in which glitter emerged as a central artistic medium and conceptual framework. Rather than simply talking *about* how glitter functioned as a method in terms of slippage, (dis)orientation and embodiment, students were invited to take glitter from a small container that was passed around the room. In so doing, they enacted elements of the method itself by quite literally *becoming* glittery, as the glitter stuck to their clothes, hands and other surfaces. 'Methods in Practice' talks are followed by workshops that deconstruct, critique and question these ontologies of art-based research to enable students to work towards their own critically grounded new languages and typologies of practice. They also facilitate discussion about developing as a researcher and individual trajectories, experiences and aspirations. The Pg.Cert. can be seen to function as a threshold space for Ph.D. students at the beginning of their doctoral journey to (un)think what they think they know, raise vital epistemological questions in negotiating practice and theory and question what research itself may mean and become. On a conceptual level, this very much aligns with the topology of 'research–practice–pedagogy' I have previously set out in that the Pg.Cert. is constituted by the relations of its parts and is very much performative and reflexive in nature, in that it enacts the concerns it addresses, simultaneously shaping and being shaped by researchers themselves.

These values feed into the PGR Studio, which comprises more informal spaces of learning and teaching and non-accredited provision for ADM Ph.D. students throughout the remainder of their doctoral journey and indeed beyond. It is an experimental, creative and practice-based space that resonates across all disciplines in ADM, where studio can be an artists' studio, a design studio, a recording studio, a rehearsal studio or a writing studio. PGR refers here to Postgraduate Researcher, a term used in the sector. Initially formed with two colleagues, I coordinate the work of the PGR Studio, which encompasses a plurality of discrete activities as part of ADM's doctoral education provision to not only support and train researchers, but also enhance the Ph.D. community and experience, forming part of the topology I have discussed. Many of these activities started as smaller funded

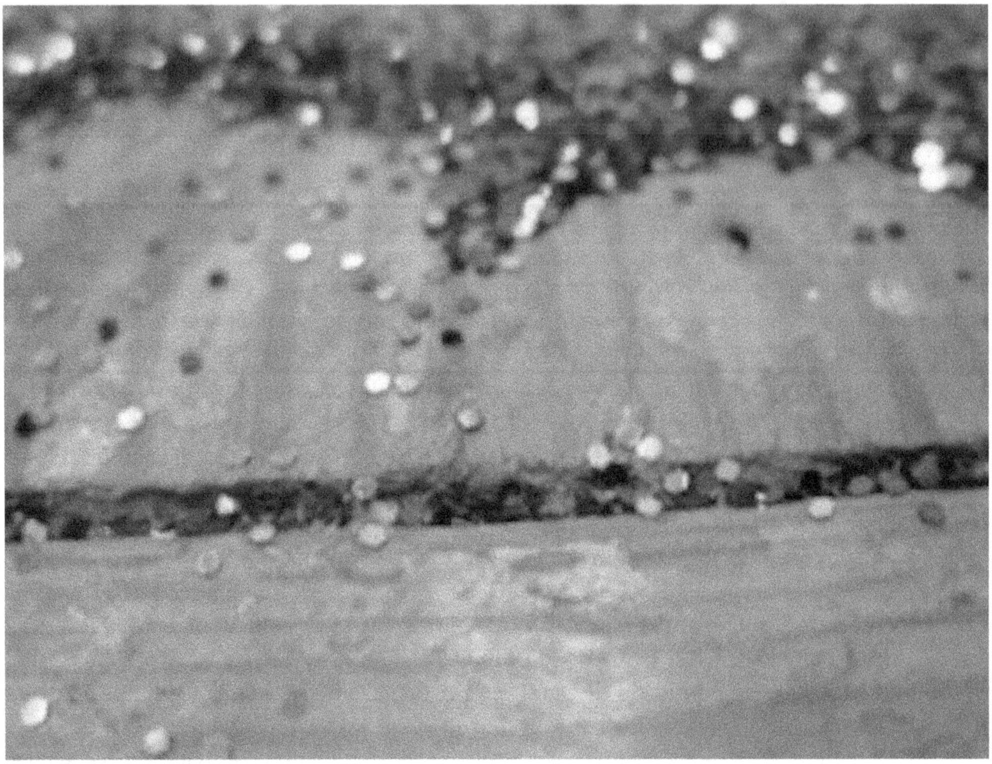

Figure 3: Lisa Metherell, detail of installation *Glitter* (2010).

pilot projects, including a peer mentoring scheme that places value on being organic, performative and creative (Boultwood et al. 2014), working with the education charity The Brilliant Club where Ph.D. students give university-style tutorials on their research in schools to widen access to highly selective universities, as well as an annual conference that seeks to dismantle traditional spaces of academia. In addition, there are a number of nomadic 'happenings' comprising social-oriented events such as walking, dancing and drawing that bring together students based on individuals' research practice. These take place alongside interactive workshops such as viva survival, experimental writing and in the past articulating research narratives through spoken word, where different concerns including well-being and 'career' support are addressed both explicitly and tacitly through practice and praxis. Crucial to the PGR Studio is an ethos of collaboration and community to bring together ADM researchers who are split across different geographical locations across the city centre. Ph.D. students are also employed each year as Research Assistants to be part of the team, and we work collaboratively with students to organize, develop and deliver events and activities so that they are informed directly by students themselves. Most importantly, provision is not developed specifically or exclusively for Ph.D. students who are engaged with art as research, but for all students in which aspects of practice are addressed in these activities, adapting reflexively to the needs and concerns of individuals.

Conclusions

The topology I have set out encompasses a multiplicity of spaces of teaching and learning; methodologically, conceptually, theoretically, epistemologically and ontologically through the intersection of what I have called research–practice–pedagogy. Resonating with Barthes in *Image Music Text* (1977) the researcher can be seen to mediate between spheres of teaching and learning, creating their own paradigms of development that inform the Ph.D. and what this may be as they become in this transitional and performative space. Rather than teaching or training Ph.D. researchers to be certain types of researchers or learning *how to do* particular skills or methods, emphasis is placed on *being* and *doing* themselves, in which knowledge and skills emerge through an expansion of understanding *as* praxis, embodied by the researcher. Opening up borderland spaces for art-based Ph.D. researchers amidst this topology and its pedagogic activities can enable the integration of academic, social, creative and professional realms where learning and self-efficacy can also take place through negotiating identity, belonging and different communities of practice, resonating with the artist-researcher or para-academic. What can be argued to be the very principles of art-based research itself, such as unknowing, performativity, reflexivity, fluidity, emergence and the experimental, can usefully function in dialogue with the values and ethos of Researcher Development as a way to establish topologies of doctoral education in the arts in which research, practice and pedagogy are intertwined. Fundamentally, this retains the richness, unruliness and possibilities of art as research yet supports researchers engaged in this discourse in a way that acknowledges different frameworks and requirements in the wider doctoral landscape.

References

Arts & Humanities Research Council (2015), *AHRC Student Experience Survey*, Swindon: AHRC, http://www.ahrc.ac.uk/documents/projects-programmes-and-initiatives/ahrc-student-experience-survey. Accessed 10 December 2016.

Bachelard, Gaston (1994), *The Poetics of Space*, 2nd trans. ed., Boston: Beacon Press.

Barrett, Estelle (2007), 'Introduction', in E. Barrett and B. Bolt (eds), *Practice as Research: Approaches to Creative Arts Enquiry*, New York: I. B. Tauris & Co. Ltd, pp. 1–14.

Barthes, Roland (1977), *Image Music Text*, London: Fontana.

Bolt, Barb (2007), 'The magic is in handling', in E. Barrett and B. Bolt (eds), *Practice as Research: Approaches to Creative Arts Enquiry*, New York: I. B. Tauris & Co. Ltd, pp. 27–34.

Boultwood, Anne, Taylor, Jacqueline and Vaughan, Sian (2015), 'The importance of coffee: Peer mentoring to support PGRs and ECRs in art & design', *Vitae Occasional Papers: Research Careers and Cultures, CRAC*, 2, pp. 15–20.

Candy, Linda (2006), *Practice Based Research: A Guide*, Sydney: University of Technology, http://www.mangold-international.com/fileadmin/Media/References/Publications/Downloads/Practice_Based_Research_A_Guide.pdf. Accessed 6 March 2015.

Elkins, James (2013), 'Six cultures of the PhD', in M. Wilson and S. van Ruiten (eds), *SHARE: Handbook for Artistic Research Education*, Amsterdam: ELIA, pp. 10–15.

Emlyn Jones, Timothy (2006), 'A method of search for reality: Research and research degrees in art and design', in K. Macleod and L. Holdridge (eds), *Thinking Through Art: Reflections on Art as Research*, Oxon: Routledge, pp. 226–40.

European Higher Education Area (2009), *Third Cycle: Doctoral Education, The Bologna Process*, http://www.ehea.info/cid102847/third-cycle-doctoral-education-2009.html. Accessed 15 January 2017.

Fisher, Elizabeth and Fortnum, Rebecca (2013), *On Not Knowing: How Artists Think*, London: Black Dog Publishing.

Frayling, Christopher (1993), 'Research in art and design', *Royal College of Art Research Papers*, 1:1, pp. 1–5.

Haseman, Brad (2006), 'A manifesto for performative research', *Media International Australia Incorporating Culture and Policy*, special issue, 'Practice-led Research', 118, pp. 98–106.

Holdridge, Lin and Macleod, Katy (2005), 'Related objects of thought: Art and thought, theory and practice', in M. Miles (ed.), *New Practices, New Pedagogies: A Reader*, Oxon: Routledge, pp. 143–53.

Ings, Welby (2014), 'Narcissus and the muse: supervisory implications of autobiographical, practice-led PhD design theses', *Journal of Qualitative Research*, 14:6, pp. 675–93.

McNiff, Shaun (1998), *Art-Based Research*, London: Jessica Kingsley Publishers.

Mottram, Judith, Rust, Chris and Till, Jeremy (2007), *AHRC Research Review: Practice-led Research in Art, Design and Architecture*, London: AHRC.

Murray, Rowena and Cunningham, Everarda (2011), 'Managing researcher development: "Drastic transition"?', *Studies in Higher Education*, 36:7, pp. 831–45.

Nelson, Robin (2013), *Practice as Research in the Arts: Principles, Protocols, Pedagogies, Resistances*, London: Palgrave Macmillan.

Newman, Hayley (2001), 'Locating performance: Textual identity and the performative', Ph.D. thesis, Leeds: University of Leeds.

Perry, Gaylene (2000), 'Water's edge and the Water's edge writing', Ph.D. thesis, Victoria: Deakin University.

Price, Elizabeth (2000), 'Sidekick', Ph.D. thesis, Leeds: University of Leeds.

Roberts, Gareth (2002), *SET for Success: Final Report of Sir Gareth Roberts' Review*, London: HM Treasury, http://webarchive.nationalarchives.gov.uk/20130129110402/http://www.hm-treasury.gov.uk/ent_res_roberts.htm. Accessed 8 June 2016.

Rubidge, Sarah (2004), *Artists in the Academy: Reflections on Artistic Practice as Research*, Australian Arts Council, http://ausdance.org.au/articles/details/artists-in-the-academy-reflections-on-artistic-practice-as-research. Accessed 21 February 2017.

Schön, Donald (1983), *The Reflective Practitioner: How Professionals Think in Action*, New York: Basic Books.

Smith, Hazel and Dean, Roger (2009), *Practice-led Research, Research-led Practice in the Creative Arts*, Edinburgh: Edinburgh University Press.

Spencer, Paul and Willey, Neil (2013), 'Using research-based learning to enhance doctoral skills development', *The Impact of Researcher Development, Vitae Occasional Papers*, 1, pp. 12–14.

Stewart, Robyn (2007), 'Creating new stories for praxis: Navigations, narrations, neonarratives', in E. Barrett and B. Bolt (eds), *Practice as Research: Approaches to Creative Arts Enquiry*, New York: I. B. Tauris & Co. Ltd, pp. 123–34.

Sullivan, Graeme (2005), *Art Practice as Research: Enquiry in the Visual Arts*, London: Sage.

Taylor, Jacqueline (2013), 'Writing//painting; *l'écriture féminine* and difference in the making', Ph.D. thesis, Birmingham: Birmingham City University.

Taylor, Jacqueline and Vaughan, Sian (2016), 'A different practice? Professional identity and doctoral education in art & design', in V. A. Storey (ed.), *International Perspectives on Designing Professional Practice Doctorates: Applying the Critical Friends Approach to the EdD and Beyond*, London: Palgrave Macmillan, pp. 127–42.

Teikmanis, Andris (2013), 'Typologies of research', in M. Wilson and S. van Ruiten (eds), *SHARE: Handbook for Artistic Research Education*, Amsterdam: ELIA, pp. 162–69.

Universities UK (2009), *Promoting the UK Doctorate: Opportunities and Challenges*, London: Universities UK, http://www.universitiesuk.ac.uk/policy-and-analysis/reports/Documents/2009/promoting-the-uk-doctorate-challenges-and-opportunities.pdf. Accessed 20 May 2017.

Vincs, Kim (2007), 'Rhizome/MyZone: A case study in studio-based dance research', in E. Barrett and B. Bolt (eds), *Practice as Research: Approaches to Creative Arts Enquiry*, New York: I. B. Tauris & Co. Ltd, pp. 99–112.

Vitae (2010), *Researcher Development Framework*, Cambridge: Careers Research and Advisory Centre (CRAC) Limited.

____ (2013), *Transforming Professional Development for Researchers: Vitae Achievements 2008–2012*, Cambridge: Careers Research and Advisory Centre (CRAC) Limited.

Wilson, Mick (2008), *The 'State of Play' in Practice-led Research in Art, Design and Architecture*, Brighton: AHRC/CHEAD.

Wilson, Mick and van Ruiten, Schelte (eds) (2013), *SHARE: Handbook for Artistic Research Education*, Amsterdam: ELIA.

Notes

1 See AHRC (2007); Barrett and Bolt (2007); Frayling (1993); Macleod and Holdridge (2007); McNiff (1998); Smith and Dean (2009); Sullivan (2005). Frayling's notion of research 'through' art practice is particularly noteworthy as he first placed emphasis on the potential of art as research.

2 Examples include Hayley Newman, 'Locating performance: Textual identity and the performative' (2001); Elizabeth Price, 'Sidekick' (2000); Gaylene Perry, 'Water's edge and the Water's edge writing' (2000); Jacqueline Taylor, 'Writing//painting; *l'écriture féminine* and difference in the making' (2013).

3 UK-based research policies and organizations include the Arts & Humanities Research Council, The Concordat to Support the Career Development of Researchers, Higher Education Academy, Research Councils UK, Quality Assurance Agency and Vitae.

Chapter 8

The 'Epistemic Object' in the Creative Process of Doctoral Inquiry

Carole Gray, Julian Malins and Maxine Bristow

Within the framework of practice-led[1] doctoral research in the art and design sector, there has long been debate about the role of the artefact/creative works in the process of inquiry and in the final submission for Ph.D. examination. Their status can be ambiguous and the concept of 'exhibition' is – we would argue – problematic in this context.

Therefore, we want to suggest an alternative way of considering the role of artefacts/creative works in a doctoral submission, by discussing the liberating concept of 'epistemic objects' – their possible forms and agencies, and the alternative display/sharing of the understandings generated from these through 'exposition' not exhibition.

Whilst our experience and expertise lies within the sector of art and design, we suggest that some ideas in this chapter may resonate and be relevant to other creative disciplines in the revealing and sharing of doctoral research outcomes. This process can be difficult and provoke many anxieties for the practitioner-researcher and their supervisors, so some clarity on this might help everyone involved in the examination of doctoral work to approach it with integrity and confidence, and see it as a valuable learning experience for all involved.

From exhibition to exposition

In 1992, Allan Watson completed one of the first practice-led Ph.D.s, for which one of the co-authors of this chapter was the main supervisor. Watson's thesis, as argument, comprised:

- new three-dimensional work generated by choice and chance;
- a digital database of concepts, processes and materials called ARP – Art as Random Process;
- an illustrated written text articulating the process of inquiry, its context and contribution to knowledge.

The Ph.D. examination partly took place in a studio, where the artefacts created through this inquiry were displayed.

These artefacts visualized and embodied the research concepts, and most importantly enabled a direct, almost somatic, experience of his argument through materials in space. For

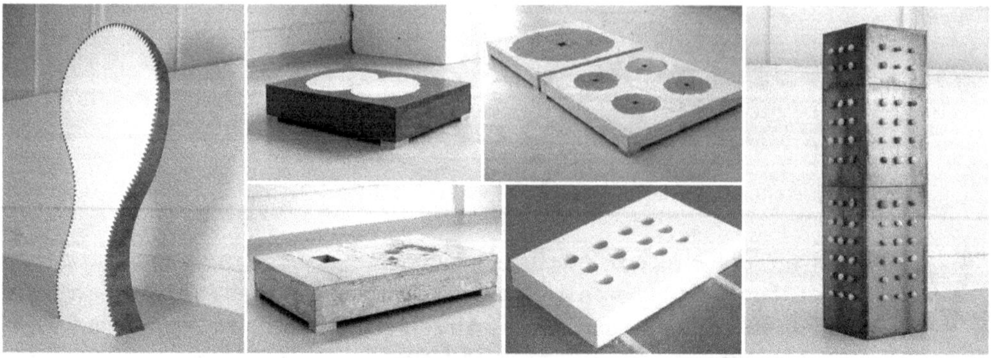

Figure 1: Artefacts presented in a studio setting (Source: Allan Watson 1992).

want of appropriate language to name this display, the candidate and supervisory team fell back on the known word 'exhibition' – although we knew intuitively this was something else.

It was not until eleven years after Watson's Ph.D. completion (and numerous others) that the first serious consideration of the role of the artwork in research was undertaken. In 2003 Michael Biggs proposed that in order to communicate this effectively, control must be exercised by providing a context for viewing/engaging. Biggs studied archaeological and museum display strategies, and drew on Peter Vergo's writing about *The New Museology* (1989). Vergo contrasts 'aesthetic' exhibitions with 'contextual' exhibitions. The former might have minimal additional information other than the artefacts themselves, and the process of understanding them is largely experiential and personal. In the latter artefacts are complementary to some accompanying 'informative, comparative and explicatory material' (Vergo 1989: 48). Biggs says:

> If the aim of research is to communicate knowledge or understanding then reception cannot be an uncontrolled process. The interpretation of embodied knowledge presented in an un-contextualised way is an uncontrolled process.
>
> (Biggs 2003: n.pag.)

Therefore, clearly in a doctoral submission the context for a display of artefacts and its careful construction and control is crucial in its reading and reception. Vergo's concept of contextualized display was given a new digital publishing framework through the establishment of the online *Journal for Artistic Research* (2011). The contributions to the journal are named as 'expositions', in an attempt to get away from the orthodox notion of 'article' or 'paper'. Examples in the various journal issues to date take a range of formats – most highly visual and some interactive, accompanied by appropriate written material. Similarly the *International Journal of Education Through Art* publishes 'visual essays', which attempt to communicate inquiries through annotated visuals.

In the context of creative doctoral inquiry, the term 'exposition' seems very appropriate, as its suggestion of exposure and explication matches very well the key characteristics of good research – accessibility, transparency, transferability (in principle if not specifics). Anne Douglas suggests that an exposition should reveal 'stages of research thinking, diagrammatic mapping of the evolving research process and its evidence in product, evidence of failure and changes of direction' (Douglas 1997: 20). Exposition events might be a regular feature throughout the doctoral inquiry, thus helping to acquire and exercise the skills needed later in the doctoral submission for Ph.D. In contrast to the 'exhibition', if we accept that the role of 'exposition' in creative inquiry is the revelation of methodology – the laying bare of the process of inquiry – then this does not necessarily require the display of completed or resolved artworks.

We would argue that in the process of any inquiry, it is crucial to track and capture (through various means) starting points, developments, changes of direction, critical moments of understandings and misunderstandings, and analytical reflections. There might be a spectrum of artefacts generated – some significant, some modest, some even deemed as 'failures' – as Paul Feyerabend writes in his book *Against Method*, 'failures are pre-conditions of progress' (Feyerabend 1998: 164). This spectrum of artefacts might visualize, materialize, embody, speculate on aspects of understandings about the focus of the inquiry. If these artefacts are not 'artworks' – what are they?

'Epistemic things'

Hans-Jörg Rheinberger gives us the liberating term 'epistemic things'. A focus of his 1997 book is the basic question of how novelty is generated in the empirical sciences. He argues for the primacy of the material arrangements of the laboratory and develops a new epistemology of experimentation, in which research is treated as a process for producing epistemic things. In a more recent book he says: 'An experiment [...] is an exploratory movement, a game in which one plays with possible positions, an open arrangement' (Rheinberger 2010: 247). For an epistemic object to have the potential to develop scientific research, it must embody a degree of uncertainty to be useful. He asserts that epistemic things 'are by nature made to be surpassed' (Rheinberger 2010: 222).

The sociologist Karin Knorr-Cetina has carried out long-term (over 30 years) studies at CERN Switzerland, examining how theoretical physicists worked with each other (Merali 2010). Knorr-Cetina identified the laboratory as the site of knowledge making. Later in her 'Objectual Practice' chapter (2001), her argument is expanded and the term 'epistemic objects' elaborated. These are described as being characterized by the ambivalence of their ontological status as knowledge bearers, being both stable and mutable at the same time. They are stable in the sense that they comprise what the inquirer currently knows so far; and mutable in the sense that they are incomplete and 'open', allowing for further exploration by the creator and/or others towards new knowledge making. Francis Crick and James

Watson's 1953 materialization of the structure of DNA using a retort stand, metal plates and rods joined with electrical connectors might be considered an epistemic object.[2]

This openness or 'lack in completeness of being' gives the epistemic object a 'capacity to unfold indefinitely' (Knorr-Cetina 2001: 181). There are resonances here with what Umberto Eco in 1962 called 'the open work', in that openness encourages engagement and interpretation. However, it does not mean that the originator (practitioner-researcher) relinquishes all control, rather s/he presents a framework within which various insightful encounters might occur (and this is taken up later in the chapter in relation to doctoral exposition).

An architecture company was the focus of Boris Ewenstein and Jennifer Whyte's study of knowledge practices in design (2009). In close observation of architects working together, the authors identified various forms of epistemic objects, from abstract concepts to concrete things; including sketches, drawings, plans, charts, photographs, project management tools – timelines, schedules, tables, virtual prototypes, scale models, and even machines and parts. They say that '[t]he object's effectiveness is defined by the context in which it needs to perform' (2009: 4). The way the team of architects worked with epistemic objects involved multiple iterations, re-workings, layerings – 'a veritable palimpsest of ideas and exploratory markings' (2009: 21). In this particular context, epistemic objects were enabling the negotiation and mediation of knowledge from different participants.

A more recent example of this process comes from Julian Malins' and Nil Melehat Gulari's design research generating innovation in small-to-medium enterprises (2011). In focus groups, individual employees select 'core value' cards – a given set of random images – to visually express particular values that they each associate with their company. This often reveals divergent perceptions of corporate identity and perceived goals, thus prompting discussion. Then through group dialogue around the images, each group negotiates an agreed set of core values, reflecting possible new future strategic company aspirations towards innovation. Depending on the group dynamics and different individuals who take part, the underlying context for this process is 'open' and constantly changing, thus providing opportunities for new thinking.

Christof Richter and Heidrun Allert's research (2011) highlights the epistemic roles artefacts play in creative design and knowledge creation, in this particular example – engineering and design education. As in the architectural example, they identify similar forms of epistemic objects: notes, sketches, models, prototypes, simulations and storyboards. Richter and Allert assert that 'the epistemic role of artefacts is under-articulated and often limited to the idea of artefacts as mere carriers and representations of information' (2011: 103). Rather, they propose that artefacts should be understood as 'epistemic instruments capable to frame, explore, catalyse, inquire [...] probe and assess ideas' (2011: 103). So the role of such 'knowledge artefacts' is not to represent what is already known, but on the contrary, to come to terms with what is not yet known. The epistemic object is defined by what it is not (or not yet) as much by what it is.

They cite Henrik Gedenryd's 1998 Ph.D. thesis, in which the term 'inquiring materials' is introduced as the capacity of artefacts to generate new insights and in themselves be 'productive things'. In this respect Antonio Gaudi's stereostatic model for the Crypt of the Church of Colonia Güell (1898–1914) brought together a set of inquiring materials – a wooden board, cords, cloth, pellets, photographs. From each catenaric arch (formed by hanging the cords from the board) small sacks of pellets were suspended. The structure was photographed. The final shape of the church's future architecture was revealed by turning one of the photographs upside-down – indeed a productive thing.[3]

Finally, Henk Borgdorff explores 'Artistic practices and epistemic things' (2012) that is the result of a conversation with Hans-Jörg Rheinberger. Picking up on the latter's ideas about the dynamics of experimental scientific practice, Borgdorff considers how knowledge is constituted in and through practice in the context of artistic discovery. He says: 'Epistemic things are [...] hybrid forms in which thinking and things are interwoven' (Borgdorff 2012: 191). This has resonances with Paul Carter's ideas in his book *Material Thinking* (2005). Focusing on the processes of creative/artistic collaborations, he uses the term 'cross-weave of thought' (2005: 5) out of which emerges a third apprehension, constituting 'material thinking'. This concept recognizes the 'creative intelligence of materials' (2005: xiii) in which 'matter becomes mobile' (2005: 182) and is 'promiscuous, eager for recombination' (2005: 188). Borgdorff (2012: 194) also considers artworks to be 'generators of that which we do not yet know' inviting us to think and thereby are epistemic agents.

Recent thinking on the concept of exposition

With these important contributions in mind, we now want to return to the concept of exposition as a means of revealing the process of inquiry for a doctoral submission. In their book *The Exposition of Artistic Research. Publishing Art in Academia*, Michael Schwab and Henk Borgdorff put forward a new relationship to knowledge, where 'the form in which this knowledge emerges, and the mode in which it is communicated, makes a difference to what is known' (2014: n.pag.). Focusing on the possibilities for publishing, the book offers perspectives on 'exposition' from a range of practitioners and thinkers in art and the performing arts (e.g. music, dance, drama, etc.) on various approaches to exposing 'practice as research'. Building on this, in the editorial of issue 7 of the *Journal of Artistic Research* (JAR), Schwab offers a description of exposition that we cannot better, so we quote it extensively here:

> Exposition is an introduction. Exposition need not tell what something is; rather, it can set the ground for a play to follow, which can be open-ended and need not be concluded in the publication itself.
>
> There is a didactic element to the notion of exposition, as far as it teaches how and as what something may be seen without determining outcomes. One may even say that there is

> something inherently gentle to exposition considered as introduction, a relief, perhaps, from the obligation of being a 'work of art', in the serious sense of the word.
>
> Although introduction suggests discursiveness, what is meant here is not so much explanation but a willingness to share materials and modes of thinking and doing.
> (Schwab 2015: n.pag.)

This gives us an excellent idea of what the purpose of an exposition might be: a laying of the 'ground', an opportunity for exploration; 'gentle' in nature, it suggests a necessary humility; the sharing of thinking processes and the revealing of methodology; and perhaps most importantly it invites participation in order to enrich and expand understandings from the inquiry.

If this is the purpose of an exposition, then Henk Slager gives us a possible metaphoric structure for it. He identifies the use of archives as a currently used display format for practitioner-researchers exploring 'art as research' and its presentation as knowledge (see *Critique of Archival Reason* exhibition curated by Slager 2010). In analysing new work by research-oriented international artists involved in this exhibition, Slager identifies that these particular works 'in different ways cut against the conventions of archival display'. In his chapter 'Counter-Archival Dissemination', he says: 'Research-oriented artists currently produce rhizomatic presentation models while presenting various constituitive segments such as photographic material, drawings, performances, video and texts in a fluent integral manner' (Slager 2014: 141). This rhizomatic model offers an excellent vision of how a doctoral exposition might be structured and materialized.

Exposition – recent Ph.D. examples

We have had some difficulty in finding good examples of doctoral expositions. Certainly in the United Kingdom, most Ph.D. examinations are still private events, so any attempts at exposition usually remain within that event, unless the candidate chooses to make a public presentation of work before and/or after the examination. Many expositions go undocumented, are not archived and tend to be inaccessible. However, some excellent examples of doctoral research in progress and completed can be found in Henk Slager's curated exhibition *Nameless Science* (2008–2009). Matts Liederstam's Ph.D. 'See and seen: Seeing landscape through artistic practice' (completed in 2006) comprised an exhibition, a web site and a text. For the exhibition – still so named – a model of the space was created. Liederstam designed tables for studying the materials presented, and placed optical instruments on the tables to enable the viewer to actually experience the act of looking. The installation guided the viewer from one experience to the next, and involved the viewer in a negotiation process that constructs the way pictures are perceived in art history. This is clearly a carefully structured and user-friendly encounter with research for the viewer/participant, enabling Liederstam's argument to be experienced directly.

Maxine Bristow's doctoral research (completed 2016) included an 'attempt' at an exposition – *Attach/Detach*, sited in the Contemporary Art Space Chester, UK. Her inquiry aimed to re-position her practice from a historical allegiance to the medium specific conventions of textiles to the current 'post-medium' condition of contemporary art – in her case through a sculptural/installation practice. Drawing on Theodor Adorno's notion of the 'constellation' (Adorno 2007: 162), she conceived the thesis, including an exposition, as a series of interrelating theoretical, methodological, contextual and practice-based 'components'. The significance of the constellation is that 'it allows sensuous resonances to intuitively emerge and conceptual connections to be temporarily illuminated but they remain fluid and are not categorical understandings' (Bristow email to co-authors, 31 December 2016).

Bristow's 'constellatory' exposition included:

- A collection of individual 'thingly'[4] sculptural elements conceived in a way that could be configured and reconfigured within a series of staged *mise-en-scène*. Offering the opportunity for continual rearrangement, the physical form of the work remains essentially mutable. Meaning is similarly contingent, mobilized through the various correspondences set in play across the different elements and the subject of the experiential encounter.

- Two parallel modes of visual documentation aimed to reveal the tension between subjective and material agency and the shifting relationship between the 'classificatory' (what Neil Leach described as 'knowledge-as-quantification') and the 'constellatory' ('knowledge-as-sensuous correspondence') (Leach 2006: 23). A 4m retail-style concertina catalogue presented the individual sculptural components in the form of a quasi-taxonomy. The gridded linear sequential format and regular folded divisions of this suggested the temporal evolution of the Ph.D. and the rational coherence and classificatory grounding from which the improvised constellatory staging of the work takes its measure.

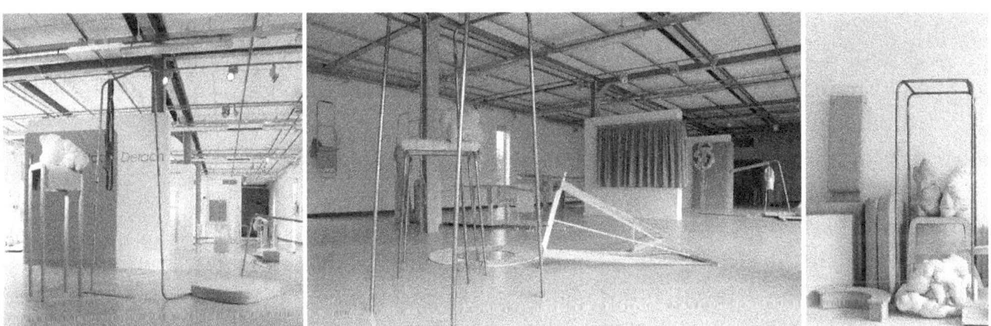

Figure 2: 'Thingly' sculptural components (Source: Bristow 2016).

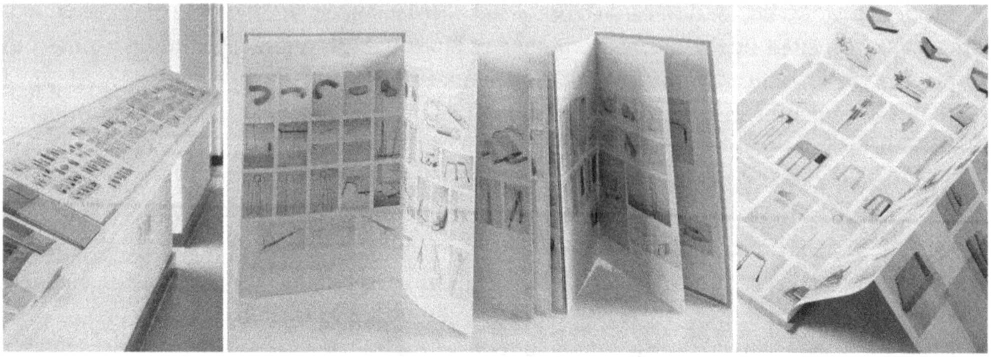

Figure 3: Concertina catalogue (Source: Bristow 2016).

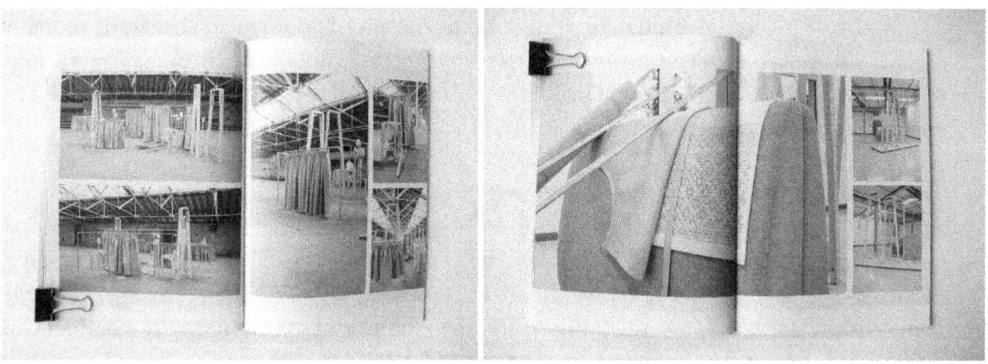

Figure 4: Catalogue documenting possible scenarios (Source: Bristow 2016).

This was accompanied by:

- A 68-page, A4, perfect-bound catalogue that documented the (re)staging of the various sculptural components within different installational scenarios and exhibition contexts.
- An illustrated written text that is itself a constellation of practice strategies, theoretical, methodological and contextual perspectives.
- A selection of supporting material including Ph.D. abstract, project maps, mind maps, photographic research, sketches, maquettes and reflective journals.

There was also work-in-progress split-screen video footage that presented a more detached walk-through of the exposition installation set against a more poetically ambiguous close caressing of surfaces.

For Bristow it was important that the exposition reflected the processually oriented nature of her inquiry and it was crucial in revealing a sensuous mode of knowledge

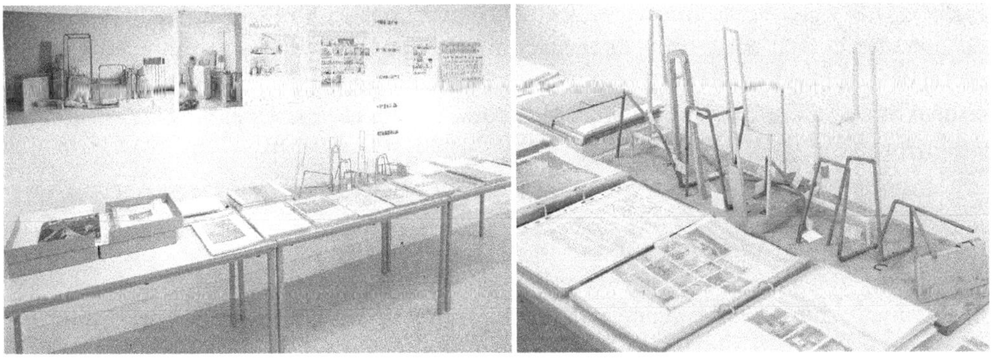

Figure 5: Examples of supporting material (Source: Bristow 2016).

production that couldn't be revealed through other means. It provided her with a further opportunity to reconfigure some of the sculptural elements from her 'thingly' taxonomy and, in allowing direct access to the practice, afforded authority to the performative nature of the experiential encounter and both the affective and cognitive dimension of materially embodied experience.

Exposing the tensions that were the focus of her research and maintaining the non-hierarchical dynamic fundamental to the constellatory methodology, the epistemic agency of the exposition resided in the precariously unfolding relationship between individual self-determination (of the artist/researcher and the viewer/beholder) and an active opening up to what she describes as the 'productive indeterminacy' of matter/material in all its sensuous fullness and complexity. Here the resonance of an abstract sculptural language is privileged over representation for the way that it can accommodate contradiction and facilitate somatic and semantic correspondences yet at the same time continually elude subjective mastery and conceptual synthesis.

Bristow observes that on reflection the detached authority of the gallery context meant that the ideological conventions of the exhibition were perhaps still dominant and the (re)staging of the work lacked the speculative nature of previous manifestations within the studio. The architecture of the gallery also created a clear separation between the staging of the practice elements and the display of what was perhaps still construed as 'supporting material'. With the benefit of critical distance, this could have been further mediated and given greater prominence.

Acknowledging these various individual attempts at exposition, more organized and explicit thinking is taking place. In this respect the Adapt-r network breaks new ground in doctoral education (Adapt-r 2013). An EU-funded international network established in 2013 involving seven European and Australian universities, Adapt-r hosts a Ph.D. research project database and organizes various residential events – Practice Research Symposia – that combine research methods training, supervisor training, research in progress reviews, seminar and examination 'auditing', exhibitions, and 'practitioners in conversation' sessions.[5]

Perhaps the most radical move is the totally open public Ph.D. examinations that are documented in their entirety on video and published on the web.[6] Such examination events encourage the researcher to articulate the Ph.D. inquiry in the presence of artefacts and/or resolved creative works, thus enabling participants the direct experiencing of the researcher's argument and its constructive interrogation.

Exposition – a 'rhizome' structure?

In this final section of the chapter we offer practical generic advice on how, within the context of a Ph.D. examination, a doctoral exposition might be shaped and what it might comprise. As Biggs suggests, context is crucial – so the first thing to consider is where an exposition might be best communicated and experienced; we think this is conditional on the focus of the inquiry. For example, the authors know of various practice-led Ph.D.s whose outcomes and outputs have been publicly accessible within the context of contemporary art centres. For example, the 'emerging artworks' from Jessamy Kelly's Ph.D. research (completed 2009) were displayed in a Crafts Council Solo Showcase at the National Glass Centre, Sunderland in 2006. Kelly argues:

> In exhibiting the artworks at Craft and Art galleries it was possible to test the viability of the new process routes and artworks against the work of others in the field.
>
> (Kelly 2009: 99)

Whilst this is an important aim and may provide ongoing contextualization of the research, within such contexts the public would naturally expect to see resolved artworks. Alternative kinds of spaces might be considered depending on the nature of the inquiry and its findings, for example an industrial unit, a furniture workshop, a community centre, a heritage site, a museum, a garden centre, etc. In such contexts public expectations will be different, and a research exposition might provide a surprising engagement with the research issues that usually the public are not party to.

Having established a proper context for the doctoral exposition through choosing an appropriate physical space and creating a particular aesthetic, as Matts Leiderstam did, what are the possible elements that the practitioner-researcher might include to fully expose the process of inquiry? We take up Slager's analogy of 'rhizome' as one useful structure to consider. There may be many more imaginative options; however, according to Gilles Deleuze and Felix Guattari (1993) the concept of 'rhizomatic' for representing and interpreting information is compelling, because of its non-hierarchical, non-linear, connective capacity. It allows for growth, fluid change and interaction. We offer the following as suggestions, not prescriptions, to be creatively interpreted. The exposition should ideally reflect the nature of the inquiry in form and content. Figure 6 presents a possible rhizomatic visualization of the probable components of a doctoral exposition.

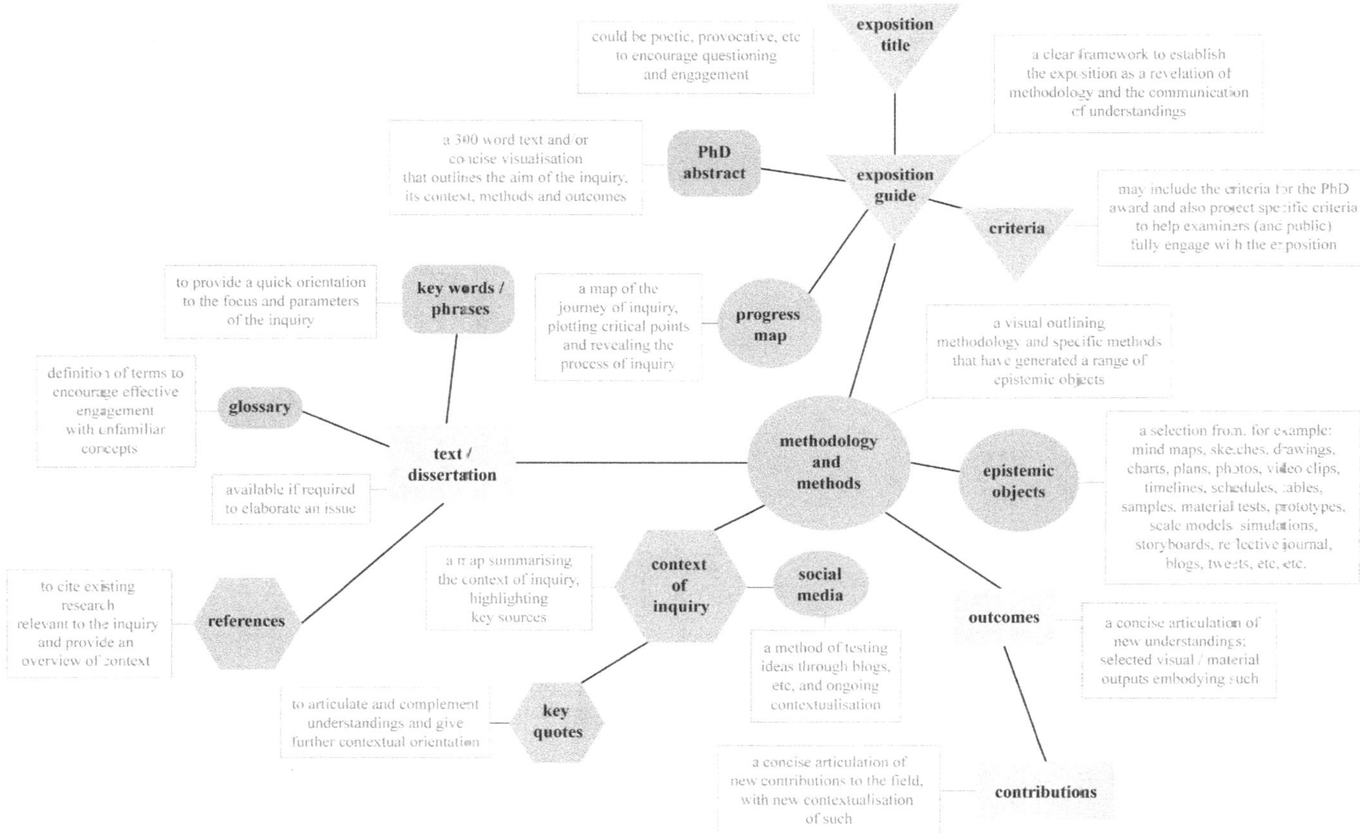

Figure 6: Exposition – a rhizome of possible elements by Gray and Malins.

Some detail is given in the figure for each component, so here we discuss the overarching concepts. It is now apparent that the exposition must be a controlled experience within an appropriate context, presumed to be a suitable physical space in which the researcher actively guides the participants. In this sense its careful construction is the obligation of the doctoral researcher, much like a contemporary curator will instigate and deliver an encounter with creative works in a gallery setting. However, the exposition is not an exhibition and the researcher must make this distinction, and provide criteria by which the materials displayed can be understood and evaluated. An abstract, keywords and a glossary of terms will help to quickly orient examiners (and public) to the focus and parameters of the inquiry. There may be a number of means by which the creative inquiry can be contextualized in terms of key thinking and practice in the defined field, for example, a mapping of the context of inquiry, key quotes and key references. Increasingly, the use of social media tools as a means of sharing and testing ideas about the questions and assumptions of an inquiry is a valuable feedback mechanism, as well as providing ongoing contemporary contextualization.

Conclusion

If we accept that the main function of the doctoral exposition is to reveal methodology, then this aspect must be given great emphasis. There might be a key visual (or set of) that maps the methodological approach and methods in the journey of inquiry, highlighting critical points of insights as well as misunderstandings. The latter might be materialized in a selected range of epistemic objects, some demonstrating what the researcher currently knows so far – knowledge constructions, and some embodying partial valuable insights, allowing for future exploration by the researcher and/or others – knowledge bearers. Epistemic objects, as Jeanne Bamberger and Donald Schön say, act as 'a materialised "log" of the making process' (1991: 192) and are part of the Ph.D.'s aim of knowledge contribution to the field.

Finally, the outcomes of the inquiry must be clearly and concisely articulated. There may be a range of new knowledge – conceptual, methodological, aesthetic, technical, etc., and these might be embodied in various output forms. Some might be considered as resolved works, but as Schwab proposes they need not necessarily be 'works of art' (2015). The new knowledge contributions must be positioned in relation to the field of inquiry, and their value, or potential value be suggested.

The exposition must be captured in some way for archival purposes, and post-examination included in the final submission for Ph.D. This then becomes accessible learning material for new researchers, and something on which to experiment and build.

The doctoral exposition should not be something that is 'tacked on' at the end of the research for the purpose of the examination. Rather it should be considered as an essential component of research training and exercised throughout the Ph.D. experience. We consider it as important and to be as carefully developed as the written text, which is always a 'partial' component of the final submission for Ph.D. The Ph.D. is constantly evolving and we should not be afraid to experiment – pushing the boundaries, challenging assumptions and searching for better ways of doing and articulating inquiry.

As Schwab admits there is a didactic flavour to exposition, and at best it should be a memorable learning experience for all involved – the researcher, the examiners, doctoral peers and public. Most importantly, one would hope that a doctoral exposition would be a highly visual/haptic and engaging encounter with the research, exploiting the creative knowledge, experience and skills of the practitioner-researcher. From this perspective the exposition can be seen as yet another exciting opportunity to make a poetic statement.

References

Adapt-r Network (2013), http://www.adapt-r.eu. Accessed 30 January 2017.

Adapt-r Practice Research Symposium (2015), 'Examination of Dimitri Vangrunderbeek', https://vimeo.com/130647624. Accessed 30 January 2017.

Adorno, Theodor (2007), *Negative Dialectics* (trans. E. B. Ashton), London: Continuum.

Bamberger, Jeanne and Schön, Donald (1991), 'Learning as reflective conversation with materials', in F. Steier (ed.), *Research and Reflexivity*, London: Sage, pp. 186–209.

Biggs, Michael (2003), 'The rôle of "the work" in research', *PARIP: Practice as Research in Performance*, National PARIP Conference, Bristol, United Kingdom, 11–14 September, http://www.bris.ac.uk/parip/biggs.htm. Accessed 24 January 2017.

Borgdorff, Henk (2012), 'Artistic practices and epistemic things', *The Conflict of the Faculties: Perspectives on Artistic Research and Academia*, Leiden: Leiden University Press, pp. 202–16.

Bristow, Maxine (2016), 'Pragmatics of attachment and detachment: Medium (un)specificity as material agency in contemporary art', Ph.D. thesis, London: Norwich University of the Arts and University of the Arts.

Brown, Bill (2004), *Things*, Chicago: University of Chicago Press.

Carter, Paul (2005), *Material Thinking: The Theory and Practice of Creative Research*, Melbourne: University of Melbourne Press.

Deleuze, Gilles and Guattari, Felix (1993), *A Thousand Plateaus*, Minneapolis: University of Minnesota Press.

Douglas, Anne (1997), 'Observations and comments on "The Viva Voce"', in J. Swift (ed.), *The Viva Voce, Research Training Initiative*, Birmingham: Birmingham Institute of Art and Design, University of Central England, pp. 20–25.

Eco, Umberto (1989), *The Open Work*, Cambridge: Harvard University Press.

Ewenstein, Boris and Whyte, Jennifer (2009), 'Knowledge practices in design: The role of visual representations as "epistemic objects"', *Organization Studies*, 30:1, pp. 7–30.

Feyerabend, Paul (1988), *Against Method*, London: Verso.

Gaudi Club (n.d.), *Model for the Crypt of the Church of Colonia Güell*, http://www.gaudiclub.com/ingles/I_VIDA/fotobras/colonia/1102.jpg. Accessed 24 January 2017.

Gedenryd, Henrik (1998), 'How designers work: Making sense of authentic cognitive activities', Ph.D. thesis, Lund: Lund University Cognitive Studies.

Kelly, Jessamy (2009), 'The combination of glass and ceramics as a means of artistic expression in studio practice', Ph.D. thesis, Sunderland: University of Sunderland, http://sure.sunderland.ac.uk/3656. Accessed 24 January 2017.

Knorr-Cetina, Karin (2001), 'Objectual practice', in T. R. Schatzki, K. Knorr-Cetina and E. von Savigny (eds), *The Practice Turn in Contemporary Theory*, London: Routledge, pp. 175–87.

Leach, Neil (2006), *Camouflage*, Cambridge: The MIT Press.

Liederstam, Matts (2006), 'See and seen: Seeing landscape through artistic practice', Ph.D. thesis, Lund: Malmo Art Academy, Lund University, http://www.seeandseen.net/dissertation/. Accessed 24 January 2017.

Malins, Julian and Gulari, Nil Melehat (2011), 'Innovation by design: A programme to support SMEs', *Swedish Design Research Journal*, 2:11, pp. 25–32.

Merali, Zeeya (2010), 'Physics: The large human collider', *Nature*, 464: 482–84, http://www.nature.com/news/2010/100324/full/464482a.html. Accessed 24 January 2017.

Rheinberger, Hans-Jörg (1997), *Toward a History of Epistemic Things: Synthesizing Proteins in the Test Tube*, Stanford: Stanford University Press.

——— (2010), *An Epistemology of the Concrete: Twentieth-Century Histories of Life*, Durham: Duke University Press.

Richter, Cristof and Allert, Heidrun (2011), 'Epistemic role of artefacts in creative design and knowledge creation', in A. Kovacevic, W. Ion, C. McMahon, L. Buck and P. Hogarth (eds), *DS 69: Proceedings of E&PDE 2011, 13th International Conference on Engineering and Product Design Education*, London, UK, 8–9 September, London: Design Society, pp. 103–08.

Schwab, Michael (2015), 'Editorial', *Journal of Artistic Research*, 7, http://www.jar-online.net. Accessed 24 January 2017.

Schwab, Michael and Borgdorff, Henk (2014), *The Exposition of Artistic Research: Publishing Art in Academia*, Leiden: Leiden University Press.

Science Museum (n.d.), 'Crick and Watson's DNA molecular model, England, 1953', Brought to Life, Exploring the History of Medicine, http://www.sciencemuseum.org.uk/broughttolife/objects/display?id=6145. Accessed 24 January 2017.

Slager, Henk (2008–2009), *Nameless Science*, apexart, New York, 10 December–31 January, https://apexart.org/exhibitions/slager.htm. Accessed 30 January 2017.

——— (2010), *Critique of Archival Reason*, RHA, Dublin, 18 February–7 March, http://www.rhagallery.ie/exhibitions/critique-of-archival-reason/. Accessed 30 January 2017.

——— (2014), 'Counter archival dissemination', in M. Schwab and H. Borgdorff (eds), *The Exposition of Artistic Research: Publishing Art in Academia*, Leiden: Leiden University Press, pp. 237–44.

Vergo, Peter (ed.) (1989), *The New Museology*, London: Reaktion Books.

Watson, Allan (1992), 'An exploration of the principle of chance as a stimulus to the creative activity known as sculpture', unpublished Ph.D. thesis, Aberdeen: The Robert Gordon University.

Notes

1 We interpret the term 'practice-led' as a methodological approach (not only in art and design fields but also in architecture, engineering, nursing, etc.) in which:

- the impetus for inquiry comes from some form of creative practice (rather than theory);
- practice (including related key thinking) provides the context for inquiry and its critical positioning;
- methods for inquiry may be those already used in practice, adopted/adapted from a wide range of related practices, and even invented;
- new insights and understandings from the inquiry should be effectively shared with peers and public.

2 For a visualization, see Science Museum, http://www.sciencemuseum.org.uk/broughttolife/objects/display?id=6145.

3 For a visualization, see Gaudi Club image, http://www.gaudiclub.com/ingles/I_VIDA/fotobras/colonia/1102.jpg.

4 The term 'thingly' or 'thingness' emerges as a practice strategy that allows for a sense of familiarity yet resistance to conceptual synthesis. In the introduction to his edited collection entitled *Things* (2004), Bill Brown makes a distinction between objects and things, suggesting that objects are delimited by concepts and cultural codes through which they become recognizable and meaningful. Things, on the other hand, exist in a suspended form of identity, in reference to the object but not in a way as to be able to necessarily identify it. Connoting a simultaneous sense of the general and particular, things operate on the threshold and suggest a liminality where they are immediately graspable but at the same time elude comprehension. As Brown observes, 'the thing really names less an object than a particular subject-object relation' (Brown 2004: 4).

5 The network includes KU Leuven, Belgium; RMIT University, Australia; University of Ljubljana, Slovenia; University of Westminster, London, UK; Estonian Academy of Art; Aarhus School of Architecture, Denmark; Glasgow School of Art, Scotland, UK.

6 For an example of a public doctoral examination in which one of the co-authors participated, see Adapt-r Practice Research Symposium (2015), vimeo.com/130647624 Accessed 1 June 2018.

Chapter 9

Finding My Visual Research Voice: Art as the Tool for Research

Megan Lawton

This is a personal story of discovery, of how I found my visual research voice. What do I mean by that? For me this is about expanding traditional research methodologies that tend to be used in my subject area. I would define my 'subject' as being learning and teaching. I am an educational developer working in a small, strategically important College of Learning and Teaching (CoLT) within a university. David Gosling suggests that educational developers emerge as:

> [...] a group of people with very different backgrounds and academic disciplines who nevertheless shared a common passion for improving teaching – their own and subsequently that of others.
>
> (Gosling 2007: 4)

I believe that my work has greatest impact when conducted via dialogue with peers underpinned by the notion of learning being a social construct (Vygotsky [1934] 1962). Therefore my use of visual research methodology impacts on learning and teaching by promoting activities such as dialogue, reflection and debate – I am also constantly curious. My perception is that researchers in learning and teaching tend to draw on social sciences and education traditions, which are many and varied. In my work, research is focused on beliefs, opinions, values and perceptions and less on absolutes. My experience is that data collection methods typically include storytelling, narrative inquiry, interviews and questionnaires that rely on text or the recording and analysis of the spoken word. What I offer here are examples of two methodologies that have key visual data collection methods and a third example where I have used art to make sense of emerging research.

In this chapter I aim to show how different visual approaches can offer the researcher a way of engaging with research participants that transcends text-based methods. For my own research, I value the visual as a way of making sense of and interpreting what I have found. By the creation of images for myself and ultimately to share with others, I believe I have found my visual research voice.

What do I mean by 'visual research'?

I know that I have always found it much easier to make sense of things if I can sketch out and clearly see relationships between different ideas in anything that I do. Until I used the established Soft Systems Methodology, which has visual elements as key components, my use of visual images was very personal. I still find that I need to visualize my thinking, but the major difference now is that I am willing and able to share my sketches with others to promote discussion and debate.

In 2015 I was asked to redesign a mandatory postgraduate course for colleagues who did not have a formal teaching qualification. The 'students' on this course were and are all employed by the university; therefore, a course of this nature has to be relevant, easily contextualized and is taken at the same time as someone who is teaching their own students. My thought processes were not linear, as can be seen in Figure 1. The actual thinking was, and is, much messier than can be articulated in text; however, in attempting to make some sense of the different aspects and to pull out some key issues and challenges, the visual concept map enabled me to look at relationships and interactions. It can be argued that one of the most important aspects of using a visual methodology is not being bound by a linear structure that is the norm in text.

For me, the use of visual metaphors, colour, spatial placing and the relationships between pictures are all part of the holistic picture. The creation of this image was a choice that I made to make sense of my course design. To redesign the course, I wanted to gain feedback

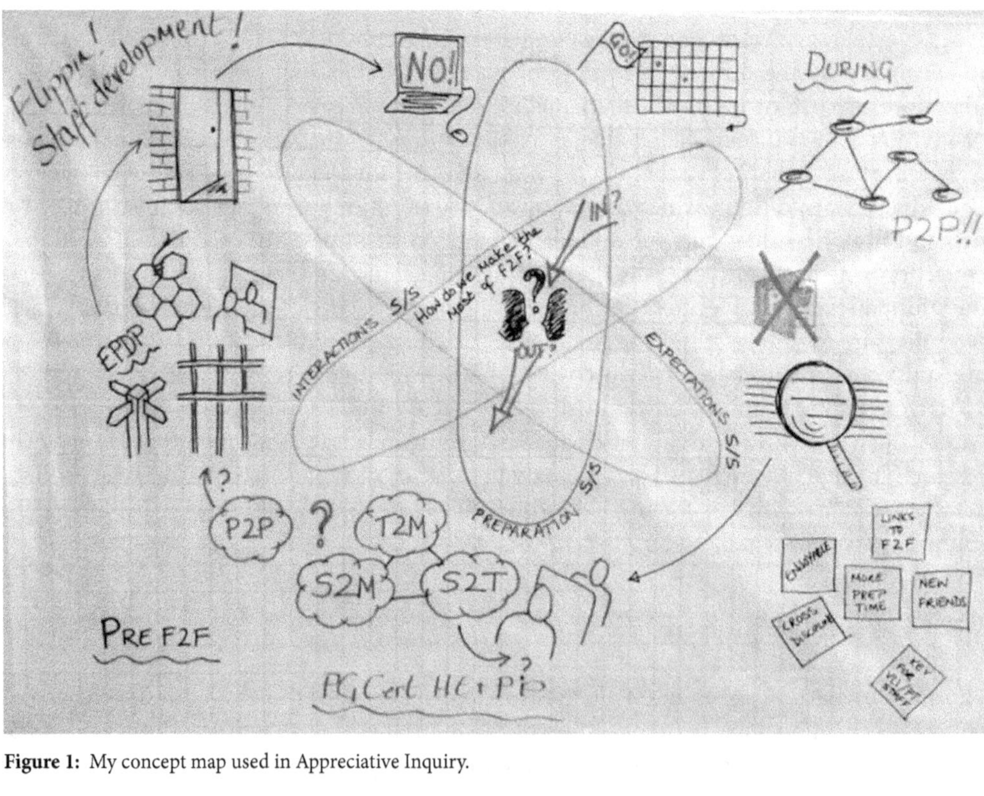

Figure 1: My concept map used in Appreciative Inquiry.

from previous participants but not in a negative way. I created the image as an enhancement to an existing research framework that I was using which is known as 'Appreciative Inquiry' (sometimes abbreviated to 'AI'). It is a solution-oriented and, most importantly, a positive research methodology. It looks at what works rather than what has gone wrong. I am a very positive, forward-looking person who likes to start with a holistic view, so this approach appeals to my own learning preferences. Glynis Cousin proposes that Appreciative Inquiry 'provides a potentially unthreatening way of researching learning environments or academic cultures' (2009: 167). My inquiry, the redesign of a new course, fitted perfectly. I wanted to look at what worked, what the future situation would be and I wanted to showcase certain aspects of the course to the students in a practical way. For example, I needed my students, who were all members of staff, to experience an inclusive curriculum design, I wanted them to experience a different pedagogic approach such as flipped learning and I wanted them to experiences how you could make the most of a blended learning experience using a new virtual learning environment. The only way I felt I could express the complexities was via a drawing.

Appreciative Inquiry has four different phases:

Discovery *(what is)*
Dream *(what could be)*
Design *(what should be)*
Destiny *(what will be)*

Though there are no defined 'tools', I found that a concept map enabled me to make sense of all the different elements and engage with research participants in all of the four different phases via the use of visual methods.

Katja Mikhailovich et al. (2015) used Appreciative Inquiry for their research with villagers in Papua New Guinea. They used a range of visual data collection medium, including maps, drawings and photographs. In their study the use of visual data collection transcended language and cultural barriers, allowing participants to express their views without written or spoken language getting in the way. The data in both this study and my own enabled participants and researchers to co-create knowledge and understanding from different viewpoints. This co-creation, Cousin (2009: 179) argues, is one of the fundamental aspects of knowledge and understanding generated by Appreciative Inquiry. She also contends that contexts are interpreted by different participants from their own perspectives. Furthermore, there is no *one* 'truth' but there may be many different solutions.

In my discovery phase I used sticky notes and flip-chart pages with the students, asking them to provide feedback on what they liked about the course as it currently was and what they would like to see in the future. I then asked them to physically arrange the notes into themes. The very act of moving and discussing where things could be placed enabled a clearer picture of what the new course structure could look like. Digital images were taken of the sticky notes and these helped me to create a concept map. I used visual metaphors, relationships, directions and colour, which would not be possible in linear text, to make sense of what should be (the design phase, Figure 1). For example, I identified that key aspects of this new course design would relate to staff and student expectations, staff and student interactions and staff and student preparedness to study in a new way. To me, these three key ideas were orbiting a central question 'How do we make the most of the face-to-face days?' This was identified from the sticky note exercise as a major concern for busy academics (both students and staff). Those ideas are still central and ever present in my image. I took this image back to my students and also to a workshop of like-minded people asking them to add to or change the image or to draw an image for themselves. In these situations the image became the catalyst for debate and discussion. Each part of the image had an impact that led to further discussion; for example, the cross through the symbol for PowerPoint raised questions for course tutors about their activities on the face-to-face days.

Wendy Luttrell and Richard Chalfen (2010) suggest that a way of looking at the impact of visual research can be linked to its position in the research process, for example, visual data collected with the aim of having a visual end point such as a documentary or photographic exhibition or illustrated book. My experience of using visual methods in Appreciative Inquiry is that they contributed to the whole research process. Therefore, I would see my use of images best described as 'participatory visual research methods' where research participants (including the researcher) use visual elements to create, reflect and make sense of any given situation. Art is therefore the tool for research rather than the topic or outcome.

The visual 'tools' for participatory research are many and varied. Visual 'tools' can include single media such as photography or a combination of visual approaches such as hand-drawn artefacts, drawing, mapping, charts, rich pictures (Checkland and Poulter 2006; Mikhailovich et al. 2015) and digital images, scans, photographs and videos (Lorenz and Kolb 2009; Bezemer 2017). The use of visual research methods is increasingly being used in a wide range of different research situations covering a vast array of topics (Pain 2012; Luttrell and Chalfen 2010). However, visual research is firmly based in a qualitative framework used to gather thoughts, views, opinions, beliefs, reflections and generating understanding. Cousin (2009) notes that visual research can connect to emotional dimensions that text-based research cannot.

An example of using a single media, in this case photography, is the research methodology known as Auto-Driven Photo-Elicitation. There are at least two research methodologies that use 'Photo-Elicitation', although that is not to say that the use of photographs does not appear in other research methodologies. One form of Photo-Elicitation is where existing images are chosen or images are made prior to any interaction with research participants. Those participants are then asked to comment on the images that are presented to them (Bezemer 2017; Callow 2012). Auto-Driven Photo-Elicitation differs, in that the research participants are asked to take their own images and then discuss their images with researchers. Charles Harrington and Ingrid Lindy (1999) call this 'reflexive photography'. There are, however, a number of studies (Meo 2010; Mikhailovich et al. 2015) that use a combination of both approaches. In both contexts what is important is not just the presentation of the image(s) but the promotion of discussion. With Photo-Elicitation there is a far greater influence on the discussion as the researcher selects the images that the respondents react to, whereas in Auto-Driven Photo-Elicitation participants take the images for themselves.

In 2009 I was part of a research team that used Auto-drive Photo-elicitation to explore international students' experiences of their first year at university. We wanted a methodology that did not rely on read or written English and an approach that gave control and power to the participants. All the research team members were staff at my university and we were conscious that we had our own beliefs and values that were affected by our own personal and professional experiences. We wanted to see what the university looked like from an international student's perspective. We thought that Auto-Driven Photo-Elicitation would suit our needs. In its simplest form, Auto-Driven Photo-Elicitation asks participants to take photographs on a given topic that are then shared with researchers who ask questions based on those images, getting the participants to reflect on the decisions, thoughts and feelings they had while taking them.

In the study that I was involved in, six participants were asked to take five images using their own equipment and to select three that they would like to discuss. In the pilot we found that discussing five images was a very lengthy process and that by adding the selection of images we were able to ask questions such as, 'Which image (of the three) is the most important from those you captured?' Followed by, 'Tell me about the image?'

Our questions were based on the use of this methodology with novice monks (Samuels 2007, in Cousin 2009: 220–21). This approach offered questions that could be used with participants when discussing their images.

In our study we asked our participants to send us their images so that we could print them off. This made it easier for the individual participant and the interviewer to see the image together as it was discussed. We agreed to video the discussions as we wanted to see how we all interacted with the image not just record the audio. We asked the question: 'If you could, how would you change this image?' In all the discussions, the students interacted with the images. Video helped keep some of the richness that this visual methodology gave us and that we felt we might have lost if we had relied on just the spoken word and text-based notes.

One major impact on choice of images was the permissions needed to take photographs with people in them as the university has a strict policy regarding taking images and recordings on university premises. Even though students were careful not to take pictures with people in them, they were still challenged by others concerned where a photo might end up. We asked the question: 'Might there be other ways of looking at these images?' This led to discussion around the use of images on social media. We were able to discuss what they might have liked to capture but could not because of the restrictions. Questions such as: 'Were there other images you wish you could have shot?', helped explore this issue.

In the research, we interviewed students individually and, with their permission, created a shared digital portfolio with the images and narratives. We had planned to exhibit the images and asked permission at the start of the research from students to do this. However the images and the narrative became quite personal for the participants who felt that they did not want this public display. They felt that the images were primarily a catalyst for discussion and that, without being a part of the discussion, others could and would misinterpret the images they took. The following are three examples of students' narratives.

> Image – a prayer room in a mosque.
> *The image of the prayer room and Mosque could represent my religion but to me they are about support and understanding. The Mosque to me is a place to go to ask for clarification about why UK people might respond in a particular way and the prayer room was a place for peer support and advice – the sharing of ideas.*
>
> (Student A)

> Image – a twisting flight of stairs.
> *It's taken on the sixth or seventh floor of the Art and Design building and it kind of represents that coming here was a big step for me. The journey from Norway to all the way to here, just feels like I've walked so many steps and I'm already quite high. I have achieved a lot and I feel people back home don't have the guts to go out and try and do it. I feel like doing this, on my own and without my family here has made me stronger and that I have walked all these steps on my own and it feels good.*
>
> (Student B)

> Image – shelves of books in a library.
> *This isn't about resources and books, it's about the fact that no one is there using them! Back home we don't have the resources that you get here and I don't think UK students appreciate how lucky they are. I like to sometimes just walk into different aisles and look at different subjects.*
>
> (Student C)

The use of Auto-Driven Photo-Elicitation was made very easy with the availability of digital devices with high-resolution cameras; though this also added concerns over where and how the images taken would be used in the future. Although we gathered visual data through photographs, the real richness came by the interaction with the images. The student narratives were compelling. The research team, myself included, were all surprised just how powerful it was to discuss the images and it is true to say that perhaps we had not appreciated the depth to which those discussions would go.

As a research team we did wonder what images we might have taken. We considered taking our own images and then comparing them to those that the participants took as an interesting twist to the methodology, particularly to see how much we were influenced by working in the research context that we were exploring. We decided not to take images as we did not want to influence or impact our participants' experience. At times it was really difficult not to get enthused and want to join in. We probably could have if we had set this up from the start, but as we had not, we thought we needed to rein in our own input.

I firmly believe that visual research is based within an interpretivist paradigm, as those who use interpretivism, 'aspire to generate *understandings and insights* in context that are held to be inherently too unstable for reliable predications to be made' (Cousin 2009: 9, original emphasis). Therefore, a key consideration of using a visual research methodology is the positionality of the researcher within the research context. Cousin argues that:

> the debate has shifted from minimizing subjectivity to thinking more about how to bring oneself into the research process through the notion of reflexivity and in the light of fresh understandings about language. These notions are informed by an acknowledgement that our knowledge of the world is mediated and interpreted from a particular stance and an available language, and that we should own up to this in explicit ways.
>
> (Cousin 2009: 10)

In using Auto-Driven Photo-Elicitation, my own views were challenged: seeing images from my particular stance was very different to those of our international participants.

This third example is very personal to me, given that I used a visual methodology for my own doctorate in Professional Studies (Learning and Teaching) entitled 'Of sea anemones and clownfish: Exploring a mutually beneficial approach to educational development through Soft Systems Methodology' (Lawton 2010). For my own academic research I decided to use Soft Systems Methodology. This is not particularly well known within social science and education research, though it appealed to me for a number of different reasons. Soft Systems Methodology was developed by Peter Checkland in the late 1960s, with a seminal work being published in 1990 that included a 30-year retrospective (Checkland and Scholes 1990). In 2006, Peter Checkland and John Poulter published *Learning for Action*, in part as a response to articles and publications that misinterpreted or misrepresented the methodology.

Checkland and Poulter define Soft Systems Methodology as: 'an organised way of tackling perceived problematic (social) situations. It is action-oriented. It organizes thinking about such situations so that action to bring about improvement can be taken' (2006: xv). Within the methodology you start with a 'finding out phase', which means that you can have a holistic approach from which to hone down your ideas to a definition of your plan or route. In this phase you are working in the 'real world' before moving into a 'concept' world where you can explore different potential solutions. The use of visual conceptual modelling plays to my strengths and gives me a freedom of expression that helps clarify my holistic, intuitive and creative thinking. When you have developed your concepts, you can then take them back into the real world, asking two key questions: *Is this desirable?* And *is this feasible?* You can go back to the concept world again as many times as you want until you reach an 'accommodation' with research participants on an action that will improve the situation.

In the methodology are a number of 'tools' including rich pictures. Checkland and Poulter explain:

> In making a Rich Picture the aim is to capture, informally, the main entities, structures and viewpoints in the situation, the processes going on, the current recognized issues and any potential ones.
>
> (Checkland and Poulter 2006: 25)

Checkland and Poulter further state that: 'Wise practitioners continually produce such pictures as an aid to thinking. They become a normal way of capturing impressions and insights' (2006: 25). Creating images enabled me to reflect visually in a way that words could not. I was able to consider relationships, directions and focus. The use of visual metaphors encouraged discussions that text alone could not.

Rich pictures are seen as immediate drawings that are raw; they show relationships, structures and help participants who create them make sense of and show what they perceive to be the key issues. I would agree with this to a certain extent, but I found within my research that, like using a sketchbook, I needed to reflect and develop my initial ideas into a worked-up image that I could then use within my doctorate thesis.

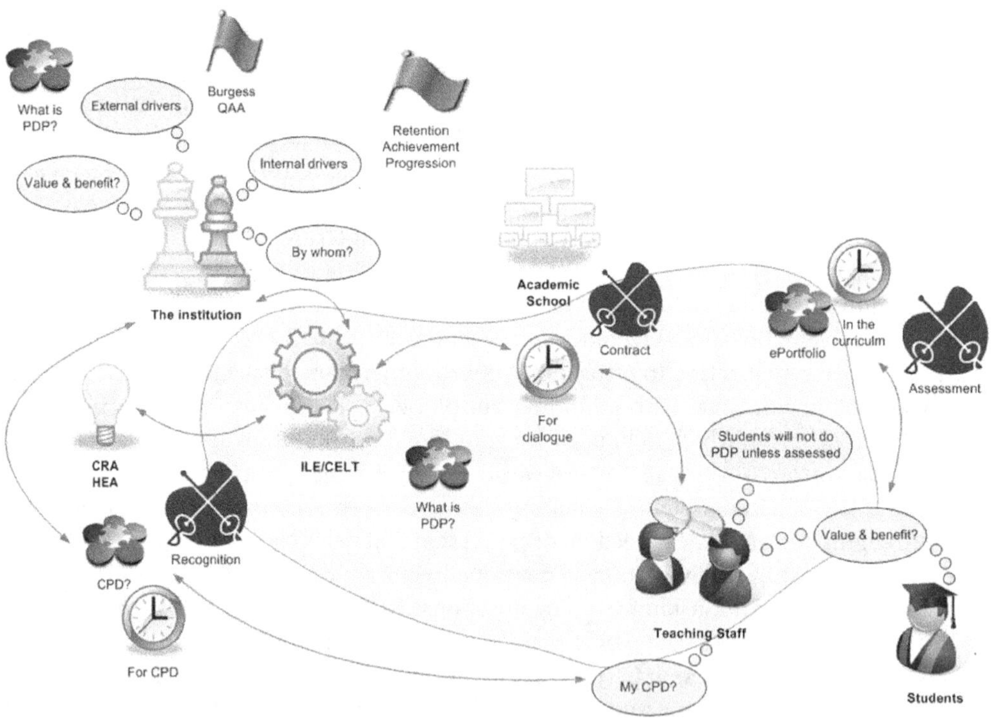

Figure 2: A rich picture from my doctoral thesis.

Checkland and Poulter might not approve of my final image, seeing it as being too controlled and clean, as they state:

> The literatures of control engineering and management science have many diagrams dominated by straight lines, right angles and rectangular boxes. These convey the impression: this is the case, full stop! The hand-drawn diagrams in the SSM literature aim to convey an organic rather that a mechanical impression. They underline that absolute certainty is forever elusive in human affairs; they are working diagrams, part of the learning process. And they look more human, more attractive than straight lines and right angles.
> (Checkland and Poulter 2006: 198)

I do agree, however, that I felt that I needed to have form, shape and colour to give my image meaning when seen for the first time. I was mindful that my doctoral thesis would become an archived document and that I would be defending and using my images in a viva voce and presentation, so therefore I felt that a more easily interpreted image for the final thesis would make my work more accessible. My image did have an end point in the way it was represented in my thesis.

My visual preferences and abilities made me question and develop the methodology, adapting it from within to suit my visual needs. In doing so, I re-awakened dormant skills in visual reflection that I had previously used as an art and design student. I have been able to modify and enrich my use of Soft Systems Methodology to give participants access to my perceptions without me being there to offer my interpretations, in a way that is accessible, engaging and conveyed a depth of meaning that I do not think could be done by just using simple line drawings.

In my final image I did draw upon (no pun intended) some conventions suggested by Andrew Monk and Steve Howard (1998), including the use of crossed swords depicting conflict or tension between stakeholders or where I felt that it was impossible and/or impractical to suggest improvement. In my image, for example, there was an issue that staff saw between the academic contract that they were on and the expectation for them to undergo continuing professional development. This was something that I could not address in my project but could acknowledge in the rich picture. I used speech bubbles for concerns expressed, such as *students will not do personal development planning unless it is assessed*, acknowledging this as a legitimate issue raised but out of the scope of my research. I used a symbol of a red flag to warn of issues such as national reports, for example *Beyond the Honours Degree Classification – The Burgess Group Final Report* (2007) that I identified as a major impact on the context of my research. My rich picture enabled me to have a holistic view of the context for my research as I saw it and then to look at what I could realistically have an impact on, which was one of the agreed outcomes for the doctorate in Professional Studies for which I was studying.

I spent some time reflecting upon what I felt represented the roles and relationships within my institution that impacted my research. For example, in my view an image of chess pieces represented the senior executive team as strategic managers and that I felt that I was a pawn being moved around in some bigger game. For my own central unit I represented working with School-based learning and teaching as cogwheels, meshed together as an entity within a bigger 'machine', neither one working without engagement with the other. The organic growth of this picture from initial simple pencil sketches led me through a visual reflective process that has made me question how I perceived my own place in my research. When I have presented my rich picture to others in my own institution and in national and international settings, many have commented on the fact that they feel they too can interpret the image.

The use of visual research methodology for my doctorate would support literature that sees the value of visual methods used to enhance: 'rapport building; facilitating communication (promotes, expressing abstract ideas, visuals as adjuncts to communication); facilitating expression of subconscious and tacit knowledge; accessing the difficult-to-reach (groups and places); and encouraging reflection' (Pain 2012).

How have I seen my approach to research changing?

Visual data collection can connect researchers and subjects in a way that removes language barriers, both in terms of literacy and lexicon. It can break down barriers between researchers and participants through a shared experience of creating, developing and interpreting images (Mikhailovich et al. 2015). Jeff Bezemer (2017), when discussing the use of visual research in clinical/medical education, highlights that subject traditions have focused on text-based learning. However, clinical practice relies on visual recognition and interpretation, and the ability to '*see, feel and talk* about the world', therefore, using visual data collection reflects the real-life experiences and skills needed in this area.

Art as a tool for research can both be explicitly part of the research methodology, as I experienced when using Soft Systems Methodology and Auto-Driven Photo-Elicitation or implicitly used by researchers and research subjects to collect data as evidenced in my use in Appreciative Inquiry. What is demonstrated by these research examples and the three research methodologies offered here is that the visual is a powerful tool to generate emotional responses, promote discussion and dialogue and capture relationships that would be difficult to do via text.

I would argue that there has been an increasing interest and use of visual research methods and methodology in recent years. For example, in 2012 the *International Journal of Research and Method in Education* produced a special edition 'Problematising visual methods: Philosophy, ethics and methodologies', and in its editorial Kate Wall, Elaine Hall and Pamela Woolner suggest that the need for this special edition 'reflects the fact that visual methodology in education research is at an important turning point'. There are in fact some weighty tomes such as *The Sage Handbook of Visual Research Methods* (2011). Over recent years, capturing and using images has become far more accessible

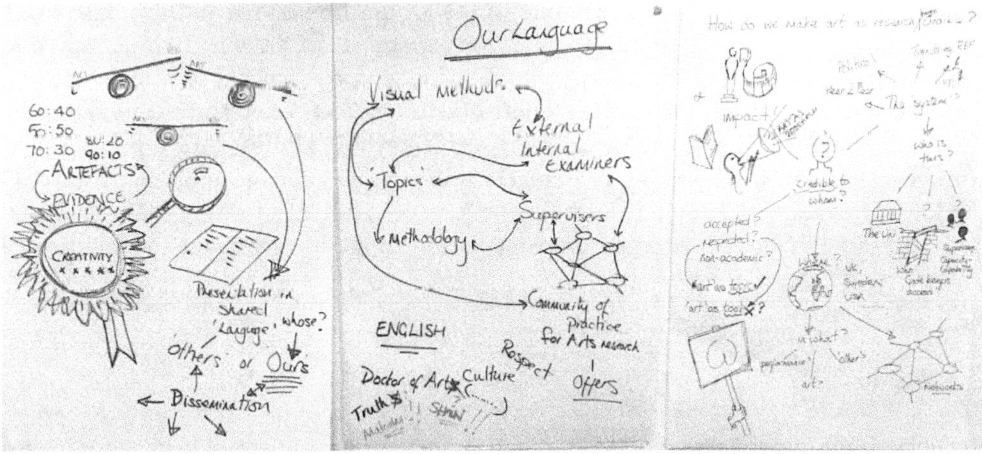

Figure 3: Concept maps, *Art as Research in Learning and Teaching Conference* (2016).

through mobile devices, thus offering greater opportunities and ease in using art as a tool for research.

In the *Art as Research in Learning and Teaching Conference* (University of Wolverhampton 2016) hosted by the University of Wolverhampton in the United Kingdom, I took part in a group discussion on 'How do we make art as research credible?' I found it impossible to make sense of the discussions without mapping and creating an image and then sharing that image with others (Figure 3).

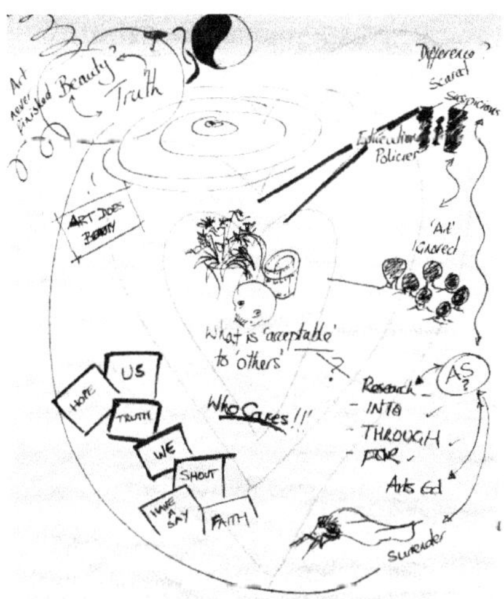

Figure 4: Artistic response to keynote address (2 September 2016).

I created these images whilst listening to the group discussions and trying to make sense of what I saw were the main themes. My experience of drawing rich pictures and concept maps empowered me to find my visual voice in a room full of researchers in a way that I would not have felt able to contribute to via text. I felt brave enough on the third day to agree to provide a visual reply to the keynote address 'Art: a procedure of truth' by Malcolm Ross. The image I created was primarily for me and I can still recall the key messages that I took away from the keynote address in a way that text-based notes could never do. I invited participants to add to my image, hence the addition of the hearts.

Conclusion

In conclusion to this chapter and to summarize my journey, I now feel that I have moved from just the personal use of images for my own benefit. By using images as tools for research, I see their value for co-creation of knowledge that transcends language and cultural barriers. Images, when shared, create discussion and debate and elicit feelings, emotions and reflections. I have discovered that art is a very powerful tool for researching, learning and teaching.

The use of images helps me recognize and accept my preference for a holistic, intuitive approach to learning and move from that position to one that adds detail, process and accountability. When studying for my doctorate I undertook a full assessment of my dyslexia and found that I have, 'visuospatial (non-verbal) reasoning ability lying in the superior range', which I think gave me the confidence to embrace and find my visual voice. Finding established frameworks and methodologies that have visual elements legitimized what I was creating for my personal use and took me on a path into using art as a tool for research. When used as a tool, the dynamics of sharing and co-creating images, I believe, takes my research to another level. I believe that I am able to engage with research participants in a way that transcends language and text constraints, respects and values different world-views, beliefs and opinions. My experience of using art as a tool for research has been focused on qualitative research approaches, particularly when looking at complex problematic situations. Co-creation of an image or images promotes dialogue and debate, different points of view and perceptions come to the fore, links and relationships between different elements are often made.

I recognize that I now feel that I have found my visual voice and that this approach may not be comfortable for all; but for too long I have been uncomfortable in a mainly language/text-based research world that has perhaps not valued art as a tool for research. I have found that there are now more examples of visual research tools being used across a wide range of research areas – some of which I have referenced here. You or your participants do not have to be an artist to find your visual voice; for me this is about owning and participating in research that is inclusive.

References

Bezemer, Jeff (2017), 'Visual research in clinical education', *Medical Education*, 51:1, pp. 105–13.

Burgess, Robert (2007), *Beyond the Honours Degree Classification – The Burgess Group Final Report*, http://www.hear.ac.uk/reports/Burgess2007. Accessed 5 June 2017.

Callow, Jon (2012), 'The rules of visual engagement: Images as tools for learning', *Screen Education*, 65, pp. 72–79.

Checkland, Peter and Poulter, John (2006), *Learning for Action*, Chichester: Wiley.

Checkland, Peter and Scholes, Jim (1990), *Soft Systems Methodology in Action*, Chichester: Wiley.

Cousin, Glynis (2009), *Researching Learning in Higher Education*, Abingdon: Routledge.

——— (2010), 'Positioning positionality: The reflexive turn', in M. Savin-Baden and C. Howell Major (eds), *New Approaches to Qualitative Research, Wisdom and Uncertainty*, London: Routledge Education, pp. 9–18.

Gosling, David (2007), 'We did it our way! Narratives of pathways to the profession of educational development', *Educational Developments*, 8:4, pp. 1–6.

Harrington, Charles F. and Lindy, Ingrid E. (1999), 'The use of reflexive photography in the study of the freshman year experience', *Journal of College Student Retention: Research, Theory & Practice*, 1:1, pp. 13–22.

Lawton, Megan (2010), 'Of sea anemones and clownfish: Exploring a mutually beneficial approach to educational development through Soft Systems Methodology', doctoral thesis, http://eprints.mdx.ac.uk/id/eprint/7980. Accessed 30 January 2017.

Lorenz, Laura and Kolb, Bettina (2009), 'Involving the public through participatory visual research methods', *Health Expectations*, 12:3, pp. 262–74.

Luttrell, Wendy and Chalfen, Richard (2010), 'Lifting up voices of participatory visual research', *Visual Studies*, 25:3, pp. 197–200.

Margolis, Eric and Pauwels, Luc (eds) (2011), *The SAGE Handbook of Visual Research Methods*, London: Sage.

Meo, Aanalía Inés (2010), 'Picturing students' habitus: The advantages and limitations of photo-elicitation interviewing in a qualitative study in the city of Buenos Aires', *International Journal of Qualitative Methods*, 9:2, pp. 149–71.

Mikhailovich, Katja, Pamphilon, Barbara and Chambers, Barbara (2015), 'Participatory visual research with subsistence farmers in Papua New Guinea', *Development in Practice*, 25:7, pp. 997–1010.

Monk, Andrew and Howard, Steve (1998), 'Methods and tools: The rich picture: A tool for reasoning about work context interactions', *Interactions*, 5:2, pp. 21–30.

Pain, Helen (2012), 'A literature review to evaluate the choice and use of visual methods', *International Journal of Qualitative Methods*, 11:4, pp. 3003–19.

Patching, David (1990), *Practical Soft Systems Analysis*, London: Pitman.
University of Wolverhampton (2016), *Art as Research in Learning and Teaching International Conference,* University of Wolverhampton, Telford Innovation Campus, United Kingdom, 31 August–2 September 2016.
Vygotsky, Lev ([1934] 1962), *Thought and Language*, Cambridge: MIT Press.
Wall, Kate, Hall, Elaine and Woolner, Pamela (2012), 'Visual methodology: Previously, now and in the future', *International Journal of Research and Method in Education*, 35:3, pp. 223–26.

Part 3

Involving Students and Others in Art as Research

Chapter 10

Making and Material Affect: From Learning and Teaching to Sharing and Listening

Mah Rana and Fiona Hackney

This chapter explores the power of creative making and film as an affectual framework and means of understanding the knowledge that emerges from arts research. Working with textiles and stitch, the chapter builds on Katie Collins' observations about the inclusiveness of such needlecraft metaphors as knitting, weaving, tapestry, embroidery and quilting to convey notions of kinship, identity, complexity, time, structure and style. These observations are used to argue for research as a 'decentred' activity, an inclusive 'piecing together' of fragments that can: integrate all sorts of sources; is part of life 'both everyday and exceptional'; and has depth and intensity rather than individuality and competition as its goal (Collins 2016). Such concerns locate the project within theories of material craft and experiential learning, and the particular forms of knowledge these generate. In particular, we draw on the notion of 'craft-based ways of knowing' or experiential knowledge in practice developed by Ross Prior (2013) in his work with actors, and the ethnographic methodology employed by Sarah Desmarais (2016) to examine the value of crafts for health. Additionally, the project builds on the outcomes from a number of Arts & Humanities Research Council UK-funded projects that have interrogated creative making as: (1) a means of community co-production; (2) promoting and evidencing well-being; and (3) a mode of being through connecting (Hackney 2014a, 2014b; Rana 2011).

Prior cites 'reflective sketchbooks' as a method for capturing 'those moment-by-moment thoughts and reflections that unconsciously spring from the improvisation of working in process' (2013: 165). This project develops and expands that method through an integrated process of making and filming that captures the material, sensory and temporal engagements, as well as the conversations, that took place in a series of sewing workshops, or 'stitch encounters' as we came to call them, undertaken by co-author Mah Rana and her mother, who is diagnosed with moderate Alzheimer's. Our aim was to examine how *making* together might help them learn from each other by communicating through the practice and process of stitch; to explore, that is, how creative making might serve as a distinctive means of sharing and listening rather than learning and teaching. As a research process the activity of making and filmmaking operated in two ways. Firstly, it served as an auto-ethnographic tool to promote embodied knowledge production through reflection, a process that we termed the 'doing'. And secondly, the raw research footage was edited into a final film, *One Day When We Were Young* (Rana 2016), which served as a creative output in

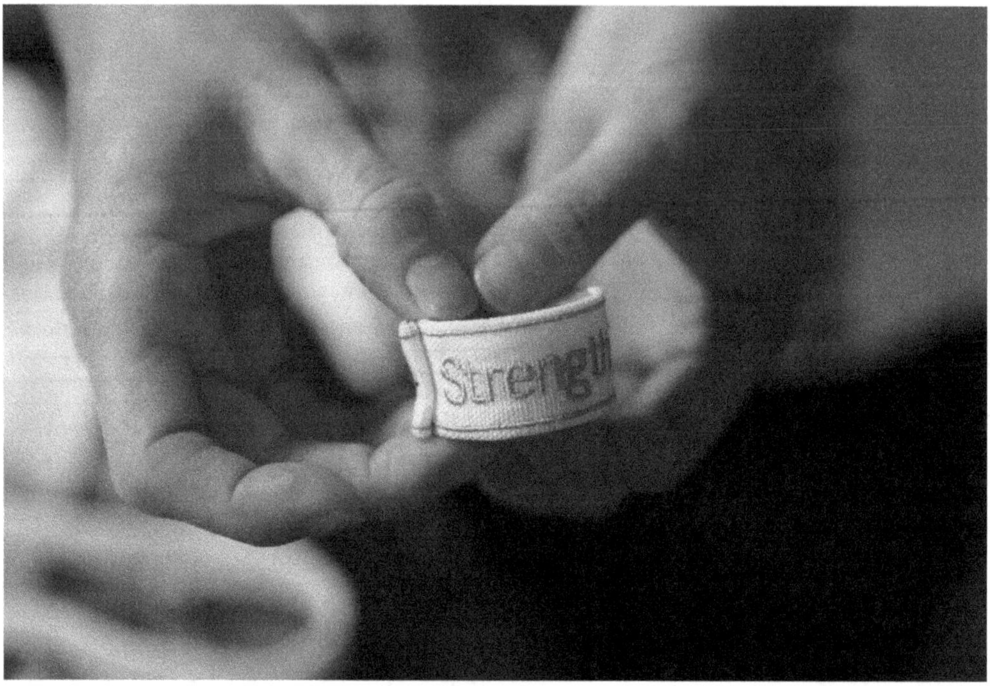

Figure 1: Stitch: Embroidered ethnography. Hannah Maughan for Co-Producing CARE: Community, Asset-Based Research & Enterprise (2014). Photography by Bryony Stokes 2014. © Bryony Stokes.

its own right and a piece of arts research that evidences and disseminates the methodology (McNiff 2008).

Through its staging of a shared, immersive, iterative process of making and filming, the project proposes an expanded, performative version of the reflexive sketchbook, which reveals small moments of change through interchange, and involves forms of embodied knowing that are at once collective and highly personal (Figure 1). It is generally accepted that arts can play a social role in health and well-being, albeit one that is hard to evidence (Chatterjee and Noble 2013). Here we propose that the learning that takes place in a social arts context, the day-to-day learning of everyday life, can serve as a model for arts research inside the academy through the process of being and doing that making together involves.

Being and doing: Reflexive making as methodology

Shaun McNiff defines art-based research as a 'systematic use of the artistic process [the making of art work] as a primary way of understanding and examining experience by both researcher and the people that they involve in their studies' (2007: 29). Ross Prior proposes the term 'craft-based ways of knowing' to describe knowledge originated in the particular meanings inherent in practice (2013: 161). This tacit or praxis-based knowledge, according to Prior, is deeply personal knowledge that is founded on 'particular meanings inherent in practice (the act of doing and the act of being), which are often difficult to communicate' (2013: 167). As such it serves as experiential knowledge beyond language, what Michael Polanyi describes as knowing more than one can tell ([1966] 1985: 4). The sociologist Richard Sennett (2012), arguing for the radical social benefits of collective making, drew on a similar understanding of the creative process when he described how, when playing together, musicians are acutely attuned and attentive to one another, responding instinctively in a felt form of embodied collaboration. John Dewey ([1916] 1968), meanwhile, foregrounded the importance of habit when he theorized a process of experiential knowledge accumulation through iterative modification that made one particular experience available in subsequent experiences, forming a predisposition to easier and more effective action in the future. While for Dewey meaning was associated with the practical act of doing and derived from one's capacity-to-do, the cognitive psychologist Jerome Bruner (1986: 12) went further, arguing that above all, learning is about uncovering meaning rather than abstract notions of seeking the truth. He proposed that the central question we need to ask is 'how do we come to endow experience with meaning?' – a question that underpins this project and continues to be central to our work.

Concerned with craft practice, with its long history of skill, hand-work and the tacit knowledge held by 'communities of practice', we are particularly interested in exploring the distinctive qualities of craft-based ways of knowing as a means to realize and communicate meaning (Frayling 2011; Greenhalgh 1997; Lave and Wenger 1991). Working with Mah Rana's mother, who engaged with craft processes of stitch from a young age, enabled us to explore how the act of sewing might serve as a trigger to uncover the meaning materialized in Dewey's notion of habitual practice. Prior suggests a further conceptual framework when he differentiated the states of 'being' and 'doing' involved in creative practice. While 'being' is manifest in a condition of total absorption in the moment, a process of 'stepping back' to engage in 'reflexively articulating knowledge' produces an 'optimum mode of doing and the consciousness of doing' (2013: 164). 'Being', during our workshops, could principally be ascribed to the act of sewing, while 'doing', with all the consciousness it implied, was aligned with the filming that provided opportunities to step back and reflect. As an artwork the final film itself, moreover, perhaps best captures the reflexive articulation of knowledge and our understanding of how we endowed this experience with meaning. This two-stage process of meaning-making by way of: (1) an unconscious process of 'being' through the experience of stitching, and (2) conscious 'doing' through the reflective process of film and editing, provides a framework for better understanding of how meaning/knowledge might emerge through a series of stitch workshops, or 'stitch encounters'. In this case the work took place between Rana and her mother in the latter's home, but the framework might be adapted to any set of participants and a wide range of learning contexts.

Before exploring the research/learning process in more detail, we want to briefly consider the knotty question how such art-based research methods function as *evidence*. Along with Prior, McNiff and others we call for a broader definition of 'evidence', and one that draws on understandings of *affect*, rather than *effect* (2013: 168). Unlike those focused on professional arts practice, our work is located in amateur creativity and the sensory world of the everyday. As such the theoretical work of Kathleen Stewart is extremely useful. Writing about affect, Stewart proposed the twin concepts of 'worlding' and 'bloom spaces' as evidence of how we can operate affectually in the world (2010: 340). Worlding refers to the condition of being in the world: a condition that is understood and lived through the senses and is particularly sharp at times of individual and communal tension and transition. It involves the emergence of bloom spaces: spaces where the senses come to the surface, new lessons are learnt, different priorities emerge, connections and adjustments are made: where we understand ourselves and others differently with new depth, clarity and calm, despite the circumstances. Seeing the world through the lens of worlding helps us pay attention to what it is to be in the world, our embodied reactions, how we live (physically, emotionally, neurologically, socially, psychologically) in the orbit of people, things, animals, processes and habits. Our lives become a series of daily, lived minute adjustments as we draw on our resources, learn new skills, address challenges, survive and even thrive, despite the stuff life throws at us.

As Rana and her mother engaged in the sewing sessions we came to understand how the action of slowing down, watching, listening and paying attention to the nuances and small interactions that occurred when they made together operated as a form of worlding in which the sewing circle or stitch encounter operated as a bloom space. The workshops took place at a time of tension and transition, when Rana's mother's illness meant that the power relations embedded in their established roles of guiding mother and obedient (for want of a better word) daughter were being reversed, with Rana as the carer and her mother as the person being cared for. As a mode of worlding, sewing offered a way of being in the world through the senses and brought new knowledge to the surface. It helped both accommodate and re-orientate the mother and daughter to their new circumstances by drawing on such resources as Rana's mother's habitual stitch knowledge, resulting in new knowledge about how to be with one another. The quality of immersion and absorption, which both experienced during the sewing encounters, signalled a felt condition of affectual *being* in the world, with all the subjective knowledge that involves. The filmmaking process and the film itself, meanwhile, helped endow experience with meaning by shaping the intuitions, feelings and observations experienced during the stitch encounters into an art object that both functions as an artefact in its own right and evidences the *being* and *doing* aspects of the making engagement. As a process that acknowledges the tensions and power relations involved in knowledge exchange and foregrounds the importance of participant assets, this model of sharing and listening through 'being and doing' has much to offer learning and teaching.

Stitch encounters: Meaningful making as shared experience

Together the twin processes of making and filming constitute an immersive research process that explores experiential 'being', reflexive 'doing' and the acquired knowledge that emerges from both. This section will examine Rana's own experience of undertaking the stitch workshops, or stitch encounters, with her mother and the next section considers how filming was integral to the research. Both draw on Rana's 'stitch diaries' that she kept to record her feelings, intuitions and observations. Although written in the first person to communicate the experiential nature of the practice, the sections were written jointly with Hackney who became a third person in the process: a sounding board and analytical interlocutor assisting with interpretation. We have organized the material into subsections to convey a sense of the *research as process* and chart the 'meaningful moments' as and when they occurred.

Planning: The project schedule was to film four consecutive weekly one-hour stitch encounters in which my mother and I sat down together in her home to make and talk. We chose embroidery as the process we would use. My mother had excelled in embroidery at school and had taught me when I was young, and I was interested to see to what extent she had retained her skills. It was a material practice freighted with meaning for us and, therefore, an ideal means to explore, more widely, the process of learning and teaching. My mother additionally has a piece of embroidery work that she made in her twenties and my intention was to use this as what Lev Vygotsky (1978: 55) described as a 'tool', a designated object to focus our attention, aiding reminiscence and sparking conversation. I was confident that the process of sewing together would trigger memories and support communication. Sewing, I hoped, would provide a safe space for us to *be* together. Advance project planning included sourcing project materials that I hoped would be familiar to my mother such as vintage embroidery iron-on transfers, something that was commonly used by amateur needle-smiths in the early and mid-twentieth century. The process of planning gave me a sense of order and feeling in control, something that had become increasingly important since my mother's Alzheimer's diagnosis in 2014. As her carer I have become hyper-vigilant and attentive to the work of problem-identifying and solution-finding and my identity as daughter has often felt diminished as a result. This is an aspect of parentification, the role reversal that takes place when a child takes on the responsibilities that normally belong to a parent, which is often experienced by the adult-child caregiver of a parent (Johnson 2013). I am acutely aware of the shift this has created in the relational dynamic between my mother and me.

Stitch Encounter 1: Despite my careful planning, halfway through the first stitch encounter my mother surprised me by introducing a new element drawn from her habitual craft-based knowledge and long-held experience. It was a disruption that temporarily undid the difficult feelings associated with parentification. I unexpectedly found myself re-experiencing being with her in ways that I recalled from my childhood in the 1970s. This process began when I suggested that we work on a sewing project together to make and embroider pillowcases. When I showed my mother the fabric I had pre-cut and hemmed she dismissed my efforts as 'ordinary hemming' rather than 'hemstitching', which was preferable being 'a bit fancy-like', as she put it. She had taught me to sew, knit and embroider but not to hemstitch, a technique she had not used since her girlhood in the 1940s. My plan had been to select a floral pattern for stitching, instead my mother took charge and taught me to hemstitch! This reversal felt comforting and reassuring; the act of teaching and the agency that went with it was now in her hands, literally. In my diary I noted down a felt sense of pleasure as I listened carefully to her instructions and watched her demonstrate. I learnt by example just as I had as a child, in the same living room, as my mother showed me a new needlework technique. I also noted how the family stories that she told during this first session were more fluid than they had been over the past three years: more focused and with less repetition. It seemed that the act of sewing together took us into a space, equivalent to Stewart's 'bloom space', in which my mother was more alert and confident, as her habitual craft-based knowledge came back into play and she began to feel grounded and find herself again.

Stitch Encounter 2: The second stitch encounter had a relaxed pace and sense of familiarity for both of us. My mother picked up the piece that she had started in the first session and continued to work purposefully. As I sat next to her and continued with my own needlework project, another extraordinary thing happened as she began to sing 'One day when we were young that wonderful morning in May', words from a Viennese waltz played in three by four time, a rhythm that complimented the rhythm of her stitching. This improvisational element was something that I had witnessed before when running 'It's Nice to Make', the project I facilitated at Headway East London, when participants spontaneously broke into a song, underscoring the rhythm of the process and establishing a felt sense of community. I made a playlist of similar songs and used them to provide a musical context to enhance the mood of future 'stitch encounters'. The lyrics and gentle melody evoked nostalgia for the past and a powerful sense of the past in the present. This became a defining feature both of future stitch encounters and the short film.

In this session I became increasingly aware of my mother's patient, meticulous handling of needle and thread: how carefully she stitched every four threads, not three threads nor five threads, but always four threads. If she made a mistake she would unpick and redo it (Figure 2). Occasionally, I heard small sounds of frustration, but these quickly passed. Sarah Desmarais in her research on crafting and mental health noted a similar response when working with amateur groups who would become frustrated by their failures, but achieved an enormous sense of confirmation and confidence when they overcame them, qualities that she concluded could be transferred to everyday life (2016). I also noticed how my mother's stitching skills were much sharper and more precise than mine, even though she has not embroidered for over sixty years. Unconsciously drawing on an embodied muscle memory and making fine adjustments as she went, she seemed to be following a sewing protocol that helped her attain a degree of certainty and clarity that I had not seen for some

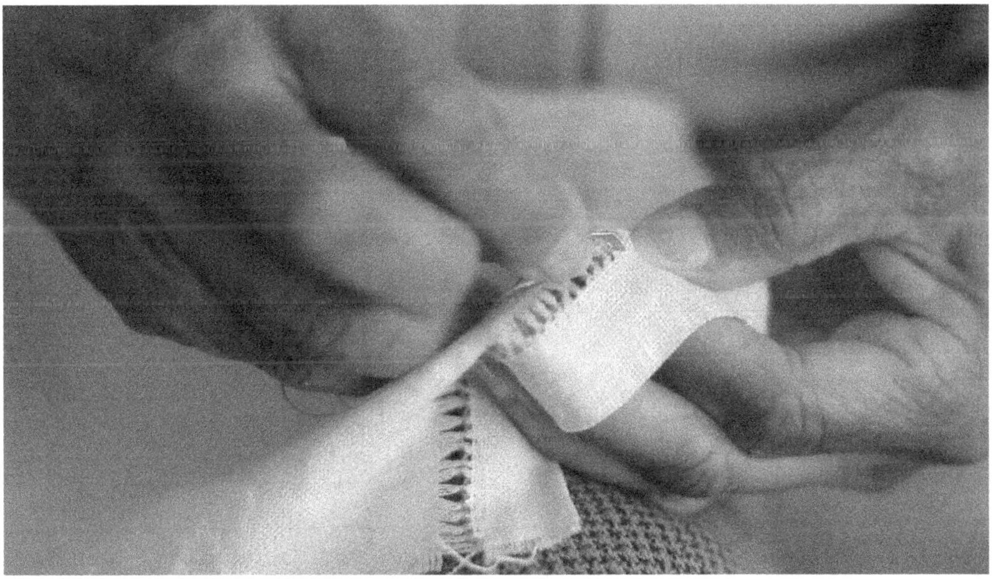

Figure 2: Four threads only: film still from *One Day When We Were Young* (2016). © Mah Rana.

time. The purposeful quality of her making, however, did not always translate into verbal communication, particularly when it came to expressing her feelings. When I asked her about how *making* made her feel, or if she enjoyed sewing, she tentatively responded with, 'umm … it's okay'. I sensed that this hesitancy was more about her reticence than her illness, a question of culturally constructed femininity perhaps rather than cognitive impairment. Her fluency in stitch, however, was beyond question. Making, it seemed, did indeed serve as a safe space, or bloom space, for us to communicate (Figure 3).

Stitch Encounters 3 and 4: In between the second and third stitch encounters I worked on my hemstitch sampler feeling a sense of achievement each time I completed a new variation, an experience that could be read as a process of skills-learning first through social interactions (*interpsychological*) before absorbing the knowledge within oneself (*intrapsychological*) (Vygotsky 1978: 57). The repetitive nature of the stitch work was calming. I kept the sampler near to me and in sight. It became a reassurance object, a tool to reduce anxiety (Winnicott [1971] 2005). During this 'stitch encounter' I showed my mother my hemstitch sampler. She praised me saying simply, 'That's good Mah!' This was a very emotional moment for me as I re-experienced what it felt like to be my mother's daughter again. It became a key moment in the narrative arc of the film and will be considered further in the following section. The fourth and final session felt like a culmination of the process as we both settled into a rhythm of working that was purposeful and mindful, a shared state of *being* akin to what Mihaly Csikszentmihályi (1999: 10) described as 'flow', when an activity is both 'challenging and enjoyable'.

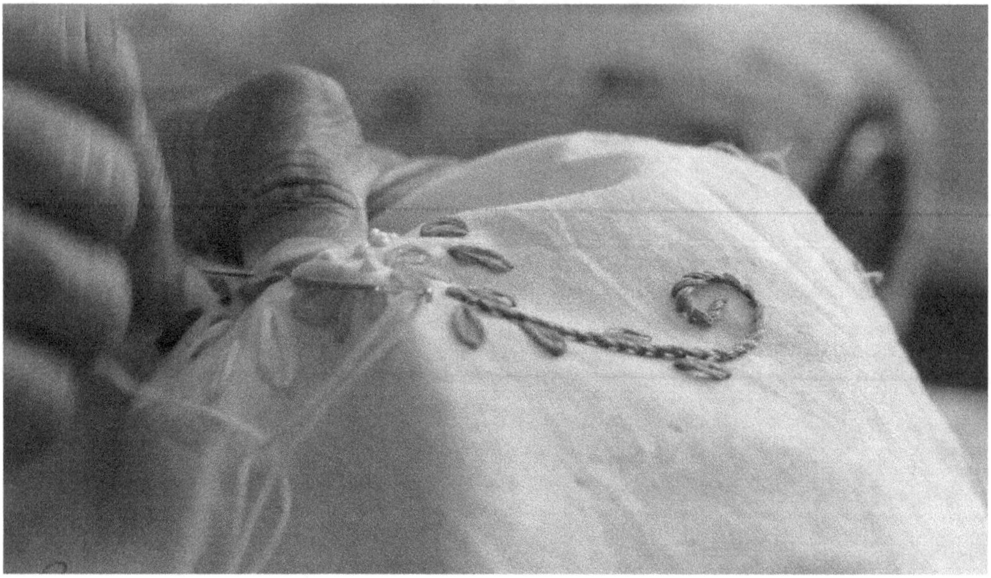

Figure 3: Embroidery stitchwork: film still from *One Day When We Were Young* (2016). © Mah Rana.

Stepping back: Reflexive filming and making

Reflective sketchbooks capture the unplanned spontaneity that occurs through creative play and improvisation where, in Prior's words, the 'process of "hap" happens' (2013: 167). For us, the combined process of filming and making provided a similar improvisational 'haptic' space as parallels and connections between sewing, filming, making and looking emerged and the action, rhythm and pace of each process responded to, reciprocated and shaped the other. This was the first time that Rana had used her DSLR camera on its film setting and she was tentative, sensing her way as she learnt a new technical process in addition to working out how to employ it as a research tool. The following section examines how filming served as a lens through which to consider the process of 'doing' through 'reflection in action' (Schön 1988) in the stitch encounters as knowledge from each creative discipline was applied to a learning situation to construct new knowledge in praxis.

Stitch Encounter 1: In the first stitch encounter I felt that I was guessing a lot, out of control and confused. What right did I have thinking that I could pick up a camera and make a film without any experience! I had watched many films before, paying attention to the frame angles and lighting, and had read some books, but this was the first time that I had put my ideas into practice. As a result I relied on what felt right, but to begin with not a lot felt right. I made mistakes such as setting the exposure too high, which was frustrating, but noted down such technical improvements as how to focus manually while handholding the camera in an attempt to address these issues. I was learning through doing and the fact that I came away with film footage was a thrill in itself. I gradually became aware of how my process of learning through making (and making mistakes) reproduced my engagement with my mother through stitch. Like her, I drew on my habitual craft-based knowledge, albeit in other mediums to make the film. I didn't know much about film technique but I had watched filmmakers: how they moved their bodies with the camera, how they would be in the moment of embodied film*making*. A quote from the director Danny Boyle (2007) where he talked about filming as a slow process resonates with me. I became increasingly aware of filming and stitching as equally slow processes that demand focus, precision, careful attention to the small details and interactions involved in being in a particular moment; I began, in other words, to view film as the means to create a mindful *mise-en-scène*.

Stitch Encounter 2: The sewing activity had its own sense of concentrated flow, and although on one level filming was an intervention, I was keen for it to be integral to the process rather than disruptive. I hadn't been sure how my mother would react to being filmed, but she took it in her stride as if it was the most natural thing in the world. While we talked and she sewed I regularly checked the camera on the tripod because it automatically stopped filming every twelve minutes. We established a repetitive rhythm of sewing, talking, filming and checking. After reviewing footage from the first stitch encounter I decided to handhold the camera so that I could get closer to my mother's hands, closer to the *making*. This reinforced the tacit qualities and craft of hand-making. Close-up shots of my mother's hands threading a needle or clasping and re-clasping as she spoke, the detail of stitches, the vibrant colour of cotton reels, and the textures of cloth, convey the haptic qualities of making and the intimacy of our relationship. The act of filming paralleled that of making in the relationship between hand and tool, whereby the tool (camera or needle) is an extension of the self that embodies, enacts and manifests knowing and intention. The close and slow aesthetic that emerged, enhanced by natural lighting and the play of lacy shadows across the screen, became a defining feature of the film, suggesting my mother's emergent sense of self and the renewed relationship between us that was developing inside and outside the camera frame.

Stitch Encounter 3: In the first and second stitch encounters, my presence was signalled solely by my voice. For the third stitch encounter I put the camera back on the tripod and stepped into the liminal space of the workshop and into the frame. I had been working on a sampler using the new stitch my mother had taught me and wanted to show her my progress. I set the camera to frame a shot of the two of us together, lower body only signalling our embodied engagement as we examine the embroidery. She praises my progress murmuring that I should be a teacher, a moment that is doubly poignant because it both takes me back to a time in the past when she was my advisor and guide, and reminds me of the present in which she no longer recognizes (knows) me as a teacher, something that is an important part of my career (Figure 4).

Stitch Encounter 4: As the workshops developed, I realized that having the camera in my hand gave me the control that I had been missing in the same way that my mother's meticulous stitching brought her a sense of calm, order and purpose. I began to choose

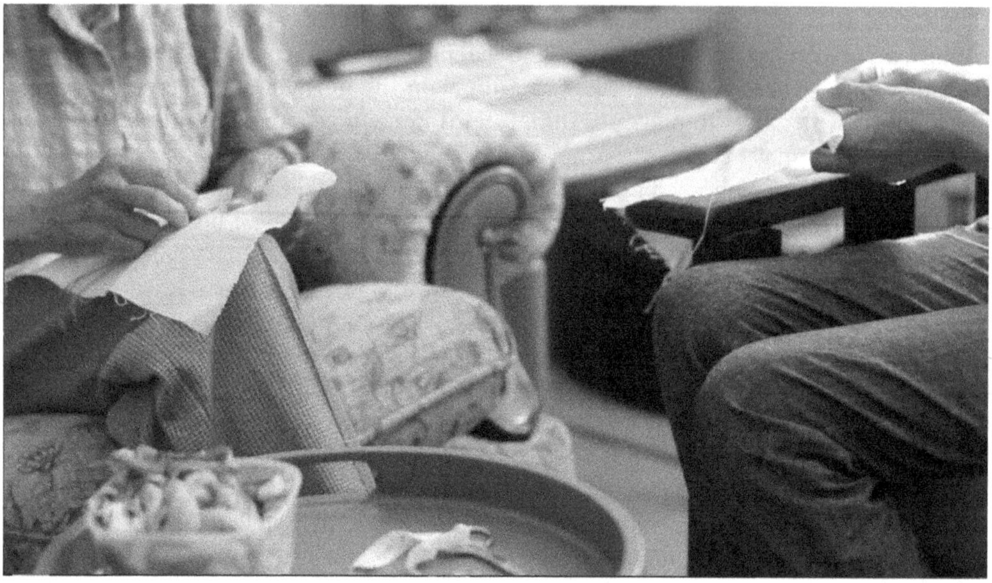

Figure 4: Making together: film still from *One Day When We Were Young* (2016). © Mah Rana.

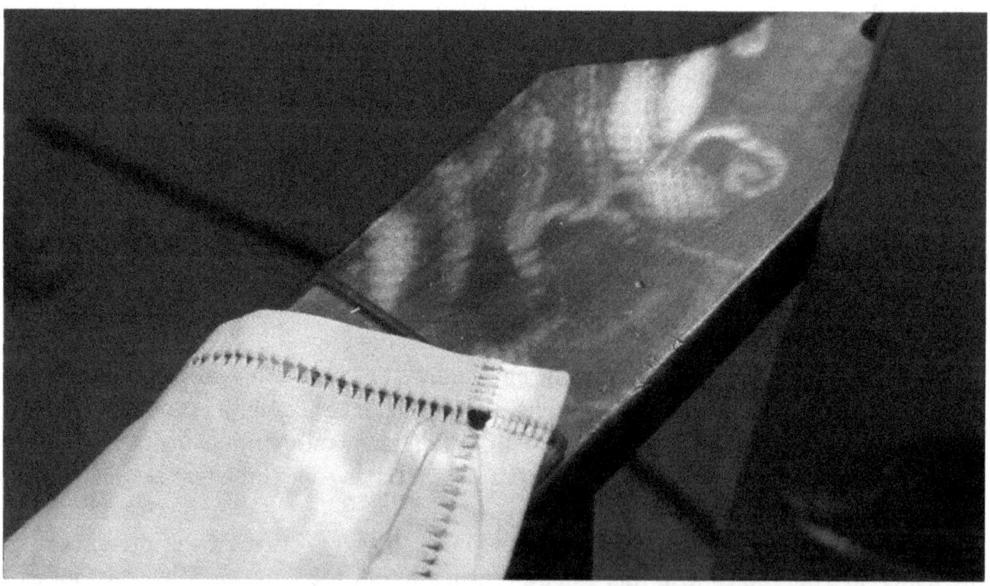

Figure 5: Hemstitch sampler: film still from *One Day When We Were Young* (2016). © Mah Rana.

moments to stand back, take stock and look around the room. I captured these small but useful reflexive pauses by filming cut-away shots of interior details such as light reflecting on a chair arm (Figure 5), or a clock face with the time and date in oversized numbers, a visual aid that helps my mother locate herself in the present, reminding us that time and memory operate according to a new logic for her. Finding a way to stand back and reflect helps one examine the essence of an experience, notice things that might have been missed and generate meaning. The film footage enabled this to happen in a rich three-dimensional way that included time, space, sound, voice, colour, texture and movement. Together with the workshop activities, film served as a liminal space in which transition and change (my mother's condition and our relationship) could be observed, understood and managed in new and reassuring ways.

When my mother examines a black-and-white photograph of her sewing that was taken by my father (Figure 6), it serves as a form of photo-elicitation and stimulates memories (Harper 2002). She comments on a Singer sewing machine in the background, recalling that she brought it with her from Barbados to London in 1954; how her mother had been a very good dressmaker and how she had wanted to be a dressmaker like her. I reflect on how my mother's memories about skills, desires, people and identities from the past are contained in and materialized through sewing, and realized how this helped her reconnect with a sense of self that was forged long before the Alzheimer's diagnosis. Later, while editing the film footage and making the film, I saw how the dual acts of sewing and filmmaking helped me experientially connect with my mother through stories of herself in the past – her sewing

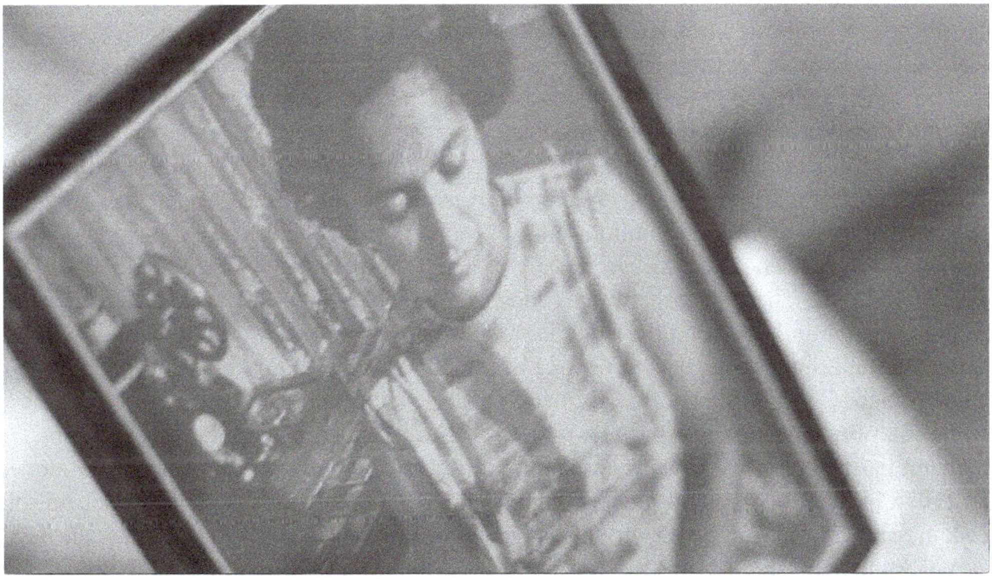

Figure 6: Reminiscing with photograph: film still from *One Day When We Were Young* (2016). © Mah Rana.

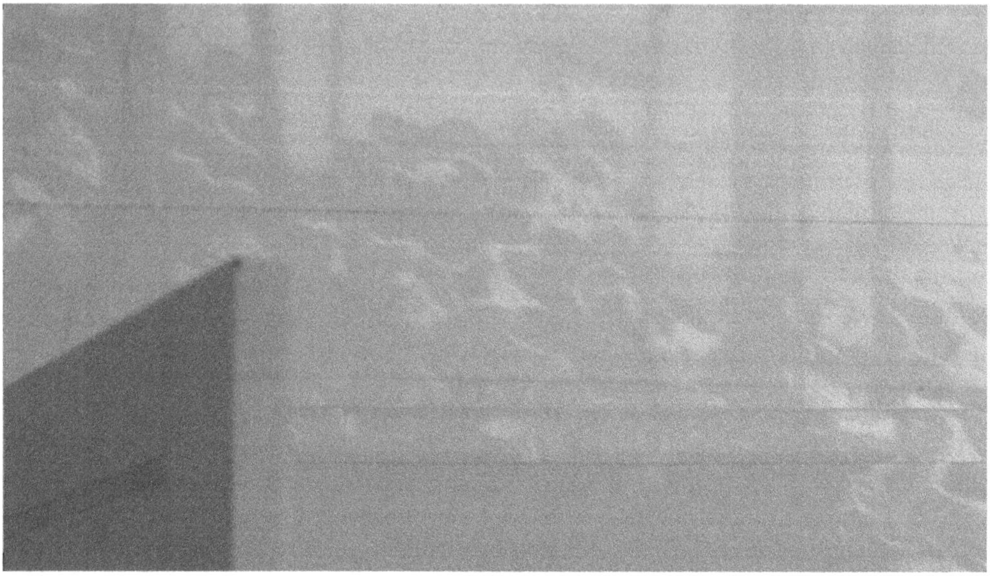

Figure 7: Shadows and light: film still from *One Day When We Were Young* (2016). © Mah Rana.

memories – and her presence in a present that was materialized in and through the act of making.

Finally, it is important to mention the editing process and how it contributed to the production of reflexive knowledge embodied in the film. We wanted to tell a story, or at least to suggest one: the story of Rana's mother, her condition, Rana's experience as carer, and how their skills and inherent abilities as creative makers could produce new knowledge about themselves and how they communicate. Each stage of the editing was shaped by and responded to the stitch encounters. The soundtrack, for instance, was inspired by the song Rana's mother sang when stitching. With its orchestral sweeping strings it references Douglas Sirk melodramas of the 1950s – films that she would have watched as a young woman. True to her lived experience, the sweet, nostalgic melody also serves as an emotional trigger for the audience. The first three frames showing: a shadow embroidery effect on the wall (Figure 7), a reminder note on the front door, Rana's mother's feet dressed in knitted slippers, serve as establishing shots, while the pace of the film mirrors the pace of the stitching and conversation. Close-up shots of hands, needles, fabric and stitch convey a sense of intimacy, while cut-away shots provide space for reflection. The decision not to include faces was made early on partly for ethical reasons and anonymity. The film ends with Rana's mother alone, absorbed in her stitching and quietly singing under her breath as she concentrates on the task in hand: a woman at peace with herself living in a present *made* meaningful by the past.

We wanted to show how the act of creative film*making* can serve as a model for learning and teaching through sharing and listening that foregrounds participant assets and the power relations involved in knowledge exchange. Although a personal history of stitch was important on this occasion, the model of knowledge generation through tacit knowledge could be applied to a wide range of activities in educational, professional and amateur contexts (Hackney 2013). A central factor is the creation of a safe space in which to improvise and a shared interest in and/or knowledge of a set of skills or creative propensities. Examples of how similar workshop models have been employed within the academy include Tandemize, a project part funded by the British Council and directed by Rana that worked with a small group of undergraduates from the United Kingdom and Sri Lanka through a series of international residencies and Live Archive, which was developed by Hannah Maughan in collaboration with Textile Design students at Falmouth University. Film as a reflexive intervention was additionally central to the Co-Producing CARE project that informed many of these initiatives (Hackney 2014a). Live Archive used sewing workshops to creatively engage with textile heritage through sewn responses to a personal archive (Hackney et al. 2016), while Tandemize worked with students and local craftswomen in the United Kingdom and Sri Lanka to create multiple material conversational spaces to flatten the tutor–student hierarchy, and realize social and cultural capital within the group.

Conclusion

Learning, Bruner (1986) argued, is about uncovering meaning in experience rather than truth seeking. Dewey ([1916] 1968) foregrounded the importance of habitualized, experiential knowledge through *doing*. While Stewart emphasized the affective value of worlding, as we pay attention to our embodied reactions, draw on our resources, learn new skills and address challenges, as life becomes a series of minute daily adjustments to help us survive, and even thrive. These concerns and insights provide a useful frame to examine Rana and her mother's experiences as they sewed, filmed and sang together, living in the past but generating knowledge about new ways to be in the present through the act of doing embodied in reflexive creative making. Rana spoke about the tasks of problem-identifying and solution-finding that she is forced to face on a daily basis when caring for her mother, life tasks that parallel our work in learning and teaching in higher education. After the project she felt that she had found a way for this work to become, at least to some degree, more of a shared process, and that her relational dynamic with her mother had changed through the experience of making, sharing, listening and reflecting. The combined process of film*making* through stitch encounters moves us to not only to engage directly with sensory and temporal experience but also to foreground research as a lived condition located in personal relationships and histories. As such, and in the best traditions of action research, it foregrounds the potential of learning and teaching methodologies that promote social participation and meaningful change. For Rana and her mother, the stitch encounters constructed a liminal, bloom space in which the latter's identity as a person with Alzheimer's became less dominant and multiple identities as a maker, a teacher and a mother re-emerged.

One Day When We Were Young was selected for screening in the Crafts Council's Real to Reel Film Festival at Picturehouse Central Cinema in London (3 May 2017). A piece of art in its own right, the film also functions as a resource for others who wish to uncover meaning in experience through a process of making, sharing, listening and reflecting that is embedded in and responds to everyday life.

Acknowledgements

This work was developed from a series of projects funded by the Arts & Humanities Research Council (AHRC) under Co-Producing CARE: Community Asset-Based Research & Enterprise (grant number AH/K006789/1). Film editing for *One Day When We Were Young* was funded by the Arts Learning and Teaching (ALTR) Research Group, University of Wolverhampton. We would like to thank all those who participated in this and related projects and particularly Mah Rana's mother, Waveney.

References

Boyle, Danny (2007), 'What I do…The director', in C. Wilkinson (ed.), *The Observer Book of Film*, London: Observer Books, pp. 10–11.

Bruner, Jerome (1986), *Actual Minds, Possible Worlds*, Cambridge: Harvard University Press.

Chatterjee, Helen and Noble, Guy (2013), *Museums, Health and Well-Being*, London: Routledge.

Collins, Katie (2016), 'Woven into the fabric of the text: Subversive material metaphors in academic writing', LSE Review of Books, http://blogs.lse.ac.uk/lsereviewofbooks/2016/05/27/the-materiality-of-research-woven-into-the-fabric-of-the-text-subversive-material-metaphors-in-academic-writing-by-katie-collins/. Accessed 4 June 2016.

Csikszentmihályi, Mihaly (1990), *Flow: The Psychology of Optimal Experience*, New York: Harper & Row.

Desmarais, Sarah (2016), 'Affective materials: A processual, relational, and material ethnography of amateur group crafts practice in two arts-for-health settings', unpublished Ph.D., London: Falmouth University and University of the Arts London.

Dewey, John ([1916] 1968), *Democracy and Education*, New York: The Free Press.

Frayling, Christopher (2011), *On Craftsmanship: Towards a New Bauhaus*, London: Oberon Books.

Greenhalgh, Paul (1997), 'The history of craft', in Peter Dormer (ed.), *The Culture of Craft*, Manchester: Manchester University Press, pp. 20–52.

Hackney, Fiona (2013), 'Quiet activism & the new amateur: The power of home and hobby crafts', *Design and Culture*, May/June, pp. 169–94.

——— (2014a), 'Co-creating CARE', https://cocreatingcare.wordpress.com/the-project/. Accessed 10 January 2017.

——— (2014b), *Beyond the Toolkit: Understanding & Evaluating Crafts Praxis for Health & Wellbeing*, https://www.falmouth.ac.uk/content/beyond-toolkit-understanding-evaluating-crafts-praxis-health-wellbeing. Accessed 10 January 2017.

Hackney, Fiona, Maughan, Hannah and Desmarais, Sarah (2016), 'The power of quiet: Re-making affective amateur and professional textiles identities', *Journal of Textile Design, Research & Practice*, 4:1, pp. 33–62.

Harper, Douglas (2002), 'Talking about pictures: A case for photo elicitation', *Visual Studies*, 17:1, pp. 13–26.

Johnson, Anna (2013), 'How adult children experience parent dependency in a caregiving/care-receiving dyad', Ph.D. thesis, Minnesota: Walden University.

Lave, Jean and Wenger, Etienne (1991), *Situated Learning*, Cambridge: Cambridge University Press.

McNiff, Shaun (2008), 'Art-based research', in J. Gary Knowles and Ardra L. Cole (eds) (2008), *Handbook of the Arts in Qualitative Research: Perspectives, Methodologies, Examples, and Issues*, London: Sage, pp. 29–40.

Polanyi, Michael ([1966] 1983), *The Tacit Dimension*, Gloucester: Peter Smith.

Prior, Ross W. (2013), 'Knowing what is known: Accessing craft-based meanings in research by artists', in S. McNiff (ed.), *Art as Research: Opportunities and Challenges*, Bristol: Intellect, pp. 161–69.

Rana, Mah (2011), It's Nice to Make, http://www.itsnicetomake.com/. Accessed 10 February 2017.

——— (2016), *One Day When We Were Young*, https://vimeo.com/180566371, London: It's Nice to Make.

Schön, Donald (1988), *The Reflective Practitioner: How Professionals Think in Action*, New York: Basic Books.

Sennett, Richard (2012), *Together: Rituals, Pleasures and Politics of Cooperation*, London and New York: Penguin.

Stewart, Katherine (2010), 'Worlding refrains', in Melissa Gregg and Greg J. Seigworth (eds), *The Affect Theory Reader*, Durham and London: Duke University Press, pp. 339–53.

Vygotsky, Lev (1978), *Mind in Society: The Development of Higher Psychological Process*, Cambridge: Harvard University Press.

Winnicott, Donald W. ([1971] 2005), *Playing and Reality*, London and New York: Routledge.

Chapter 11

Using Art to Cultivate 'Medical Humanities Care' in Chinese Medical Education

Daniel Vuillermin

Ziyou said: 'My friend Zizhang is a man of rare ability, but he has not reached the fullness of humanity.'

– The Analects of Confucius 19.15[1]

In the Song Dynasty (960–1279) the Chinese court established the imperial examinations (*keju* 科举), a meritocratic system of teaching and learning that until its abolition in 1905 centred on ethics and the arts. Aspiring civil servants were required to be highly versed in the classics but also skilled at poetry and calligraphy. Whereas the civil service examinations integrated ethics and aesthetics, today's National Higher Education Entrance Examination (*gaokao* 高考) divides the sciences and the humanities. This divide, which in a Western context C. P. Snow (2012: 1–21) described as 'the two cultures', is particularly pronounced in the field of medical education in China. One step towards bridging this divide is a course – Medicine and Visual Culture – taught by myself at the Institute for Medical Humanities at Peking University Health Science Center and Vivienne Lo, convenor of the China Centre for Health and Humanity, at University College London (UCL). Medicine and Visual Culture is the only course on offer to medical students in mainland China that incorporates analysis of the visual culture of medicine together with the use of art as research in learning. This elective course is available to second- and third-year medical students and is the only opportunity for students to engage in visual arts practices as a form of research. Suzy Wilson (2006: 15–16) argues the arts play three primary roles in medical education: practical skills; examination of cultural and ethical issues through the arts; and an introduction to artists working in health. In a Chinese context the examination of specific cultural practices, social attitudes and an emerging ethics of care are central to the use of art as research in learning and teaching.

This chapter analyses the use of Medical Art Projects (MAPs), a core component of the Medicine and Visual Culture course, to explore the processes of using art as research in learning and teaching in medical education in China. The MAPs are conducted in three stages: research, praxis and exegesis and are designed to enable students to creatively and critically engage with how the processes of disease, healing and health are visually constructed and portrayed. Moreover, creative arts research aims to cultivate ethical practice or what Guo Liping et al. (2016: 29) describe as 'medical humanities care' (*yixue renwen guanhuai*

医学人文关怀), that is, 'humane care [...] in biomedical research and healthcare'. This chapter outlines the broad development of the role of art in Chinese education in relation to the emergence of the medical humanities in contemporary medical education in mainland China, details the content of the Medicine and Visual Culture course, surveys the requirements of the MAPs and explores the use of the MAPs as part of students' research and assessment. MAPs serve to augment the established medical curriculum and seek to engage students in experiential learning and knowledge through arts practice and exegesis. As the Medicine and Visual Culture course and the MAPs are the first of their kind to be implemented into China's medical degree system, research into art and medical education in mainland China has yet to be conducted. This introductory study is a first step towards mapping the field and aims to provide a foundation for further research in using art as research in learning and teaching in Chinese medical education.

Towards using art to cultivate 'medical humanities care'

> Zilu asked what makes a gentleman. The Master said: 'Through self-cultivation, he achieves dignity [...] Through self-cultivation he spreads his peace to all the people.'
>
> (Confucius 1997: 72, 14.42)

For more than 1,500 years China's imperial examination system was not so much an accumulation of a set of professional skills but rather a system of social advancement based on personal cultivation. Although aspiring students of ancient times dedicated much of their time to rote learning, according to the sinologist Simon Leys (Confucius 1997: xxix), the purpose of education was 'primarily moral: intellectual achievement was only a means towards ethical self-cultivation [...] Confucian education was humanistic and universalist'. Historically in China, a person's sensibility was refined through the study and practice of art and poetry. As Shihkuan Hsu (2015: 10–15) writes, art played a vital role in Chinese education of the 'whole person' from the familial, professional, ethical, moral, to the spiritual. Yet over the course of the twentieth century, through war, civil war and revolutionary zeal, such principles were severed, resulting in what Confucian bioethicist Fan Ruiping (2010: 231–50) describes as the contemporary 'moral vacuum' of the People's Republic of China.

Increasingly medical schools in the United States and Europe are drawing upon the visual arts to supplement the training of students' observation and diagnostic skills (Shapiro et al 2006: 263–68) with a broader aim of 'humanizing' medical education (Bleakley 2015: 2–5). Numerous studies on using arts in medical education over the past decades have explored how the praxis of art creation not only 'sharpens trainees' skills in observation, description, critical thinking and communication' (Kumagai 2012: 1138) but also fosters self-care, empathy and shared values. In the contemporary Chinese medical education system, however, using art as a means of learning and research remains in its infancy.

This is to be expected, given China's tumultuous history during the twentieth century, in particular, events such as the Cultural Revolution (1966–76) in which 'medical education essentially ceased' (Wu et al. 2014: 19). According to Wu et al. (2014: 19), the Cultural Revolution profoundly hindered the development of a modern medical academic degree system. In addition to uprooting the 'capitalist' middle classes, including urban 'bourgeois' doctors, the Cultural Revolution centred upon the destruction of ancient Chinese culture and education (or the so-called Four Olds [*sijiu* 四旧]: Old Customs, Old Culture, Old Habits and Old Ideas), which for centuries had emphasised the centrality of the arts in education. Although the arts – traditional, modern and post-modern – have flourished since Deng Xiaoping's Reform and Opening-Up policies (*gaige kaifeng* 改革开放) of the late 1970s, more recently the ruling Chinese Communist Party (CCP) has appropriated aspects of ancient Chinese education in an attempt to align traditional Chinese culture with socialist core values; art should be a public service to improve the values of the CCP, society and the individual in order to achieve the so-called great rejuvenation of the Chinese nation.

In contemporary Chinese medical education, there is a growing recognition of the role of the medical humanities, which is leading to further economic investment and integration into the existing curriculum by means of compulsory and elective courses. The medical humanities are being prescribed as a treatment for the ailments of the doctor–patient relationship at China's monolithic, under-resourced and over-crowded public hospitals where violence against doctors (Pan et al. 2015: 111–116) and bribery are common occurrences (Xu 2013: 1). In order to address issues of the doctor–patient relationship in China, Peking University Health Science Center (PUHSC), one of China's elite medical institutions, has taken the lead on implementing medical humanities and bioethics courses that address 'the social context[s] of illness' and provide 'practical training in communication and conflict resolution' (Lancet 2014: 1013). The intellectual and ethical framework developed at PUHSC is based upon the contemporary Chinese conceptions of medical humanities (*yixue renwen* 医学人文), which underpins the course content.

Medical humanities care

In a Chinese context, medical humanities have multiple inter-related meanings that centre upon the Confucian concept of benevolence (*ren* 仁). 仁 is variously translated as benevolence, compassion, altruism and goodness. According to Vivienne Lo (cited in Vuillermin 2016: 3), this fundamental Chinese ethical principle is 'what makes individuals and society "human" or "humane"' and it 'illuminates the principles and practice of medicine and health care, past and present'. While 仁 bears some resemblance to ancient Greek ideals of medical practices, Fan Ruiping (2011: 7) argues that personal health in China is a 'state of complete physical, mental and social well-being' and that moral virtues are integral to a Confucian definition of a healthy person. Such a model of health, which integrates the human body with the metaphysical, cosmological and moral, differs greatly from Western individualized, materialist conceptions of the self and self-care. One framework for Chinese medical humanities, developed by Guo Liping et al. (2016: 29), proposes a hierarchy that encompasses the ethical and the practical:

1. Medical humanities spirit (*yixue renwen jingshen* 医学人文精神), the ultimate care for man and the respect for life;
2. Medical humanities care (*yixue renwen guanhuai* 医学人文关怀), meaning beneficence in biomedical research and health care;
3. Medical humanities as a branch of learning (*yixue renwen xueke* 医学人文学科), the interdisciplinary cluster of the humanities and social sciences that scrutinizes medicine from their own unique perspectives;
4. Medical humanities competence (*yixue renwen suzhi* 医学人文素质), the ability to take benevolent actions in biomedical research and clinical care.

Based on the principle of medical humanities care, the MAPs seek to bring together critical learning processes that centre on understanding the world through active research, engagement, exploration, inquiry, self-expression and communication to encourage ethical Chinese virtues in students: benevolence (*ren* 仁), justice (*yi* 義/ 义), knowledge (*zhi* 智) and integrity (*xin* 信) (Li 2012: 105–52). Students are tasked to examine the role of visual culture in representations of illness in order to develop medical humanities competence by cultivating medical humanities care. As Wang Yu, a Biomedical English major, states:

> I think that the role of art in medical education is to provide a totally new approach to understanding medicine and patients. The current medical education pays too much attention to medical knowledge but ignores the importance of medical humanities care. Art can provide a way for medical students to understand what is most important in medical treatments for patients.
>
> (Wang Yu 2016)

While Wang Yu claims that using art in medical education is a 'totally new approach', the cultivation of medical humanities care can be said to be a reclamation of Chinese virtue-oriented learning practices. According to Chang Ruilun (2005: 228) in ancient China, 'kind-heartedness' was the 'highest quality humans can possess' and arts practices were integral to the process of cultivation of the 'whole person', not simply a set of skills. By reintegrating historical learning practices into contemporary medical education, doctors in China are encouraged to not only treat their patients' physical ailments but also attend to their emotional and spiritual experience of illness. Art is a vital means that not only allows medical students to critically engage with how the processes of disease, healing and health are visually constructed and portrayed but also serves as a process of self-cultivation, empathy and professional development.

Medicine and visual culture

One step towards implementing art-based research in a Chinese medical context is an elective course at the Institute for Medical Humanities at PUHSC: Medicine and Visual Culture, which is taught by Vivienne Lo and myself. The course serves to examine representations of medicine in the visual arts – anatomical drawings, paintings, photography, graphic memoirs and cinema, among others – from Anglo-European and Chinese sources. The broad pedagogical aims of this course are to foster visual literacy, to highlight the significance of visual culture in medical history, culture and education in relation to various experiences of illness and to reflect upon the notion of the Medical Gaze, that is, how medical knowledge, technology and practice objectifies the body and dehumanizes the patient as a case study. This elective course is available to two clusters of students: Biomedical majors (Clinical Medicine, Nursing, Dentistry, among others) and Biomedical English majors. Most science-major students during their high school years did not have opportunities to learn or practise their art as the demands of the National Higher Education Entrance Examination do not allow for extra-curricular activities. As Wang Jiawen, a Biomedical English major, states:

> When I was young it was compulsory for me to play Chinese and Western musical instruments and learn traditional Chinese painting and calligraphy although now it all seems to be lost.
>
> (Wang Jiawen 2016)

Like most children in China, Wang Jiawen learned art at kindergarten and primary school, but by middle school, students who want to earn top grades and enter elite institutions such as Peking University focus on science subjects; art is considered for weaker or less ambitious students.

The course is designed to provide two ontological stages of knowing: theoretical (declarative knowledge) and practical (tacit) knowledge (Prior 2012: 93). The first half of the Medicine and Visual Culture course is dedicated to theoretical training by examining key works in the visual history of medicine, from Leonardo da Vinci's anatomical drawings (1510–11) to films such as *Blind Massage* (*Tuina* 推拿) (Ye 2014) through a standard academic lecture (50 minutes) and analysis of artworks in small groups (50 minutes). The second half of the course focuses on the praxis of art creation as a means of learning wherein students engage in a range of artistic practices, including creating drawings, graphic medicine strips, class performances and the MAP.

Medical Art Project

The primary task of the Medicine and Visual Culture course is the Medical Art Project (MAP). The purpose of the MAPs is to cultivate students' creativity and expand their critical engagement with medical art and how disease, healing and health are portrayed visually. As Kerry Freedman writes:

> Artistic production is a critical path to understanding, partly because the process and the product of art-making enables students to experience creative and critical connections between form, feeling and knowing. It empowers students through their expression of ideas and construction of identities as it gives insight into the artistic motivations, intentions and capabilities of others.
>
> (2003: 147)

Based on qualitative and performative research the MAPs have manifold aims: to decentre teacher-centred pedagogy and rote memorization, to initiate independent research, to increase self-reflexivity and personal knowledge, to develop practical artistic techniques and to encourage interpersonal and organizational skills (Prior 2012: 91), with a broad aim of cultivating 'medical humanities care' (*yixue renwen guanhuai* 医学人文关怀).

MAPs are intended to disrupt established pedagogical practices of Chinese medical education to produce new forms of explicit and tacit knowledge based on four key dimensions (Prior 2012: 91–2):

1. Inter/Personal (*personal experience, auto-didacticism, reflexivity*)
2. Intellectual (*developing analytical and problem-solving skills*)
3. Practical (*praxis of art creation*)
4. Social (*ethical, cultural*)

Groups of two to five students (depending on the class size) are required to create a work(s) of art in any visual medium to examine any aspect of disease, healing and health. Given that MAPs require a range of skills – from praxis to exegesis – students tend to distribute the skills base. For example, one student may take the lead in identifying and conceptualizing what aspect of health and healing they will examine, another student with artistic skills may be responsible for creating the work, while the student with the best English-language skills will lead the MAP presentation. To date, students have embraced the opportunity to delve into various artistic practices. For most students, the MAP is the only creative project they will undertake during their medical degree as typically students are confined to exams, essays and presentations.

The open scope of both the medium and the subject is designed to encourage students to work together to devise their own approach and to collectively decide their subject. The research methodology employed for the MAPs is not focused on the material product of artistic creation – be it a sculpture, a painting, a documentary – but rather the process of artistic production. In this way the MAPs are heuristic and empirical as students must work from a blank canvas, lump of clay or a new electronic document and be involved in each stage of the development of the work from its conception and execution to its exegesis. The students are not given any direct instructions on what the artwork should explore, what medium they should use or what aspect of illness they are analysing or contesting. This approach encourages students to use art as a means of research through each stage of the creative and critical process.

To date, students have worked in the following media: documentary, short film, photography, oil painting, sand painting, drawing, graphic memoir and sculpture. The research underpinning many of the MAPs is based on students' real-world experiences as interns at one of Beijing's public hospitals or personal interactions with their fellow students and family, while others explore illness in more abstract terms. For example, Huang Cui from the group Waver drew upon the experience of procrastination among students and used the project to research how this condition adversely affects the education and physical and psychological health of students. Huang Cui (2016) states that, 'The topic of procrastination stemmed from our ordinary life where many students, including ourselves, suffer from procrastination. We want to create such art project to help solve the problem.'

Augmenting established pedagogical practices, however, offers some initial challenges. For example, when I describe in the introductory lecture of the Medicine and Visual Culture course that one of the main tasks for students is to create a work of art, a wave of gasps washes across the room. Art is feared. Creativity is a step into the uncharted. Wang Jiawen states:

> At the beginning of the Medical Art Projects we were very troubled because as Chinese students we have never done this before. At first we decided we wanted to do something different but the problem with simply wanting to be different is that you may not have a feasible idea. So we tried to link our purpose to our interests and experiences because we are all medical students and we are all females. We care about feminine health. This project linked our personal experiences and academic interests.
>
> (Wang Jiawen 2016)

Assigning students to work in small groups addresses some concerns about their individual creative abilities, as students are able to work through their ideas collectively and then delegate tasks according to particular skillsets. As Shaun McNiff notes that a:

> change in the general perception of creativity may be the most viable way of expanding participation. Rather than focusing on what you do not have or what you are not capable of doing, concentrate on what is uniquely yours.
>
> (McNiff 2003: 5)

In addition to anxieties about artistic ability, the prospect of art creation raises issues of identity. As medical students they identify with a prescribed role as a 'medical student'. MAPs disrupt this identity, recasting the role of the medical student; a transformation that sees them shift their scholastic identity from that of medical student to medical artist-researcher. The students are now in unfamiliar territory, both in terms of learning and identity. This is a jolt to this elite group, who over the course of their primary, middle and high school years became highly adept at learning through well-worn, expedient modes of learning and testing (often exam based), which for the purposes of the Chinese education system is a proven, safe formula.

In Chinese medical education, MAPs are an atypical approach to using art that engages students in new acts of research and learning. As Ross Prior (2013: 57–65) writes, 'Art-based research recognizes the valuable role that different art forms have in exploring and responding to personal experiences, the meanings that they have and the choices that can be made.' Chinese medical students have few opportunities to engage in research activities as the primary means of evaluation is examinations. Using art as research in a medical context transgresses stale pedagogical practices and challenges students to present their own critical and creative responses to create new forms of meaning in relation to real-world health-related issues.

Presentation

The work(s) are presented as part of a 30-minute formal exegesis of the research topic and art-making process. The exegesis format is adapted from Estelle Barrett's 'Developing and writing creative arts practice research: A guide' (2007: 186–99). Barrett's guide provides the students and the teacher with a rigorous and clear framework for presenting art-based research. Each group prepares a PowerPoint presentation that details:

- the subject to be investigated;
- the creative and intellectual origins of the work(s);
- the mediums, materials, methods and conceptual frameworks;
- a formal analysis including its symbols, motifs etc.;
- what aspect(s) of illness, healing and health the students are analysing or contesting;
- what is the outcome and significance of the work(s).

Lastly, the students engage in a 10-minute Q&A with their classmates and the lecturer. The purpose of the presentation is not only to provide a platform for students to explicate the process of conception, research and execution but also to delineate the primary arguments of the artwork.

Assessment

Currently, MAPs comprise 50 per cent of the overall grade and are jointly assessed by me and peers by using a point-based criteria sheet. I make additional qualitative notes about the work and the presentation; however, the peers provide a quantitative grade. The MAPs are not assessed according to the aesthetic quality of the artworks as most students did not receive any formal training or have not practised art since their childhood. To my surprise, however, many groups produce innovative, well-crafted works, yet for the purposes of assessment the focus is on the execution of ideas rather than technique or craft. The primary criteria are based on:

- innovative and well-presented work(s) displaying reflection on the progressive development and exploration of ideas and concepts from the initial exploratory work through to their refinement and execution;
- skilled and effective use and manipulation of visual language to comprehensively communicate artistic responses, ideas, concepts and observations;
- the body of work that presents a clear relationship between the concept(s) and the finished artwork(s).

The quality of the delivery of the presentation is also assessed, according to the following criteria:

- does the speaker maintain appropriate eye contact with the audience and is suitably animated;
- was the information well communicated (language skills and pronunciation);
- were the visual aids well prepared, informative, effective and not distracting;
- was the length of the presentation completed within the assigned time limit of 30 minutes.

The aim of the MAPs is not to transform medical students into artists, rather the project offers the opportunity for students and teachers to explore new modes of research and learning by engaging in creative and reflexive practices with the broad aim of 'humanizing' the practice of medicine in China or the cultivation of medical humanities care.

Sample Medical Art Projects: *Body and Soul, Wax Women*

> I think art makes us empathetic because I feel I'm no longer an outsider of the patients' suffering [...] Empathy rather than a 'medical gaze' makes the interaction and communication between the patient and the doctor more harmonious.
>
> (Pan Xuru 2016)

The following selection of MAPs seeks to demonstrate the range of media, topics and themes to show evidence of how students use art to become what Suzy Wilson describes as 'empathic problem-solvers' (2006: S15–S16). In many cases the MAPs were the first instance of students engaging with the community and their peers in a health-related context. By employing creative, critical and reflexive visual arts practices, select groups sought to reaffirm ancient

Chinese values such as perseverance (*Body and Soul*) or challenges to contemporary social attitudes towards women in China (*Wax Women*).

Body and Soul

This 12-minute documentary explores the social model of disability and the ancient Chinese virtue of perseverance (*hengxin/yili* 恒心/毅力) by focusing on Chen, a young man with osteogenesis imperfecta who lives alone in Beijing working as a customer service consultant for the online shopping platform Taobao. Chen is originally from Jilin province but moved to Beijing to seek an independent life. First-tier cities such as Beijing, Shanghai and Guangzhou offer migrant workers across China the promise of higher wages, professional opportunities and a more open social and cultural environment. The documentary follows Chen as he makes his way from the supermarket to his tiny 3-square-metre apartment. Chen is a wheelchair user in Beijing, one of China's most congested cities. The focus of this documentary is not Chen's impairment but rather the disabling effects of Beijing's built environment and transportation system. Chen instructed the students that they should not assist him in any way as he wanted the team to capture the various obstacles and mobility challenges that he encounters on the streets, inside buildings and on public transport. On occasions Chen receives voluntary assistance from security guards and members of the public. The students follow Chen holding the camera at his head-height so as to see the environment from his perspective. This angle reorients the viewer's gaze towards a more horizontal perspective. For example, Chen's visual and physical engagement with supermarket products is largely horizontal as he cannot reach items that are stacked above the bottom two shelves. Both the research activities of the students and the documentary film itself serves as what Arthur Kleinman (1988: 10) describes as 'empathic witnessing', that is, how narratives construct the meanings of illness in relation to disease or impairment.

While the Chinese government and organizations such as the China Disabled Persons' Federation have made considerable efforts and achievements over the past decades to improve access to education and employment, wheelchair users such as Chen cannot wait until major cities such as Beijing develop accessible infrastructure; therefore, they must take it upon themselves to venture through its urban landscapes. This leads to one of the major themes of the documentary: perseverance. This virtue is extolled in the ancient classic divination text the *Book of Changes* (*yijing* 易经). According to the hexagram 'Waiting/Nourishment' (*xu* 需):

> Perseverance brings good fortune.
> It furthers one to cross the great water.
>
> (I Ching 2017)

One commentary of the 'Waiting/Nourishment' hexagram from the Richard Wilhelm translation elaborates:

> One is faced with a danger that has to be overcome. Weakness and impatience can do nothing. Only a strong man can stand up to his fate, for his inner security enables him to endure to the end [...] It is only when we have the courage to face things exactly as they are, without any sort of self-deception or illusion, that a light will develop out of events, by which the path to success may be recognized. This recognition must be followed by resolute and persevering action.
>
> (I Ching 2017)

This MAP frames Chen's disability in terms of the western social model of disability but characterizes Chen's endeavours in classically Chinese terms, which is that perseverance is a virtue.

Wax Women

In another MAP – *Wax Women* – three female Biomedical English majors Wang Jiawen, Liao Meixia and Long Jingmiao sought to confront the taboos of women's health in a Chinese context by visualizing the pain experienced by what the group describes as the 'Other Gender'. Through a series of crayon drawings and sculptures, the team examined the pain of menstruation (Girls' Open Secret), pre- and post-natal depression (Blue Delivery), the pain of beautifying the body (Dangerous Elegance) and *Touch Me. Touch Me* addresses breast cancer, feminine health and sexuality, is made from two mounds of polystyrene and melted crayon. In between the breasts is a pink ribbon that symbolizes breast cancer. The right breast is covered in melted orange and red crayon, representing a healthy breast; the splashes of colour are intended to portray the health and vigour of the organ. The left breast, however, is deformed, blackened and incomplete. This breast serves as a warning to the public about breast cancer. 'Maybe this artwork is an exaggeration of what a cancerous breast may look like but we want to warn people about the health risks' (Wang Jiawen 2016). According to Wang Jiawen (2016), in China there are campaigns to promote awareness about breast cancer but 'not many'. 'People are now more open about talking about breast cancer', says Jiawen 'but in China if people feel unwell they won't go to the hospital as they think they will be healed in a few days. Because there are so many people waiting at the hospitals they would rather not go. So sometimes the disease will get worse.' In addition to addressing health concerns during the class presentation, the all-female group took the extra step of confronting the sexualization of breasts. One of the members took the sculpture around the classroom and asked the boys to touch the sculpted breasts. This brought about a great deal of laughter and awkwardness in the class room; however, as a subversive act it also sought to break the taboo of speaking openly about sexuality in China. Wang Jiawen states:

> We want people to pay attention to women. From ancient times Chinese women have been discriminated against. Even now in their careers or in public spaces many women are looked down upon, particularly in less developed areas.
>
> (Wang Jiawen 2016)

The creation of this series of images and sculptures enabled a dialogue and debate about the male gaze, the medical gaze and female health in a Chinese context. In traditional and contemporary representations of the Chinese female body, the breasts are fully covered, signifying sexual and aesthetic modesty. This modesty extends to medical examinations. For Chinese women breast cancer is the most common cancer (Zuo et al. 2017: 214–18), and one barrier to reducing incidence and mortality is confronting the sexualization of the female body. By creating works of art that address women's health issues, this group used the presentation format to directly confront taboos in Chinese culture, society and education, with the aim of improving female health.

Conclusion

> Art is an essential part of being human. If doctors cannot find beauty in people or in the things around them this will impede their ability to be good doctors. Art needs to be cultivated during medical education otherwise healthcare workers won't have the opportunity when they are in the field.
>
> (Wang Jiawen 2016)

From a historical perspective the MAPs are a return to a system of learning in China that integrates art-based practice with the study of medicine and ethics. Yet today medical students in mainland China, as elsewhere, are primarily trained to understand the biological, physiological and psychophysiological aspects of the body and disease, paying little attention to the personal, social and cultural dimensions of experiencing illness. The MAPs signal a shift in pedagogy and research in mainland Chinese medical education, augmenting the disease-based model of medicine by encouraging students to use art as a means of researching and representing the sociocultural and humanistic aspects of health care. Together with problem-based learning programmes offered at PUHSC, the MAPs augment both theoretical and practical knowledge by offering students the opportunity to learn through new or unfamiliar skillsets, in this case, using art as research. As the MAPs are the first art-based research projects to be implemented into medical education in China, there is significant room for development and further research. One aspect of the MAPs that requires further development is that although the open scope is intended to allow students to freely inquire and devise their topics, a clearer framework is required to help guide students through the processes of conception, research, execution and exegesis. Moreover, a more rigorous system of evaluation is required to measure how using art as research in learning may improve medical humanities care. Further research into the use of art as research in learning and teaching in a Chinese context may entail further examination of the ethical dimensions of the MAPs, such as medical humanities care or cross-cultural comparative study between related MAPs in the United States and Europe and mainland China. As an experimental art-based research project the MAPs offer tremendous potential to engage students in innovative acts of learning that allow students to engage in the intuitive and emotional aspects of medical education; as Huang Cui (2016) states, 'Art … inspires me to undertake more research on illness, healing and health.'

References

Barrett, Estelle (2007), 'Developing and writing creative arts practice research: A guide', in E. Barrett and B. Bolt (eds), *Practice as Research: Approaches to Creative Arts Enquiry*, London: I. B. Tauris & Co Ltd, pp. 186–205.

Bleakley, Alan (2015), *Medical Humanities and Medical Education: How the Medical Humanities Can Shape Better Doctors*, New York: Routledge.

Chang, Ruilun (2005), 'Culture and art education in China', *International Journal of Education Through Art,* 1:3, pp. 225–36.

Confucius (1997), *The Analects of Confucius* (trans. Simon Leys), New York: W.W. Norton & Company Inc.

Cui, Huang (2016), Biomedical English major, PUHSC, interviewed by Daniel Vuillermin, Beijing, 13 October 2016.

Fan, Ruiping (2010), *Reconstructionist Confucianism: Rethinking Morality after the West*, New York: Springer.

——— (2011), *Confucian Bioethics*, Dordrecht: Springer.

Freedman, Kerry (2003), *Teaching Visual Culture: Curriculum, Aesthetics and the Social Life of Art*, New York: Teachers College Press.

Guo, Liping, Wei, Lihong, Li, Yanfeng and Li, Han (2016), 'Medical humanities and empathy: An experimental study', in D. Vuillermin and L. Guo (eds), *Chinese Medical Humanities Review 2016*, Beijing: Peking University Medical Press, n.pag.

Hsu, Shihkuan (2015), *Education as Cultivation in Chinese Culture*, London: Springer.

I Ching (2017), *I Ching* (trans. Richard Wilhelm), http://www2.unipr.it/~deyoung/I_Ching_Wilhelm_Translation.html. Accessed 23 May 2017.

Kleinman, Arthur (1988), *The Illness Narratives: Suffering, Healing and the Human Condition*, New York: Basic Books.

Kumagai, Arno (2012), 'Acts of interpretation: A philosophical approach to using creative arts in medical education', *Academic Medicine*, 87:8, pp. 1138–46.

Lancet (2014), 'Editorial: Violence against doctors: Why China? Why now? What next?', *The Lancet*, 383:9922, p. 1013.

Li, Jin (2012), *Cultural Foundations of Learning East and West,* Cambridge: Cambridge University Press.

McNiff, Shaun (2003), *Creating with Others: The Practices of Imagination in Life, Art, and the Workplace*, Boston: Shambhala.

Prior, Ross W. (2012), *Teaching Actors: Knowledge Transfer in Actor Training*, Bristol: Intellect.

——— (2013), 'Knowing what is known: Accessing craft-based meanings in research by artists', *Journal of Applied Arts & Health*, 4:1, pp. 57–66.

Shapiro, Johanna, Ruckner, Lloyd and Beck, Jill (2006), 'Training the clinical eye and mind: Using the arts to develop medical students' observational and pattern recognition skills', *Medical Education*, 40:3, pp. 263–68.

Snow, Charles Percy (2012), *The Two Cultures*, New York: Cambridge University Press.

Vuillermin, Daniel (2016), 'Introduction', in D. Vuillermin and L. Guo (eds), *Chinese Medical Humanities Review 2016*, Beijing: Peking University Medical Press, n.pag.

Wang, Jiawen (2016), Biomedical English major, interviewed by Daniel Vuillermin, Beijing, 13 October.

Wang, Yu (2016), Biomedical English major, PUHSC, interviewed by Daniel Vuillermin, Beijing, 13 October.

Wilson, Suzy (2006), 'What can the arts bring to medical training?', *The Lancet*, 368:S15–S16, http://www.thelancet.com/pdfs/journals/lancet/PIIS0140-6736(06)69909-1.pdf. Accessed 23 May 2017.

Wu, Lijuan, Wang, Youxin, Peng, Xiaoxia, Song, Manshu, Guo, Xiuhua, Nelson, Hugh and Wang, Wei (2014), 'Development of a medical academic degree system in China', *Medical Education Online*, 19, https://www.ncbi.nlm.nih.gov/pmc/articles/PMC3895259/. Accessed 23 May 2017.

Xu, Zhanwen (2013), 'The distortion of the doctor-patient relationship in China', *SGIM Forum*, 37:2, http://www.sgim.org/File%20Library/SGIM/Resource%20Library/Forum/2014/Feb 2014-01.pdf. Accessed 23 May 2017.

Xuru, Pan (2016), Biomedical English major, PUHSC, interviewed by Daniel Vuillermin, Beijing, 13 October.

Ye, Lou (2014), 推拿 ('Blind massage'), China: Shaanxi Culture Industry, Dream Factory, Les Films du Lendemain.

Yu, Pan, Xiu, Hongyang, Jiang, Pinghe, Yan, Honggu, Xiao, Lizhan, Hui, Fanggu, Qing, Yanqiao, Dong, Chizhou and Hui, Minjin (2015), 'To be or not to be a doctor, that is the question: A review of serious incidents of violence against doctors in China from 2003–2013', *Journal of Public Health*, 23:2, pp. 111–16.

Zuo, Tingting, Zheng, Rongshuo, Zeng, Hongmei, Zhang, Siwei and Chen, Wanqing (2013), 'Female breast cancer incidence and mortality in China, 2013', *Thoracic Cancer*, 8:3, pp. 214–18.

Note

1 Confucius (1997: 96).

Chapter 12

Entanglement in Shakespeare's Text: Using Interpretive Mnemonics with Acting Students with Dyslexia

Petronilla Whitfield

This chapter prioritizes the major role of the reader as 'actor creator' in the performance of Shakespeare and explores the multidimensional roles of art in facilitating the challenges of dyslexia. It considers how the creative process of reading can become destabilized for acting students with dyslexia, and presents examples of art-based interdisciplinary practice, which can circumvent an individual's difficulties in engaging with the written text. When intersected into the established curriculum in the teaching of acting Shakespeare, these methods can enhance inclusive strategies of pedagogy, expanding opportunities for multi-literacies towards performance.

Firstly, in order to establish how we make sense when reading – particularly in the reading of Shakespeare – I begin from the premise that there is no external reality presented by the printed marks on the page that might be assumed to contain Shakespeare's intended meanings. However, through a convoluted process involving the reader's interaction with the written words and the literary form presented by Shakespeare (and his myriad of editors) as 'a shared system of rules [...] so understanding will be uniform', the alphabetical symbols and grammatical form are cognitively processed by the reader (Tompkins 1994: xviii). Meanings are constructed through word recognition, mental images, feelings, memory and selective ideas (Rosenblatt 2005: xxv). Analogous with acting, Vivienne Smith labels this dynamic process of reading as the interpretive framework, breaking it down into three tiers: the emotive, experiential and intertextual (2010: 66–68).

When lifting the words from the page into performance, an actor's task is to convey their individual interpretation as they experience and understand it in the moment of speaking. The communication of the 'I myself' of the actor through their manner of voicing, articulating, reading and delivery of text is at the centre in presenting identity, ability and artistic expression. The actor's persona is always there, underpinning the character and author's words. As theatre director John Harrop emphasizes, '[n]o matter how actors act, they cannot expunge themselves from the performance [...] this "I-ness" is a necessary part [...] the playwright's intention only comes into being through them' (Harrop 1992: 6). The reader-response theorist Wolfgang Iser (1978: 131–32) employs the term *entanglement* to describe the reader's experience when they are wholly involved and present within the presence of the text. For the acting student with dyslexia, there is a painful contradiction in Iser's depiction of the *entangled* reader. For those with dyslexia, the word *entangled* commonly encapsulates a more troubled meaning, that of being ensnared or tangled-up in their interaction with the text. The individual is thereby impeded from discovering any presence, either of him or herself as the author or the text. These fundamental elements inherent in the reading and performing of a complex text such as Shakespeare highlight the vulnerable status of the acting student with dyslexia.

The background context

There is an increasing number of students with dyslexia in higher education (Brunswick 2012: 1; Pavey et al. 2010: 28). In my experience of teaching voice and acting in higher education actor-training institutions, every cohort of acting students invariably includes a number of individuals assessed as dyslexic by an educational psychologist. There is some discrepancy in the umbrella term used to label dyslexia. The UK Equality Act (2010) defines dyslexia as a disability, while some others refer to it as a learning difficulty or difference (Brunswick 2012: 4). David Pollak underlines that these terms are loaded with assumptions. He highlights that the words 'disability' or 'difficulty' suggests the problem lies within the learner, while 'difference' suggests that the teaching should be adjusted (Pollak 2012: 59–60). At the university I teach in, and at several of the British drama training institutions, those with dyslexia are recorded under a general title of 'Specific Learning Difficulty'. Amalgamated with the records of other occurring types of SpLD, exact statistical numbers of students assessed as dyslexic are unclear. In discussion with the Student and Academic Service departments in four major drama schools, they report that every year there are a percentage of dyslexic students in each cohort, and in some courses, the numbers are increasing substantially (personal communications 2016).

What is meant by the term 'dyslexia'?

The word 'dyslexia' comes from two Greek words: *dys* meaning difficulty and *lexia* referring to words or language. There are many differing definitions of dyslexia and our understanding of what the concept of dyslexia might mean continues to evolve (McLoughlin and Leather 2013: 2). Despite extensive research, the causes, identification and approaches of support for those identified as dyslexic remain diverse and sometimes conflicting. The very existence of dyslexia is questioned by some professionals as having no scientific differential diagnosis for identification of who is dyslexic vs. who is a poor reader (Elliott and Gibbs 2009: 127). However, others argue vigorously for its existence, as 'a highly prevalent, socially important and individually traumatic condition' (Nicolson 2015: 5). The British Dyslexia Association states that:

> Dyslexia is a specific learning difficulty that mainly affects the development of literacy and language related skills [...] It is characterised by difficulties with phonological processing, rapid naming, working memory processing speed and the automatic development of skills that may not match up to an individual's other cognitive abilities [...].
>
> (British Dyslexia Association 2007)

The problem

Acting students with dyslexia have often worked very hard to overcome difficult experiences during their school years and to progress into higher education. Generally, they are highly motivated, in spite of (or because of) their dyslexia and frequently demonstrate strong abilities, although these can be masked by the features of their dyslexia. Because of this, dyslexic individuals can be perceived as lazy or not trying by their teachers (Pollak 2005: 73; Thomson 2009: 216). In actor-training environments, those who teach will have encountered talented individuals where the process of reading (in conjunction with other characteristics) presents inexplicable challenges, which appear resistant to conventional techniques for improvement. These difficulties become particularly noticeable when working on Shakespeare. Shakespeare's unfamiliar language and multi-layered meanings can interfere with the process of guessing of words (a tactic sometimes used by those with dyslexia), comprehension and the fluent communication of the text. I am referring to the act of reading classical text aloud, in scene rehearsals and class exercises. It is notable that some individuals have an inability to read with an unbroken flow. The participants provide a variety of reasons for this, explaining sometimes that they do not recognize a word, do not understand the word, have to process the word letter by letter, the small words move about and sometimes they cannot explain why they cannot read the words. These difficulties can permeate beyond reading, such as the ability to process sounds received aurally, adapt one's speech from a habitual model, break out of embedded intonation patterns, dual task and articulate the precise syllables within the word.

In describing their reading experiences with Shakespeare, my dyslexic students accentuate that they frequently panic when facing the text, that they need to read it several times before they can recognize the words, and that the words seem to them as meaningless marks (participant interviews 2008–2017). My annual teaching of the Shakespeare unit with second-year acting degree students has highlighted the hurdles that dyslexic individuals can encounter, and that established approaches to working on Shakespeare make little provision for those with dyslexia who might function more effectively using modalities outside of conventional procedures.[1] Furthermore, my research has uncovered a paradox. Although Shakespeare's language can initiate considerable obstacles for those with dyslexia, his abundant visual images, wrapped within metaphor, simile and personification can stimulate a cross modal innovation in style, combined with a passionate enthusiasm for acting Shakespeare amongst those with dyslexia.

The rationale for the study

My study is motivated by my conviction that the problems experienced by those with dyslexia need to be more effectively supported by the teaching approaches in actor-training, which has also been recognized by Deborah Leveroy (2013a, 2013b). My former Ph.D. study explored the premise that some acting students identified as dyslexic demonstrate a preference for processing the written text through non-verbal, visually led media (Whitfield 2015a). There is a body of literature that supports this theory of visual preferences in dyslexics (West, T. 1997; West, O. 2007; Grant 2010; Bacon and Handley 2010; McLoughlin and Leather 2013; Leveroy 2015).

In his book *The Year of the King* (1985), the actor Anthony Sher presents examples of his drawings, which help to build his vision of his character and physical appearance when playing Richard III in Shakespeare's play. This cross-disciplinary approach to acting is idiosyncratic to Sher's multiplicities of talents. Ross Prior has also referred to the crucial role of 'the reflective sketchbook' for some performers, in illuminating, recording ideas and analysing blocks. Through the use of a 'non-verbal, pictorial, idiomatic, symbolic and metaphoric' living document created throughout their devising journey, they can refer back to this pre-verbal, unplanned manuscript, enabling the process of re-examination and future creation (Prior 2013: 61). Although both of these practices bear a relationship with my participants' visual languages, there are also differences underlying their primary purpose.

Using art within action research

There have been many science-led studies of dyslexia, but the utilization of an art-led study as a producer of data, theory and practice will speak directly to those who share similar artistic environments. Utilizing art as research focuses on the phenomenological experience: the stimulation and processing of feelings, sense awareness and intuitive thinking, enabling a capturing of meanings that measurement cannot (Barone and Eisner 2012: 167–68). An engagement with the aesthetic sensibilities in Shakespeare's sensuous writing and the interpretive nature of acting does not seek to uncover objective, quantifiable answers that exist in generalizable outcomes. The acting community will be familiar with Stanislavski's description of artistic truth created from the imagination. When acting a role, Stanislavski stated:

> Of significance to us is: the reality of the inner life of the human spirit in a part and the belief in that reality. We are not concerned with the actual […] existence of […] the reality of the material world! […] Try always to begin by working from the inside […] Put life into all the imagined circumstances and actions until you have completely satisfied your sense of truth.
>
> (Stanislavski 1980: 129)

In my study, art exists as the object, the working experience and the research, ascertained through four interrelated pathways. Firstly, art as the object is inherent in Shakespeare's writing as the fundamental material; secondly, there is a technical art required, and acquired, through the experience of speaking and acting Shakespeare; thirdly, the act of drawing as the process and producer of art expands the experience and conveyance of meaning, evolving into research; and fourthly, the conducting of a conscious pedagogy emerges through the examination of the art as object, experience and research. In consideration of its worth, Shaun McNiff argues that art-based research is evaluated by its usefulness to other people, leading to professional change (McNiff, S. 2013: 6). Through dissemination of my research in this study, I aim to encourage ideas for changes in inclusive practice amongst similar communities working with dyslexic individuals.

My methodology uses a mixed methods approach where alongside using art as research, this particular project is one of case-study interlinked with action-research. While case-study enables a close observation of the participants, recording their voices so they might be heard in the world, action-research allows the research directions to be both participant and researcher-led. The nature of action-research, wherein a problem is identified, possible solutions are imagined and action taken, with an evaluation of outcomes, provides the structure to explore ideas for change in teaching approaches (McNiff, J. 2013). In this chapter, I share examples of some of my work with two dyslexic research participants who were second-year acting degree students, during my teaching of a nine-week Shakespeare unit at the Arts University Bournemouth in England. Combining the roles of teacher and researcher, my interaction with my participants utilized interviews, observation of class work, rehearsal of Shakespeare scenes, filmed action research workshops and in-depth recorded reflection and discussion. The examples of work presented in this chapter are supported by illustrations of the participants' process and their recorded comments, in conjunction with analysis and theory about dyslexia and the discipline of acting. Both participants focused on in this study have signed consent forms agreeing to be involved in my research, and have given written permission for their work to be included in this chapter, with the use of their first names. In doing this, they state that they have pride in their work and their contribution to assisting others with dyslexia. One participant emphasizes:

> I don't feel it's something I need to hide, or feel ashamed of. I went through sixteen years of schooling without my dyslexia being picked up on, and that was hard because I felt stupid a lot of the time. But after being diagnosed [at university] I realised that it wasn't stupidity, it was just that I had a different way of way of learning and responded better to a less conventional way of teaching. This made me more confident as a person as well as in my work. So I'd like to help anyone else who may have gone through a similar situation.
>
> (personal communication 2017)

The use of a visual storyboard

Participant: Abigail

In an action-research trial, I was working with research participant Abigail on a Shakespeare scene from *Measure for Measure* (Act III, Scene i) in which she was playing Claudio. This was a small section of the scene, which she had previously prepared, learnt and rehearsed with another dyslexic research participant; therefore, she had plenty of time in advance to become familiar with the language and content. In her performance of the scene, her acting and speaking of the text initially appeared effective in being emotionally driven with a convincing psychological realism. However, in observation of her performance, it gradually became clear that she did not understand all of the language, which was demonstrated by her manner of delivering important phrases without much thought accompanied by vague gestures, or stumbling over the formation of the words. When questioned, she admitted that she had originally known what the more unusual words had meant, but could not retain their meaning in her mind. When looking at a Shakespeare text, Abigail described seeing only jumbled words in a block, with little meaning attached to them. She gave a convoluted explanation of her dyslexic reading experience explaining:

> *It's big words I get stuck on … the other day I read a word and it was a word I couldn't read, but I could remember that I read it before and knew what it said, but I couldn't read it … I couldn't sound it out …*

Abigail said that she is 'like a child, taking a long time to read each word' using her finger to follow the words on the page. If she does not do this, she cannot take the information in. Despite my giving Abigail an explanation of the meanings of the words in the scene, which she said she had forgotten, she continued to have difficulty with anchoring the information in her mind, and then speaking and physicalizing the language with credibility.

Forming a bridge into reading and speaking the text: Abigail's drawing of Claudio's speech (*Measure for Measure* Act III scene i)

I decided to explore if the act of drawing the text might assist Abigail. In taking this approach, I was mirroring methods utilized by other dyslexic acting students in my classes, who drew scribbled symbols and signs onto their text. Remaining with the same scene, I chose to use Claudio's speech, 'Ay but to die and go we know not where' as the working material in an action-research workshop. This is a speech where Claudio, who is condemned to death, is expressing his fear of dying. As the speech is packed with images, intricate language and is emotionally demanding, it was an appropriately challenging one to trial.

> *Claudio's speech*:
>
> Ay, but to die, and go we know not where;
> To lie in cold obstruction, and to rot;
> This sensible warm motion to become

A kneaded clod; and the delighted spirit
To bath in fiery floods, or to reside
In thrilling region of thick-ribbed ice;
To be imprison'd in the viewless winds
And blown with restless violence round about
The pendent world: Or to be worst than worst
Of those that lawless and incertain thought
Imagine howling, – tis too horrible.
The weariest and most loathed worldly life
That age, ache, penury and imprisonment
Can lay on nature, is a paradise
To what we fear of death.[2]

Action-research trial: What I did and what the participant Abigail did

This was a filmed action-research workshop where I, as the teacher/facilitator, guided Abigail through the procedure, whilst also recording the process.

Firstly, I asked Abigail to sight-read Claudio's speech aloud. As she read, she revealed her insecurity with the text, tripping over several of the words as she worked through it. We then discussed the overall meaning and individual word meanings in the monologue. When I was convinced that she had absorbed this information, I gave her a large drawing pad, with a selection of coloured pens. I explained that I was going to read the important words from the text aloud to her in short sequenced chunks, and she was to draw an intuitive personal response/representation of the meaning onto the page. Secondly, I read the crucial phrases in the monologue aloud one by one in a staggered sequence, endeavouring to use a neutral, expressionless voice, so as not to 'colour' her perception of the words. As Abigail repeated the words aloud, she drew her interpretation of the meaning/associations with the words onto the page, exploring their sounds kinaesthetically and aurally, noting the sounds and the arising feelings evoked by the words. Then, when each drawing was concluded, she wrote the phrase below the drawing, again speaking it aloud, linking meaning, phonological sound attached to the alphabet, and the muscular action of the articulators in shaping the words. Thirdly, when we had concluded working through the speech, Abigail spent some time 'reading' her drawing interpretations back to me, describing what they represented to her and her rationale for drawing them, connected to Shakespeare's words. Finally, she read the speech aloud from the text. Her sight-reading fluency and ability to engage with Claudio's experience of terror had improved enormously, resulting in a security with the words, accompanied by a freedom in an emotional delivery. At the end of the trial, Abigail stated that although she had initially worried that her lack of drawing skills (as she perceived them) would curtail her creativity, she discovered they assisted her in gaining a

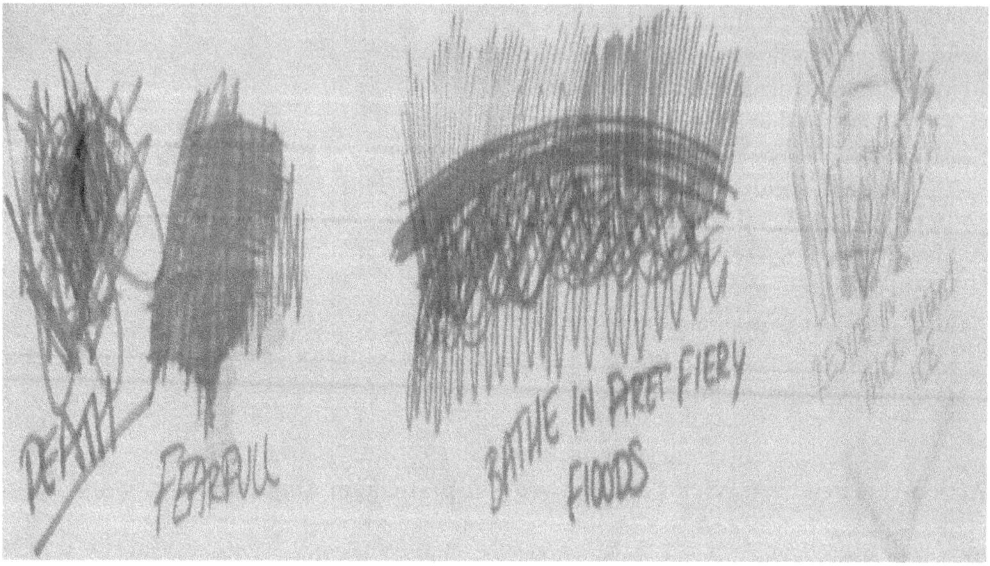

Figure 1: A clip from Abigail's storyboard for Claudio's speech, 'Ay, but to die and go we know not where' (*Measure for Measure* Act III, scene i).

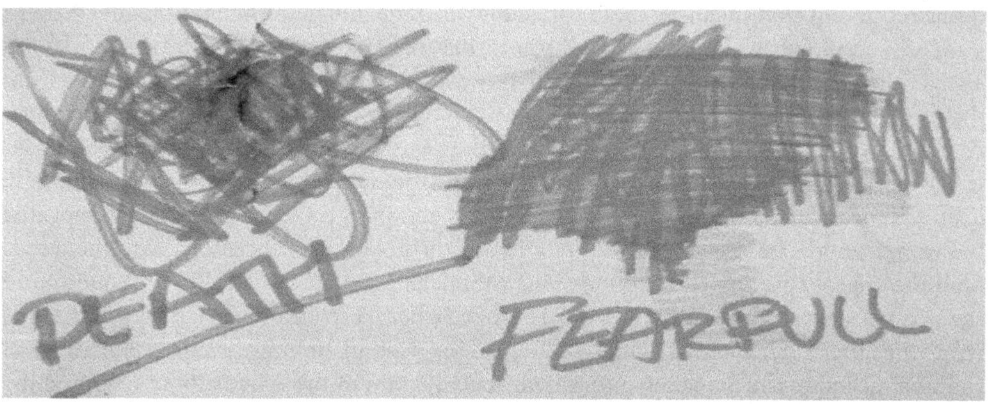

Figure 2: Phrase: 'Death is a fearful thing'.

much greater comprehension of the psychology of the character and meaning in the text. She concluded:

> There are many benefits to this work for a dyslexic student. It really helps to build detail and understanding when approaching Shakespeare's text. The text itself is what's most daunting, so analysing it first using drawings helps to build the confidence.

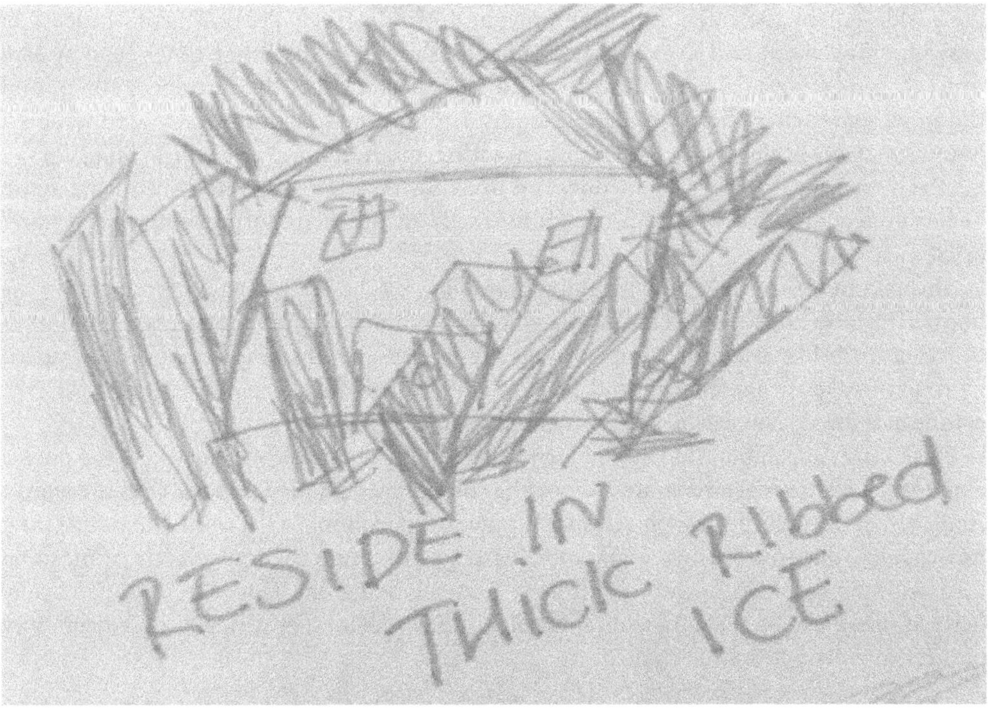

Figure 3: Phrase: 'Reside in thrilling region of thick-ribbed ice'.

Analysis of Abigail's drawing

In her physical acting of Shakespeare's text, Abigail's actions had been predominantly emotionally and psychologically driven. In her drawings, she used a similar approach, with a recurring use of emotional arousal, delineated through expressive pen use. I have examined two of her pictures individually, their properties, function and the feelings and ideas they express. I consider the pictures below.

Abigail used a forceful scribbling for the word 'Death' as she repeated the words. She tore the paper by committing to heavy, frenzied pen strokes, revealing the intensity with which she engaged with the meanings behind the words. For both the words 'death' and 'fearful', she included a layering of colours, signifying the strength of her feeling attached to the words, and the analogous emotions evoked through her perception of the colours red, dark-blue and brown.

The art and drama therapists Sue Jennings and Ase Minde accentuate the power of the arts to draw out the 'inner self': that which is known through the hidden self before we can articulate it. This 'knowing' can be expressed through a discovery of mental images emerging from within or movement expressed outside the body, working either from the inside-out or the outside-in (Jennings and Minde 1993: 118). Abigail's process of drawing, movement and speaking presents an example of the inner/outer loop system in which outer physical actions and voiced sounds can affect the interior feelings, and the inner experience then can affect the physical response, as utilized by art therapists Jennings and Minde (1993: 118) and in acting methods by Constantin Stanislavski. Stanislavski argued that 'if a part does not of its own accord shape itself inside an actor, he has no recourse except to approach it inversely, by proceeding from externals inward' (1988: 149).

This picture encapsulates the meaning of *residing*, by the idea of an existence within the house. The term 'thick-ribbed ice' is created by the figurative representation of thick chunks of ice in a rib-like enclosure, imprisoning the house. The 'thrilling region' is delineated by rough strokes in the background. A grey, silver colour has been chosen to capture the coldness of the ice and the *thrillingness* of the region.

Observing Abigail building up the picture section by section while she spoke the phrase aloud revealed how each separate entity of her design was coupled directly with the words. Abigail then acted the piece with a fresh assurance in her coining of the words, demonstrating how a single picture, which is easily memorized, can capture the multi-layers of meaning held within one of Shakespeare's phrases, particularizing the language. The personally derived image can be instantaneously recalled in the memory, ensuring a rooted certainty of the semantics within the whole.

Customizing the text and acting through drawing

Participant: Hollie

Although Hollie sometimes appeared to read aloud with ease in the exercise work on the text during the Shakespeare unit, the unpredictability of her dyslexia meant this fluency was variable. A striking example of this insecurity is an account of an incident in a voice class I was teaching. When reading a Shakespeare monologue aloud with some passion, Hollie abruptly stopped, stating she was unable to proceed. She explained that although she could see the black marks of the print on the page and understood in her mind that they were words, she could not 'read' them. They became like meaningless, incomprehensible shapes. At the time of being swept up in the emotion of the piece in her reading, and then losing her place on the paper, the words became unreadable to her. Hollie then abandoned her reading of the monologue, unable to continue, despite her initial success in fluency and freedom of expression.

When working on Shakespeare's poem *Venus and Adonis* towards a final Voice assessed performance, Hollie's communication was weakened by her imprecise articulation of some words, with consonants often dropped, giving some words a 'fuzzy' quality. Despite possessing a strong ability in acting and intelligent grasp of classical text, she skimmed through her pronunciation of many of the words in the sentences, so the observer was unable to absorb the sense of her text. This suggested to me that the imprecise quality revealed in her speech represented how her brain was assimilating the alphabetic letters of the words and their associated phonological sounds, connected with her dyslexia. The phonological deficit is one of the principal theories concerning dyslexia, which, simply put, is problems with phonological awareness and poorly conceived phonological representations, retrieving phonological information from long-term memory, and difficulties with verbal short-term memory (Snowling 2002: 61). It is also recorded in some of the dyslexia literature that children and adults with dyslexia can have problems with articulation of words and muddling of syllables, although it is unclear if this is due to a phonological deficit, auditory processing or weak procedural motor skills (Nicolson and Fawcett 2010: 110–13; Goswami 2010: 112; Griffiths and Frith 2002).

What I did and what the participant Hollie did

I recalled that in a recorded interview with me, Hollie had recounted that when she was taking notes in lectures, she could absorb the content more deeply when she 'doodled all over the words' with drawings, symbols or variations in graphic style. I suggested she might try that method when working on her *Venus and Adonis* text outside of rehearsals with her fellow actors and me. As rehearsals continued, Hollie's clarity of word improved; each component of the word began to be more fully met in her pronunciation and ownership of the language. In her final performance, some words remained under-articulated, but there was a significant advance in clarity and preciseness of word overall.

After the final live performance was concluded, Hollie showed me her rehearsal script and how she had worked on her articulation by customizing many of the words in tremendous detail. She had generated her own method for overcoming her problem of seeing only 'meaningless black marks on the page' by translating much of the text into 'little word pictures' – a term coined by Spurgeon when investigating Shakespeare's abundant linguistic images (Spurgeon 1935: 9). The written word form was no longer the solo carrier of meaning for Hollie. Using her drawing and associative colours, she had interwoven the written word and her devised images together into one sign, thus making the image/word concrete and immediately accessible to the eye and her memory. According to Dawnene Hassett, this recombination of signs fashioned into one symbol is known as 'synergy' and offers a tool for expanding meanings. 'These meanings are not "in" the text; instead they are "in" the interpretation' (Hassett 2010: 95). This use of pictures interlinked with the key words also correlates with Sadoski and Paivio's (2009: 63) 'Conceptual Peg Hypothesis', a mnemonic device where imagery serves as a mental peg on which information is deposited and saved into memory.

Hollie emphasized the value of this method for her, specifying in a recorded interview that the 'the words no longer remained two dimensional, but instead they evolve to become

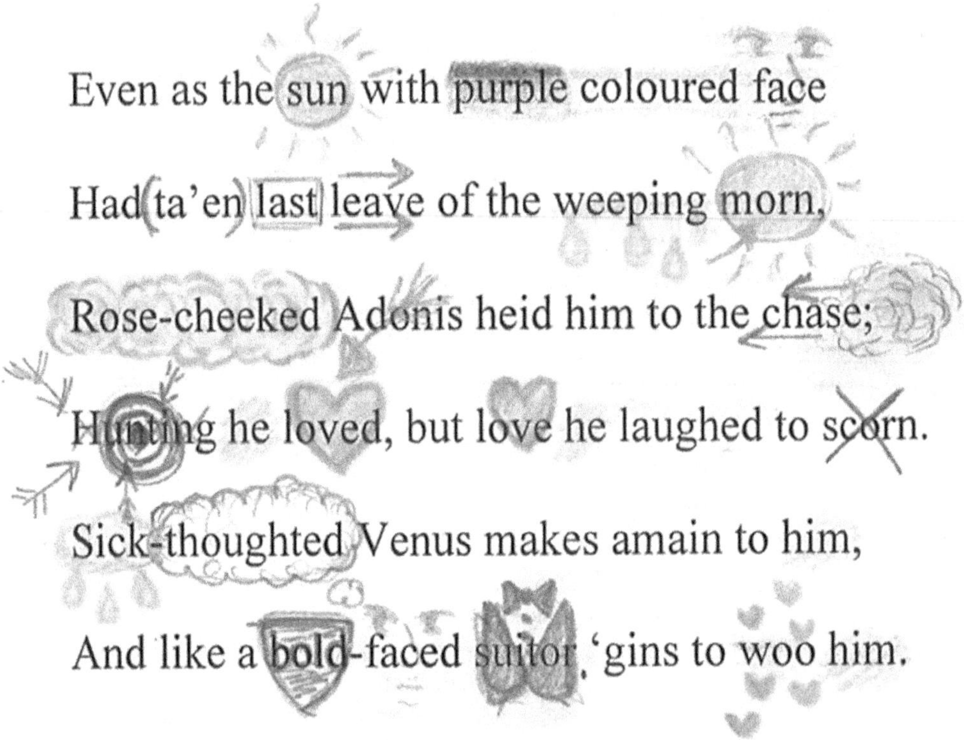

Figure 4: Hollie's iconic symbols drawn onto her text in Shakespeare's poem *Venus and Adonis*.

interactive, exciting and rich'. Invoking a synaesthetic dimension, she continued, '... it helps my articulation as I can visualise the word, its textures, colours and shape. It helps create the word shapes in my mouth distinctly.'

Hollie also used her drawing faculty to develop her grasp of the character of Venus that she was playing. In the discipline of acting, an exploration of the psychological and emotional needs of the character are commonly investigated through physical actions. Hollie used her dominantly visual sense to produce images of the physical actions of her interpretation of Venus's desire for Adonis, onto the page. This stimulated a feedback loop where the image speaks back to the creator as it comes into life, through the emergence of the drawing, transferring inner mental images or feelings into a tangible 'thing', existing on the page. In examining the purpose of Hollie's drawings of physical actions, I recognized a direct link with the acting practitioner Michael Chekhov and his use of *The Psychological Gesture*. Michael Chekhov developed a method of 'enticing, provoking and coaxing feelings' from the actor in their embodying of their character's

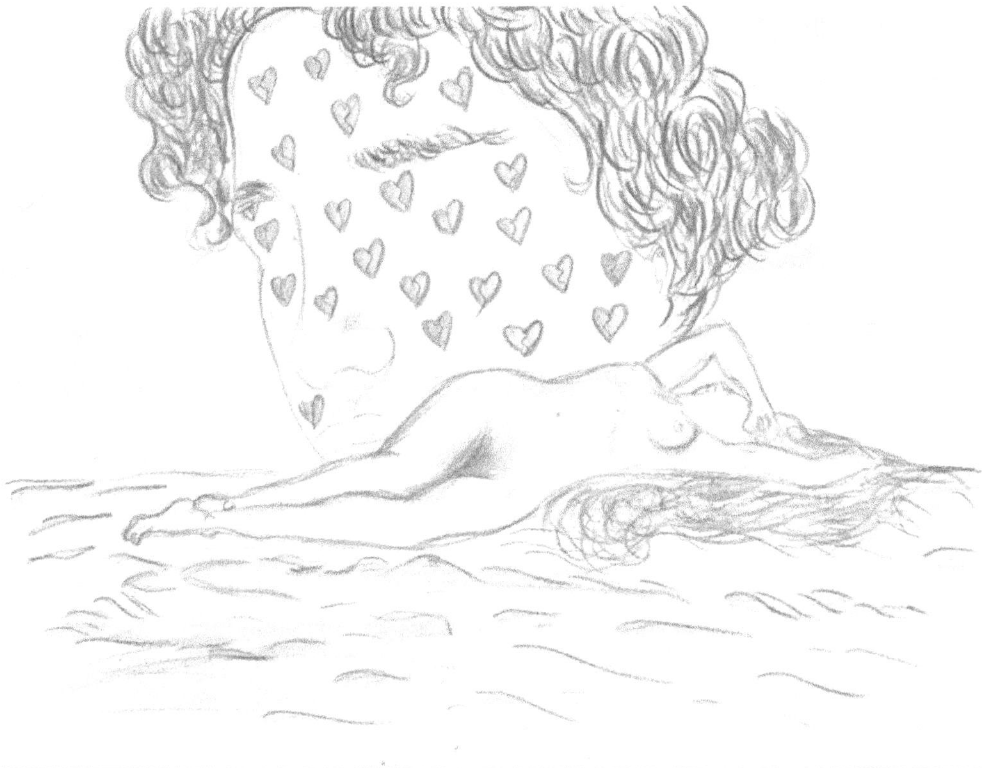

Figure 5: Hollie's vision of Venus, displaying her longing for Adonis through the external physical action.

experience by carrying out 'a strong gesture' that can encapsulate the character's state (Chekhov 2002: 64–65).

Thinking-through-drawing

It is evident that the building of visually processed models produces a parallel text, distanced from the alphabetical symbol as the dominant signifier of content. The pressure of reading the words directly from the page in class exercises and the expectations of getting them 'right' is reduced. Unlike the written word, wherein information is imparted progressively, the pictorial form allows a holistic layering of meanings captured within single illustrations, which can then be translated into the live performance. The process of thinking-through-drawing can stimulate a succession of referential prompts arising from the text and anchor concrete concepts and specific words and meanings.

In constructing an overall schema made up from the text, the focus remains on the crucial question: what exactly am I saying? This calls for an examination of each word – to be 'on the word' and 'realize the value of each word', as is the necessity when acting Shakespeare (Berry 2001: 122). Rand Spiro labels this as a 'bottom-up approach' (Spiro 1980: 265). In constructing meaning from the text, Spiro stresses that an over reliance of 'top-down' approaches (the overall global meaning) can be detrimental to those who have difficulty with taking in the words. This encourages a guessing of unfamiliar words, based on context rather than de-coding of what is actually there. However, too much reliance on 'bottom-up' processing – literally breaking the text up letter-by-letter and word-by-word – can detract from a comprehension and retention of the whole (Adams 1980: 16–17). Marilyn Adams recommends that an interplay between a 'top-down' and 'bottom-up' process is necessary to obtain fluent reading and comprehension, but stresses that this can most successfully occur when word recognition is overlearned (1980: 18). The term 'overlearning' describes the additional work often carried out by those with dyslexia, in order to develop an automaticity in a skill, reinforce what has been learnt or simply to achieve what those without dyslexia can do with apparent ease (Morgan and Klein 2000: 151). Overlearning can include repetition, multi-sensory practices that cross modal channels and breaking tasks down into small steps (Reid 2003: 151–52). The extra work entailed in the participants' transference of the word from its alphabetic form into pictures is an example of multisensory overlearning, reinforced through repetition of the words and kinaesthetic actions.

One of the prevailing aspects of dyslexia reported in the literature (and highlighted by the majority of my research participants in interview) is a weakness in verbal working-memory.[3] Moreover, the psychologist Rod Nicolson, a principal researcher into dyslexia, has recently presented a theory, based on empirical tests, which argues that dyslexics can have difficulty with their procedural learning, whilst possessing distinct strengths in areas of declarative learning (Nicolson 2015: 55–60). Briefly explained, procedural memory involves automatic skills, such as tying a shoelace and habit-based language skills, while declarative memory concerns the embedding of detailed knowledge into long-term memory. Declarative memory has two areas: that of semantics (word meaning) and that of the episodic (events and facts) (Thomson 2009: 168–69). Although Thomson highlights that semantic memory is a component that has impact on dyslexics' difficulties, the participants' analogic visual text does appear to remove the danger for weakness in their procedural learning (i.e. sight-reading, automatic understanding, just 'knowing' how to do something). The visual symbols assist in off-loading working-memory by externalizing the information onto the page, facilitating a construction of a mental model of the words' meaning and the embedding of the whole text into long-term memory (semantic memory). Additionally, the process sifts through information, organizing it into manageable chunks and into linear sequences (episodic memory).

Conclusion

Investigating how to support those with dyslexia in our teaching can be time-intensive and demanding. In actor-training environments, the curriculum commonly comprises of much repetition of methods, albeit encompassing highly specialized knowledge and skills. Many of us, as teachers of acting and voice, are trained professional performers and teach our subject as we were taught it, at drama school, in the theatre or in our teacher-training. The received ideas and routines of others are regularly implemented and often unquestioned. In his study of actor-trainers, Ross Prior emphasizes that actor-training concentrates on methods of acting, whereas areas concerning *how* to learn to teach and to develop practice, and then to make that practice explicit, are under-researched. Prior underlines that teachers should ask themselves: 'how do I know if I am an effective trainer? How do we teach more effectively?' How do we structure our classes to benefit all students? (Prior 2012: xxi, 50–56). When working in an environment of unexamined pedagogy, there is a risk that the individual learner, such as those with dyslexia, can be judged as inadequate in their abilities or personal effort, if they are not able to perform within the boundaries presented by the teacher.

In her study of dyslexia and learning styles, Tilly Mortimore (2008: 276) has cautioned that identifying a learning style preference in an individual does not mean that they will favour the same style across all learning situations, and a larger study than this one might reveal more variation in dominant learning styles. However, in my own explorations, these visual tools have proved to enable some individuals with dyslexia to become more accurately and imaginatively 'entangled' within Shakespeare's text so that their expression of the 'I myself' of the Actor Creator can materialize with freedom, and confidence, so they can be fully present within the 'dynamic of the language' (Berry 2001: 3). Furthermore, these methods can be integrated into the established curricula and utilized with dyslexics and non-dyslexic students, in group exercises or with single individuals. Generated from art-based research, theory and practice, these strategies allow flexibility in a variety of uses for those teaching, extending inclusive strategies for the study of acting Shakespeare (or other complex texts) for all individuals.

References

Adams, Marilyn Jager (1980), 'Failures to comprehend and levels of processing', in R. J. Spiro, B. Bruce and W. F. Brewer (eds), *Theoretical Issues in Reading Comprehension*, New Jersey: Lawrence Erlbaum Associates, pp. 11–32.

Bacon, Alison and Handley, Simon (2010), 'Dyslexia, reasoning and the importance of visual-spatial processes', in N. Alexander-Passe (ed.), *Dyslexia and Creativity*, New York: Nova Science Publishers, pp. 25–49.

Barone, Tom and Eisner, Elliot (2012), *Arts Based Research*, London: Sage.

Berry, Cicely (1993), *The Actor and the Text*, London: Virgin Books.

——— (2001), *Text in Action*, London: Virgin Publishing.

British Dyslexia Association (2007), 'Definition of dyslexia', http://www.bdadyslexia.org.uk/dyslexic/definitions. Accessed 13 April 2017.

Brunswick, Nicola (2012), 'Dyslexia in UK higher education and employment', in N. Brunswick (ed.), *Supporting Dyslexic Adults in Higher Education and the Workplace*, Chichester: John Wiley & Sons, pp. 1–10.

Chekhov, Michael (2002), *On the Technique of Acting*, London: Routledge.

Department for Education and Skills (2004), *A Framework for Understanding Dyslexia*, London: DFES.

Elliott, Julian G. and Gibbs, Simon (2009), 'Does dyslexia exist?', in R. Cigman and A. Davis (eds), *New Philosophies of Learning*, Chichester: Wiley Blackwell, pp. 115–30.

Elliott, Julian G. and Grigorenko, Elena (2014), *The Dyslexia Debate*, New York: Cambridge University Press.

Elliott, Julian G. and Nicolson, Rod (2016), *Dyslexia: Developing the Debate*, London: Bloomsbury Academic.

Goswami, Usha (2010), 'Phonology, reading and reading difficulties', in K. Hall, U. Goswami, C. Harrison, S. Ellis and J. Solar (eds), *Interdisciplinary Perspectives on Learning to Read*, London: Routledge, pp. 103–16.

Grant, David (2010), *That's the Way I Think*, 2nd ed., Oxon: David Fulton.

Griffiths, Sarah and Frith, Uta (2002), 'Evidence for an articulatory awareness deficit in adult dyslexics', *Dyslexia*, 8, pp. 14–21.

Hall, Peter (2003), *Shakespeare's Advice to the Players*, London: Oberon Books.

Harrop, John (1992), *Acting*, London: Routledge.

Hassett, Dawnene (2010), 'New literacies in the elementary classroom', in K. Hall, U. Goswami, C. Harrison, S. Ellis and J. Solar (eds), *Interdisciplinary Perspectives on Learning to Read*, London: Routledge, pp. 87–100.

Iser, Wolfgang (1978), *The Act of Reading*, Baltimore: Johns Hopkins University Press.

Jennings, Sue and Minde, Ase (1993), *Art Therapy and Dramatherapy*, London: Jessica Kingsley Publishers.

Leveroy, Deborah (2013a), 'Enabling performance: Dyslexia, (dis)ability and "reasonable adjustement"', *Theatre, Dance and Performance Training*, 4:1, pp. 87–101.

——— (2013b), 'Locating dyslexic performance: Text, identity and creativity', *Research in Drama Education: The Journal of Applied Theatre* and *Performance*, 18:4, pp. 374–87.

——— (2015), '"A date with the script": Exploring the learning strategies of actors who are dyslexic', *Theatre, Dance and Performance Training*, 6:3, pp. 307–22.

McLoughlin, David and Leather, Carol (2013), *The Dyslexic Adult*, 2nd ed., Chichester: Whurr Publications.

McNiff, Jean (2013), *Action Research*, 3rd ed., Abingdon: Routledge.

McNiff, Shaun (2013), 'Opportunities and challenges in art-based research', in S. McNiff (ed.), *Art as Research: Opportunities and Challenges*, Bristol: Intellect Books, pp. 3–9.

Morgan, Ellen and Klein, Cynthia (2000), *The Dyslexic Adult in a Non-Dyslexic World*, London: Whurr Publishers.

Mortimore, Tilly (2008), *Dyslexia and Learning Style*, 2nd ed., Chichester: John Wiley & Sons.

Nicolson, Rod (2015), *Positive Dyslexia*, Sheffield: Rodin Books.

Nicolson, Rod and Fawcett, Angela (2010), *Dyslexia, Learning and the Brain*, London: MIT Press.

Noble, Adrian (2010), *How to Do Shakespeare*, London: Routledge.

Office for Disability Issues (2010), *Equality Act 2010*, London: Office for Disability Issues.

Pavey, Barbara, Meehan, Margaret and Waugh, Alan (2010), *Dyslexia-Friendly Further and Higher Education*, London: Sage.

Pollak, David (2005), *Dyslexia, the Self and Higher Education*, Stoke on Trent: Trentham Books.

——— (2012), 'Supporting higher education students who are dyslexic', in N. Brunswick (ed.), *Supporting Dyslexic Adults in Higher Education and the Workplace*, Chichester: Wiley-Blackwell, pp. 59–73.

Prior, Ross W. (2012), *Teaching Actors: Knowledge Transfer in Actor Training*, Bristol: Intellect Books.

——— (2013), 'Knowing what is known: Accessing craft-based meanings in research by artists', in S. McNiff (ed.), *Art as Research: Opportunities and Challenges*, Bristol: Intellect Books, pp. 161–69.

Reid, Gavin (2003), *Dyslexia: A Practitioner's Handbook*, 3rd ed., Chichester: John Wiley.

Rosenblatt, Louise (2005), *Making Meaning with Texts*, Portsmouth: Heinemann.

Sadoski, Mark and Paivio, Allan (2009), *Imagery and the Text*, London: Routledge.

Shakespeare, William (2010), *Measure for Measure* (eds J. Bate and E. Rasmusse), London: Palgrave Macmillan.

——— (2007), 'Venus and Adonis', in K. Duncan-Jones and H. R. Woudhuysen (eds), *Shakespeare's Poems*, London: Arden Shakespeare, pp. 131–1194.

Sher, Anthony (1985), *Year of the King*, London: Nick Hern Books.

Smith, Vivienne (2010), 'Comprehension as a social act', in K. Hall, U. Goswami, C. Harrison, S. Ellis and J. Solar (eds), *Interdisciplinary Perspectives on Learning to Read*, London: Routledge, pp. 87–100.

Snowling, Margaret J. (2002), 'Dyslexia: Individual and developmental differences', in R. Stainthorp and P. Tomlinson (eds), *Learning and Teaching Reading*, Leicester: British Psychological Society, pp. 61–73.

Spiro, Rand J. (1980), 'Constructive processes in prose comprehension and recall', in R. J. Spiro, B. Bruce and W. F Brewer (eds), *Theoretical Issues in Reading Comprehension*, New Jersey: Lawrence Erlbaum Associates, pp. 245–78.

Spurgeon, Caroline (1935), *Shakespeare's Imagery*, Cambridge: Cambridge University Press.

Stanislavski, Constantin (1980), *An Actor Prepares*, London: Methuen Drama.

——— (1988), *Creating a Role*, London: Methuen Drama.

Thomson, Michael (2009), *The Psychology of Dyslexia*, West Chichester: Wiley-Blackwell.

Tompkins, Jane P. (1980), *Reader-Response Criticism*, Baltimore: Johns Hopkins University Press.

West, Oliver (2007), *In Search of Words: Footnotes Visual Thinking Techniques*, London: Oliver West VMT.

West, Thomas (1997), *In the Mind's Eye Visual Thinkers, Gifted People with Dyslexia and Other Learning Difficulties, Computer Images and the Ironies of Creativity*, New York: Prometheus Books.

Whitfield, Petronilla (2009), 'Shakespeare, pedagogy and dyslexia', *The Moving Voice: The Integration of Voice and Movement, The Voice and Speech Trainer's Review*, 6, pp. 254–62.

——— (2015a), 'Towards accessing Shakespeare's text for those with SpLD (dyslexia): An investigation into the rationale for building visual constructs', Ph.D. thesis, Warwick: University of Warwick.

——— (2015b), 'Towards an emancipatory praxis of pedagogy: Supporting acting students with dyslexia when working on Shakespeare', *Voice and Speech Review,* 9:2&3, pp. 113–38.

——— (2016), 'A facilitation of dyslexia through a remediation of Shakespeare's text', *Research in Drama Education: The Journal of Applied Theatre and Performance*, 21:3, pp. 385–400.

Notes

1 Many of the specialist techniques on the acting and speaking of Shakespeare assume fluent reading skills and an ease with an intricate examination of language demonstrated through practical exercises. They have an emphasis on correct technical skills in the speaking of Shakespeare. These methods can trigger a cognitive overload and anxiety in those with dyslexia. Theatre director Adrian Noble specifies that in order to learn how to act the text, the 'rules' must be learnt; the 'dos and don'ts of the craft' (Noble 2010: 5). This involves an intellectual study of the literary form and an accurate adherence to the conventions of speaking the form. Likewise, the director Peter Hall's method involves a close study of the 'clues in the text' extrapolated from Shakespeare's literary discipline. Hall underlines that 'Shakespeare's text is a complex score that demands to be read as a piece of music, learned like the steps of a dance, or practised like the strokes of a dual. The form of the text is the end result' (Hall 2003: 18).

2 This version is taken from the Arden Shakespeare of *Measure for Measure.*

3 Memory plays a fundamental role in the process of reading, decoding letter symbols and remembering their related sounds, recognizing whole words, processing meaning and the storage and retrieval of information. There are several differing models of memory, and for a comprehensive overview of the current models of memory and theories of dyslexia at a cognitive level, see Elliott and Grigorenko (2014: 56–63) and Thomson (2009: 165–202). In his book on the psychology of dyslexia, Michael Thomson states that '[…] one of the key features of the dyslexic learner is problems with memory. In particular, these centre around short-term memory in its relationship to classroom instructions and organization and in particular to aspects of written language learning' (2009: 165). Dyslexia consultants David McLoughlin and Carol Leather underline that '[o]ur practice in assessment, counselling, teaching and training has for some years been based on the assumption that all the behavioural difficulties experienced by dyslexic people stem from an inefficiency in working memory […]. This view is based on the scientific literature, but also on our practical experience. It is reinforced by the feedback provided by our clients' (2013: 19). To know more about dyslexia, see *A Framework for Understanding Dyslexia* (DFES 2004), a resource for teachers, which offers a description of the nature of dyslexia, the current theories of dyslexia (including the *Working Memory Hypothesis*) and the principal researchers in the field.

Chapter 13

Dancing as a Wolf: Art-Based Understanding of Autistic Spectrum Condition

Kevin Burrows

This chapter presents how expressive art-based research tools have been applied to form a heuristic understanding of autistic spectrum condition (ASC) perception, which differs from my own and non-autistic neural typical perception.[1] The research project presented here looks at the potential for the non-autistic or neural typical researcher-facilitator to access autistic perception through outdoor and art-based activities that can inform the development of autism-inclusive teaching and therapy models. The research project involved students who were aged 16 to 19 with autism and took place in a forest school (Knight 2011), held in the natural woodland annexed to a further education college campus. As an artist, educationalist and therapist, I had noted that my own art-making in nature facilitated a calming effect on myself and I observed similar calming effects with my students with ASC whilst they made art in natural woodland forest school.

The non-autistic researcher, who I shall refer to as 'neural typical', needs to be mindfully aware of Nancy Minshew et al.'s (1997: 303) findings that autistic perception is routed mainly through the senses of the brain's primary cortex as sensate perception. Neural typical people further process similar sensate experiences through what Temple Grandin (2010: 65), a person with autism, calls 'inattentional blindness'. This is the neural typical filtering of sensate experience through the brain's 'associate cortex' into concepts and schemas.

Participants and ethics

This project fieldwork took place between 2008 and 2012 in a special education college, with seven sixteen-to-nineteen-year-old within the autistic spectrum. The participants were chosen from my regular special educational needs art and performing arts teaching groups. Mask-making and the performing of these masks formed part of the combined arts syllabus and produced 'art' and 'performing arts' entry-level exam evidence. I noted that the practical aspect of these lessons, i.e. the creation of a mask through visual art and moving the same mask through the performing arts mirrored the first two phases of the expressive arts intermodal or multimodal process. This observation brought about the beginning of a research programme to find a heuristic understanding of autistic perception. However, before I could start my research, the National Health Service research ethics committees (NHS REC) wanted me to clarify two areas of the 2005 Mental Capacity Act (MCA):

1. Whether my adult participants were able to consent for themselves.
2. That I was eligible to train for Mental Capacity Act (MCA) and conduct MCA tests to assess the capacity of my adult participants to give *consent*.

I completed the Essex approach MCA training and NHS ethics approval was applied for and granted. The masks made by the students with autism would be danced, drawn and finally formed as poetry by neural typical co-researchers as art-based research tools.

Finding a research language

In order to find a research methodology that accommodated both autistic and neural typical perception, I had to weave a methodological path that unpicked the assumption that my neural typical thinking, feeling or behaviour and was a valid and accurate assessment of what was going on for my student participants with autism. Art-based research tools that employ expressive art therapies' multimodal (McNiff 1992) or intermodal (Knill 1978) approaches – where the participant is engaged in an imaginal, playful state of non-ordinary reality and sequentially moves through several art processes – can equip the neural typical researcher with a non-filtering phenomenological perception held in the senses of the primary cortex. This enables the neural typical researcher to bypass 'associate cortex' filtering and engage with what they experientially sense, rather than forming a heuristic understanding from pre-experienced internal truths or concepts filtered from their raw sensate experience. Likewise, outdoor psychotherapist and ecotherapist Martin Jordan (2015: 64) discusses how when in natural spaces his ecotherapeutic participant clients attune to an embodied experience of the senses in nature as they 'seek out smells and make sensual contact with the plant life'.

Amanda Baggs (2007), who is a person with autism, has posted on YouTube a two-part film entitled *In My Language*. The first part of the film shows Baggs interacting with her environment through sung modulated notes and the tactile sounds of her kinetic enacting with her environment, which she states is her own language. Although Baggs (2007) is mute with no verbal language, she is able to make herself understood by typing the written word. She states: 'my language is not about designing words or even visual symbols for people to interpret. It is about being in a constant conversation with every aspect of my environment'.

In her YouTube film, Baggs filmed herself communing with her environment through her senses. She explains that she experiences the world through the language of her sensed experience; 'I smell things. I listen to things, I feel things, I taste things, I look at things'. Bagg's (2007) film shows her moving, touching, singing, tasting and looking at her environment in a coherent way through the senses. She appears to be in harmony with herself and the space she occupies as if she is a relational and reciprocal part of her environment. This would seem to be a phenomenologically attuned way of being, which to an observer would seem to be a kind of ritual shifting of consciousness into an attuned state of being all around and inside her.

One comment on her YouTube entry suggested that in a more nature-conscious society what she did might be considered as a reciprocal shamanic communication with the universe. Shaun McNiff (1992: 13) expounds the parallels with shamanic and expressive arts experiences of other realities '[w]hatever a person paints, dances or sings has significance when we restrain the ego's value judgements'. Through the expressive arts, the neural typical person can experience a reciprocal and unfiltered sensate world of raw sensation, neurologically held in the brain's primary cortex, similar to Baggs' (2007) autistically perceived world. This is a phenomenological sensate world similar to the weak or local central coherence perception experienced by people who have autism. Francesca Happe and Uta Frith (2006: 17) discuss the difference between local sensed and unfiltered coherence of understanding in autism and the neural typical access to 'a higher order cognitive ability' executive function, where the neural typical global central coherence can be seen to 'encompass processing information in context for global meaning i.e. central coherence' – that is the making of schemas, abstracts and concepts from raw sensate experience. This 'shifting between local and global levels' from the primary to associate cortex is usual in neural typical processing. The expressive arts enable the neural typical person sustained access to the experiential world of the sensate primary cortex, which is a phenomenological world similar to Baggs' (2007) autistically perceived world, and as she states, her film's intentions are:

> [m]eant as a strong statement on the existence and value of many different kinds of thinking and interaction in a world where how close you can appear to a specific one of them determines whether you are seen as a real person or an adult or an intelligent person.

She challenges notions that her inability to verbalize in neural typical language indicates that she is dysfunctional:

> Failure to learn your language is seen as a deficit but failure to learn my language is seen as so natural that people like me are officially described as mysterious and puzzling.

What comes across so clearly here are the limitations of a neural typical perceived world-view alone, yet filtered neural typical perceptions form the basis of scientific and medical model research tools and coding that have historically formed much of our understanding of autism.

Expressive arts therapist Paolo Knill (1978) discusses art as language, and how expression, feelings and aesthetics are interconnected and, I believe, exist alongside live moments of creating the embodied image. Knill's (1978) intermodal approach to art therapy asks the participant to move from one art form directly to another as a series of sensed experiential processes. For example, the participant may begin with embodied movement or dance and move into painting or drawing without objective discussion or analysis, making a further intermodal shift into poetry as an experiential form of art expression. This process might be thought of as a combination of the embodied life held in the picture or art object being witnessed and re-experienced by the creator or the audience as a live process through another art form. I further suggest that by using Knill's (1978) expressive arts therapy intermodal process, an embodied 'scapegoat transference' (Schaverien 2000) can be witnessed, or physically re-experienced, by another participant in their making of a new art form as a heuristic experience. Knill (1978: 106) states that the intermodal process facilitates reflective and integrative processing, 'instead of going into a colloquial feedback' as psychodynamic analysis might. Knill (1978: 106) suggests that the participant 'transfer[s] into another modality of art expression', which he termed 'intermodal processing'. This parallels with Baggs' (2007) statement about her ASC perception: 'my language [...] is about being in a constant conversation with every aspect of my environment'.

To enable the neural typical person access to this unfiltered, primary cortex, unconscious experience of expressive arts therapy and expressive arts education, McNiff (1992) and Knill et al. (2005) look to phenomenological and experiential concepts. They draw on the concepts of 'active imagination' (Jung 2000) and what James Hillman (1974) calls the 'imaginal' where participants stay within what is sensed and experienced through their imaginal and creative processes. Knill's (1978) concept of intermodal transference into another art modality ensures that the participant's experience is a phenomenological and sensed experience. This has key relevance in finding a heuristic understanding between my neural typical self and my students with autism through my own intermodal transference as a way of sustaining access to the experiential plane of the primary cortex. The perceptive parallels with Knill et al.'s (2005) intermodal expressive arts *decentring* – into an altered phenomenological state – can coexist with the phenomenological world of Baggs' (2007) 'existence and value of many different kinds of thinking and interaction in a world'.

Sensed experience of arts in autism and neural typical perception

To form an understanding of my research participants' autistic perception as captured in their art-making, I needed to find a research approach that bypassed filtering and classification of the senses through the neural typical lens of non-autistic people. I attempted to understand autistic perception by limiting the neural typical bias of my own and other neural typical co-researchers by remaining in the primary cortex sensed experience. This was achieved by embarking on a relational and sensate approach of multimodal/intermodal expressive arts where the intermodal processing from one art form directly to another remains in the primary cortex of the experiential senses.

Minshew et al. (1997) suggest that this phenomenological world is typically processed in the 'primary cortex' of sensate experience. This primary cortex 'Inattentional blindness' (Grandin and Johnson 2005) in neural typical people is dependent on the executive functioning filtering (Ozonoff et al. 2002: 160) of information from sensate experience in the primary cortex into concepts, abstracts and schemas in the associate cortex. Weak central coherence (Happe and Frith 2006) in participants with autism prevents this further executive functioning filtering into concepts held in the associate cortex; hence for the person with autism, sensate experience in the primary cortex is the dominant form of perception.

In my research investigations, students with autism made and danced with masks in the woodland as part of an ongoing ecotherapeutic and expressive arts pedagogy. Knill et al. (2005) tell us that intermodal expressive arts practice, such as mask-making and dancing, increases the potential for experiential decentred shifts into altered phenomenological realities that become embedded into art. This can empower social change, relationality, communication, feelings of belonging and self-worth. Ellen Levine (2015: 62) comments that the person with autism 'must have others to speak for them' in the aesthetic analysis of their art work – an analysis made within the sensate, phenomenological and experiential perception. To address this, I invited three groups of (neural typical) co-researchers who practised in expressive arts therapy, to take part in the aesthetic analysis of my autistic students' mask artwork. The co-researchers firstly attuned to the masks made by my autistic students, gaining access to the feelings embedded in the masks. The co-researchers then intermodally transferred feelings held in the masks through attuned dancing. Joy Schaverien (2000) calls this attuned transfer of feelings from artwork 'scapegoat transference'. This transferring of feelings from one art form to another enabled the co-researchers to process the experiential and sensed data held in the masks – firstly through dancing, then drawing and finally poetic writing. Knill (1978: 84) suggests:

> When we work in a particular communication modality and directly move into another modality, using the experience and the products of the preceding process, I call that change an intermodal transfer.

McNiff (2013: 156) comments on his re-drawing another artist's work as a way of experiencing an 'empathetic connection that could only arise from a restoration of the place of creative enchantment'. Likewise, intermodal art based research tools allowed the co-researchers to experientially attune to the 'life of the picture' held in the ASC participants' art objects/masks and intermodally shift the live art process through a series of art processes – the final live art sequence residing in the form of poetry. Schaverien (1999: 87) states that the embodied image of the 'life in the picture' 'transcends what is consciously known […] the physical act of painting takes precedence […] to […] reveal previously unconscious aspects of the client's intra-psychic life'.

A heuristic understanding of that held in the art work of the ASC participants' masks was processed through the expressive arts therapy process in phase two of this research by three independent neural typical groups of co-researchers (Westcliff, Oxford and Kilkenny). All of the three groups of co-researchers understood and had practised expressive arts therapy. They worked with Halprin's (2003) dance orientated 'life art process' expressive arts therapy inter/multimodal process of dance/movement, visual art-making and poetic free-writing. The Westcliff group had already partaken in an introductory expressive arts therapy course and understood the practice of transference and Knill et al.'s (2005) expressive arts therapy architecture of the session. The Oxford group were all play therapists and as such were also au fait with the expressive arts therapy process, and the Kilkenny group were international practitioners of expressive arts therapy who thoroughly understood the process.

Multimodal and intermodal processes

The co-researcher groups were asked to be aware of their own feelings and to put them to one side, so that the initial ASC felt intention embedded in the mask image could 'speak' through the co-researchers' intermodal transfer. The co-researchers were all from a therapeutic background and as such were able to identify and bracket off their own projections. I have chosen a photograph from the Westcliff group (Figure 1) that illustrates the attunement and interaction between participant as dancer and witness and represents the intermodal process. The resultant poems made in the final intermodal phase hold the data of the expressive art-based research as intermodal transfer.

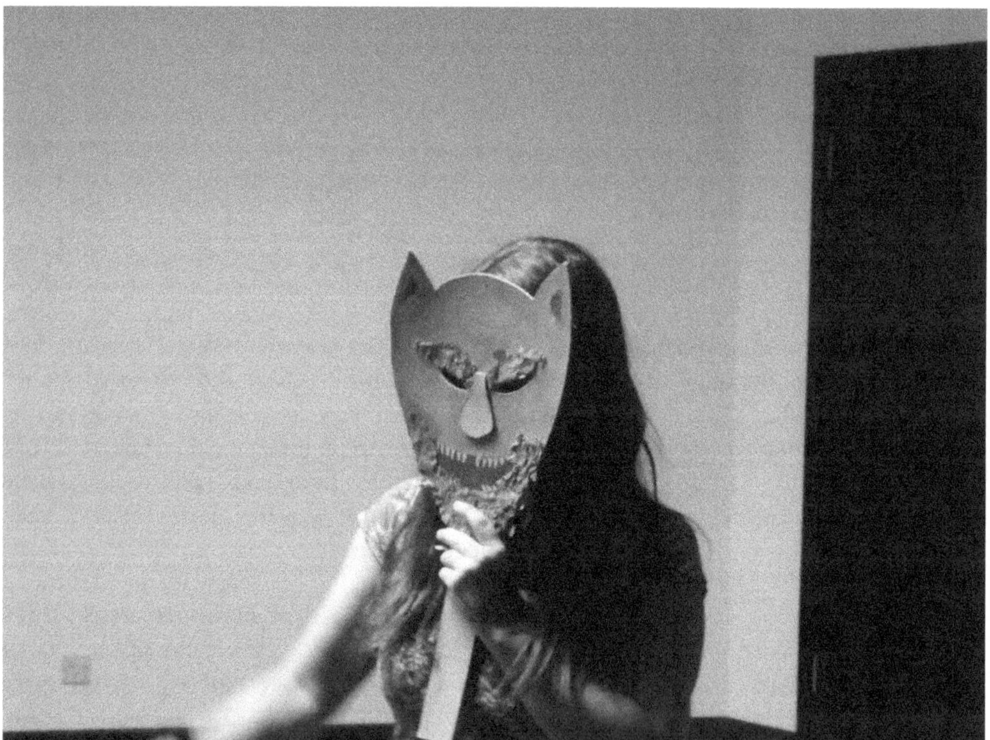

Figure 1: Westcliff Group (8 August 2015).

To begin, each neural typical co-researcher paired up and attuned to the ASC participants' mask that was worn by their neural typical co-research assistant partner, except for those in the Westcliff group who attuned to the mirrored reflection of the mask that they were wearing. From the outset of the activity, the co-researchers were briefed to bracket off their own experience and to attune and channel what was held in the autistic created mask. As they moved and danced the masks during their attunement, the co-researchers 'decentred' into a 'non-ordinary reality' (Figure 1). During this heightened sense of attunement, the co-researchers re-experienced the masks through an aesthetic analysis and re-interpretation into other art forms, from movement to visual, and finally poetic art forms.

At the point of their decentring through movement, like a bird moving into flight, the embodied dance moves the mask's dancer into a place of altered reality and perception. As movement and decentring increased, the movers became embodied in their dance until the dance naturally moved into visual art-making. Neural typical co-researcher Tessa (pseudonym) describes her intermodal experience and subsequent 'shift' into an embodied 'non-ordinary' reality through dancing, painting and making a poetic response to an autistic made mask:

> *Deep feeling place that had this incredible swinging and moving and experiencing form and reality and heart, and dark, and deep, and flying. I think it was, I became, I became an entity of something, you know it was like it was inside me, it was also a natural spirit of something else.* – Tessa.
>
> (Reported by Kilkenny)

Fellow neural typical co-researcher (dancer of the autistic person's mask), Koo (pseudonym) describes the shift as:

> *I have a very deep body sensation. Into really unknown places, places that I wouldn't go usually and it was very striking to work with the mask. I got really close, in a way that you usually don't get there and in a way unless? The mask has this magic, I can't, it would be nice to be able to put into words what the mask actually does, but it de-personifies (taking the person away) multiplies the experience so much.* – Koo.
>
> (Reported by Kilkenny)

In the study Koo states that she felt 'de-personified (taking the person away)' and Tessa describes: 'I became an entity of something', which I suggest means they have 'let go of the controlling mind' (McNiff 1992: 17) through 'active imagination', a method of investigating the 'unconscious psychic process' (Jung 1968: 4). This suggests that an expressive arts intermodal process can give neural typical people access to altered perceptual states through acquiring a 'sensory gating deficit' to become heuristically attuned to a place of coexistence with autistic perception as described by Baggs (2007).

The multi/intermodal process required co-researchers to attune to the ASC mask and move into an intermodal sequence of embodied movement followed by drawing without speaking or communicating with one another. They stay within the primary cortex of the experiential, unconscious/collective state and phenomenological space so as to avoid a cognitive analysis of what is going on in the creative process. The process then moves into poetic free-writing. At this point a parallel processing can be drawn with Giorgio Vallortigara et al.'s (2008) suggestion that analysis is formed through the creative right brain where raw experiential heuristic data emerges in a creative written form – poetry – giving potential for an 'aesthetic analysis' to take place. This is where an aesthetic of the senses is formed in writing, perhaps similar to André Breton's (1933) surrealist notion of automatic drawing and automatic writing coming directly from the embodied unconscious.

Embodied interpretation tanka poems

Sensing that a traditional textual discourse analysis would destroy what was intrinsic in the live art process of these poems, I sought a more sensate form of coding. Monica Prendergast et al. (2009: xxii) state that Poetic inquiry 'is to synthesise experience in a direct and affective way', which encapsulates and crystallizes a heuristic understanding of experience held in text. Educationalist Anna Craft (2015: 167) speaks of embodied feelings, experience and expression as the 'biological engine of action'. It is through the embodied experience that I have sought to code or frame the intermodal research findings. Sandra Faulkner discusses poetry as a methodology and describes her research tankas as a form of coding derived from Japanese *tanka* (短歌) (short poem), a distilled five-line poem, as she explains:

> First, one author wrote autobiographical poems, and then, another author used the poems as data to create research tankas [...] Finally the third and fourth authors wrote responsive poems to the grounded theory analysis and original poems.
>
> (Faulkner 2009: 27–28)

Kathleen Galvin and Les Todres (2009: 308) present a similar process to Faulkner's research *tankas*. They call their poetic inquiry and phenomenological research 'embodied interpretation', describing this as a 'phenomenological descriptive analysis of transcribed text'. They elaborate what they call 'embodied interpretation', explaining the process as 'a body based hermeneutics that goes back and forth between language and the felt sense of the text carried in our bodies'.

It has always been my intention to retain the live art process held in the masks made by the ASC participants. Knill's (1978) concept of intermodal transference has ensured that the live art process is still held within the resultant intermodal poems. Faulkner's (2009) 'research *tankas*' and Galvin and Todres' (2009) 'embodied interpretation' present a form of coding that distils rather than fragments the live art process held in the extensive and triangulated intermodal poems. Galvin and Todres argue that their embodied interpretation does 'present that aliveness in ways that don't kill it' and can 'awaken not just logical understanding, but also the sense of it as it lives' (2009: 309).

I coded my intermodal poems/research findings with my clinical supervisor Ellen Levine in a similar way to Faulkner's (2009) *tanka* research and Galvin and Todres' (2009) embodied interpretation. We arrived at a distilled version of the live art process as a series of embodied interpretation *tanka* poems that evoke in the reader of these poems, the heuristic essence of my ASC participants' live art process. To employ what is felt from these findings as an intervention in pedagogy, I re-visit Craft (2015: 167) when she states that schools traditionally 'tend not to acknowledge the body (the embodied) in teaching' – something that a positivistic, reductionistic curriculum denies. Art-based researcher Stephanie Springgay coins the term *A/r/tography* where the a/r/t connect artist/researcher/teacher, 'attends to the spaces between artist, researcher, teacher' (Springgay et al. 2008: 158–59). Springgay et al. (2008: xx) further posit that *A/r/tography* relates to Gilles Deleuze and Felix Guattari's (1987) 'rhizome' and as Deleuze (1997: 111) states: 'Creative stuttering is what makes language grow from the middle, like grass; it is what makes language a rhizome instead of a tree'. The educational metaphor that a tree forms roots from existing knowledge drawn through the trunk to flourish in the crown ensures that understanding is retained within the 'outside in' status quo of existing knowledge. Conversely, the rhizome allows growth from an 'inside out' person-centred perspective where the senses direct outcome.

Oxford co-researcher: distilled *tanka* poem as coding:

Looking at first with curiosity
I feel a longing to engage.
I can't figure it out.
I cannot offer you my full self
There is a barrier to our connection.
Only when I dance as a wolf in the forest can I meet you in a world of mystery.

Kilkenny co-researcher: distilled *tanka* poem as coding:

Playful curiosity
Is trapped inside fear
Trust has punched out
To touch, break through
And protect the web of souls

Westcliff co-researcher: distilled *tanka* poem as coding:

'Biting the softness'
My trapped teeth

My trapped teeth
Scary and scared
Sending sparkly rays of aliveness
Going step by step
Gently into
The soft nothing

My own experiential process

During a research conference on using art as research at the University of Wolverhampton in 2016, I presented and discussed this project in terms of expressive art-based research. I was asked by Shaun McNiff, a conference keynote speaker, 'why didn't you process the masks multimodally yourself?' At the same conference Malcolm Ross, another keynote speaker, independently asked this same question. I was stumped for an answer! The best

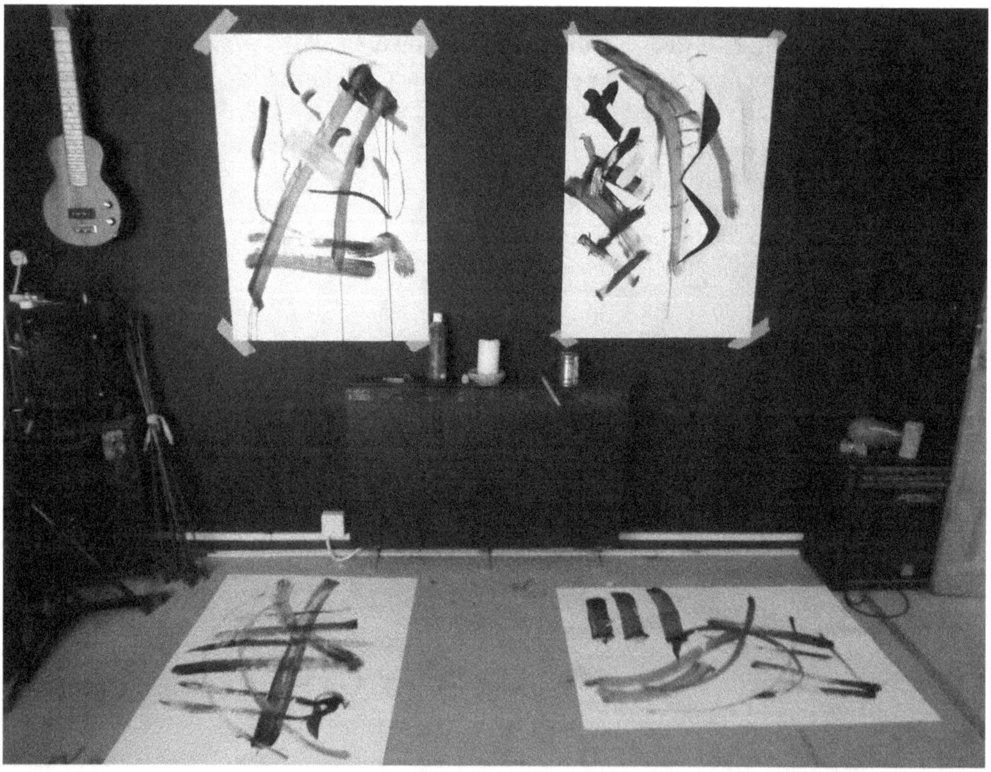

Figure 2: My expressive art-based research tools as intermodal embodied/action painting/dance (2016).

I could give was impartiality, transparency and not wanting to bias outcomes. These are all givens for a positivistic paradigm approach of minimizing felt response in favour of objectivity. Yes, why was I not processing my experiential journey with the mask? So I did.

I asked one of the co-researchers from the Westcliff group to witness my own expressive arts intermodal art-based research with the ASC mask. The resultant intermodal poem was taken into my clinical supervision. An intermodal coding/frame of my dance–paint–poem of mask was made with my clinical supervisor Ellen Levine. Like the Japanese *tanka* poems, a second reader/poet reflected on action words and meanings and messages held in the original (intermodal) poems, using open coding. To do this I highlighted parts of my intermodal poem that called to me or caught my eye as an embodied aesthetic analysis still held in the felt and sensate as embodied interpretation. Galvin and Todres (2009: 308) describe embodied interpretation as a 'phenomenological descriptive analysis of transcribed text'. They state that by moving between their embodied sense and the meanings held in texts as potentials for embodied sensate and intermodal transference, '[i]t is the body based hermeneutics that goes back and forth between language and the felt sense of the text conveyed in our bodies' (Galvin and Todres 2009: 308).

This process is emergent and requires a phenomenological and embodied immersion into the live art of the text. It is not analysed through a systematic grouping exercise in objective classification into preordained meanings of text as thematic textual analysis might. In the embodied interpretation/coding/framing of my own intermodal poem from the mask made by an autistic participant, Levine noted my body-based hermeneutic phrases as they took form in a new poem as coding through embodied interpretation as would Japanese tankas poetry, channelling the enigmatic and cryptic live art process through embodied interpretation of the felt and sensate.

Resultant intermodal poems:

The drum was our engine the dance our pilot
Completes the greeting
Folds and rips bring a soft growl into the room
Safe in darkness you hold something precious
I can dance between the trees in the forest
Building a wary trust.

Galvin and Todres (2009: 309) speak of their intention through embodied interpretation to 'represent that aliveness' that is held in this project as the intermodal poem 'in ways that don't kill it' and that 'connect to people in a heartfelt way' that awakens in the reader 'the sense of it as it lives'. Likewise, my findings as a form of *tanka* poems are an embodied interpretation of the intermodal process. The resultant text is a distilled essence of the live art process held in the *tanka* poem as a heuristic sense of the autistic participants' live art process held in the artwork of their mask.

Conclusion

During this research project, I experienced a shared sensate world where expressions between the autistic and neural typical perception can coexist. The co-researchers' poetic line 'Only when I dance as a wolf in the forest can I meet you in a world of mystery' gives an idea about this shared experiential world. There are potentials for realizing relational pedagogy and therapy models that draw on the experience of losing the objective self in the creative moment. I did not find scientific truths about what autism is or is not, but I felt a deep sense of connection with the live art experience of another's artwork – who happened to be autistic.

These deeply felt experiences expressed in my own and in my co-researchers' *tanka* poems challenge existing compensatory medical and social interventions for autism. Diagnostic styles that treat autism as an illness rather than a different way of perceiving unintentionally exclude the individual and inform compensatory social interventions – such as applied behavioural analysis (ABA) – where the autistic person's uniqueness is compromised to fit into neural typical patterns of behaviour. Scientific truths defined through neural typical lenses are redefined by art-based research into emergent expression, where the senses are explored and inform praxis.

The heuristic experience of stepping into the shoes of a person with ASC can inform new understanding and acceptance for planners and facilitators in developing creative pedagogy that includes neural typical and autistic world-views in education and therapy. Rather than 'be like us' models of education and therapy, we could begin with the premise of 'allow me to step into *your* world' and just see what emerges and grows from the centre of the rhizome of sensate experiences that we share in natural expression. Only with this understanding can we offer a truly congruent pedagogy for those within the ASC.

References

Baggs, Amanda (2007), *In My Language*, YouTube, https://www.youtube.com/watch?v=JnylM1hI2jc. Accessed 21 April 2016.

Bogdashina, Olga (2010), *Autism and the Edges of the Known World*, London: Jessica Kingsley Publishers.

Breton, André (1933), 'The automatic message (Le Message Automatique)', *Minotaure Magazine*, 3&4, n.pag.

Craft, Anna (2015), *Creativity Education and Society*, London: IOE Press.

Deleuze, Gilles (1997), *Essays Critical and Clinical*, London: Verso.

Deleuze, Gilles and Guattari, Felix (1987), *A Thousand Plateaus: Capitalism and Schizophrenia* (trans. Brian Massumi), Minneapolis: University of Minnesota.

Faulkner, Sandra (2009), *Poetry as Method, Reporting Research through Verse*, London: Routledge.

Galvin, Kathleen and Todres, Les (2009), 'Poetic enquiry & phenomenological research', in M. Prendergast, K. Leggo and P. Sameshima (eds), *Poetic Inquiry: Vibrant Voices in the Social Sciences*, Rotterdam: Sense Publishing.

Grandin, Temple (2010), *Penny Stamps Lecture: The Art of Translation*, Michigan. University of Michigan, School of Art and Design, http://www.youtube.com/watch?v=J 3ueIBH5DI. Accessed 8 August 2013.

Grandin, Temple and Johnson, Catherine (2005), *Animals in Translation: The Woman Who Thinks like a Cow*, London: Bloomsbury.

Halprin, Daria (2003), *The Expressive Body in Life, Art and Therapy*, London: JKP.

Happe, Francesca and Frith, Uta (2006), 'The weak coherence account: Detail-focused cognitive style in autism spectrum disorders', *Journal of Autism and Developmental Disorders*, 36, January, https://www.ncbi.nlm.nih.gov/pubmed/16450045. Accessed 20 December 2016.

Hillman, James (1974), *The Myth of Analysis*, New York: Harper Torchbooks.

Jordan, Martin (2015), *Nature and Therapy, Understanding Counselling and Psychotherapy in Outdoor Spaces*, London: Routledge.

Jung, Carl (1968), *Analytical Psychology: Its Theory and Practice, The Tavistock Lectures*, London: Routledge and Kegan Paul Ltd.

——— (1997), 'Tavistock lectures', in J. Chodorow (ed.), *Jung and Active Imagination*, London: Princeton, pp. 143–53.

——— (2000), *Psychology and Alchemy*, 2nd ed., Guildford: Routledge.

Knight, Sara (2011), *Forest School for All*, London: Sage.

Knill, Paolo (1978), 'Intermodal expression', Ph.D. thesis/doctoral thesis, Cincinnati: The Union Graduate School.

Knill, Paolo, Levine, Ellen and Levine, Stephen (2005), *Principles and Practice of Expressive Arts Therapy*, London: JKP.

Levine, Ellen (2015), *Play and Art in Child Psychotherapy: An Expressive Arts Therapy Approach*, London: JKP.

Limb, Charles and Braun, Allen (2008), 'Neural substrates of spontaneous musical performance: An fMRI study of Jazz improvisation', *PLoS One*, 27 February.

McNiff, Shaun (1992), *Art as Medicine Creating Therapy of the Imagination*, Boston: Shambhala.

——— (2013), *Art as Research: Opportunities and Challenges*, Bristol: Intellect.

Minshew, Nancy, Goldstein, Gerald and Siegel, Don (1997), 'Neuropsychologic functioning in autism: Profile of a complex information processing disorder', *Journal of the International Neuropsychology Society*, 3:4, pp. 303–16.

Ozonoff, Sally, Dawson, Geraldine and McPartland, James (2002), *A Parent's Guide to Asperger Syndrome and High-Functioning Autism: How to Meet the Challenges and Help Your Child Thrive*, New York: Guildford Press.

Pellicano, Elizabeth (2010), 'Individual differences in executive function and central coherence predict developmental changes in theory of mind in autism', *Developmental Psychology*, 46:2, pp. 530–44.

Prendergast, Monica, Leggo, Carl and Sameshima, Pauline (2009), *Poetic Inquiry Vibrant Voices in the Social Sciences*, Rotterdam: Sense Publishing.

Schaverien, Joy (1999), *The Revealing Image: Analytical Art Psychotherapy in Theory and Practice*, London: Jessica Kingsley Publishers.

——— (2000), 'The triangular relationship and the aesthetic countertransference in analytical art psychotherapy', in A. Gilroy and G. McNeilley (eds), *The Changing Shape of Art Therapy*, London: Jessica Kingsley Publishers.

Simons, Daniel and Chabris, Christopher (1999), 'Gorillas in our midst: Sustained inattentional blindness for dynamic events', *Perception*, 28:9, pp. 1059–74.

Springgay, Stephanie, Irwin, Rita, Leggo, Carl and Gouzouasis, Peter (2008), *Being with A/r/tography*, Rotterdam: Sense Publishers.

Vallortigara, Giorgio, Snyder, Allan, Kaplan, Gisela, Bateson, Patrick, Clayton, Nicola and Rogers, Lesley (2008), 'Are animals autistic savants?', *PLoS Biology*, 64:5, pp. 455–67.

Note

1 This chapter is drawn from Kevin Burrows' Ph.D. study at Anglia Ruskin University: 'Expressive arts in ecotherapeutic contexts: A social intervention for autism', where he developed a research methodology that embraces art-based research as a way of experientially understanding autistic perception.

Part 4

Current and Future Issues in Arts Learning and Teaching

Chapter 14

Making Art and Teaching Art: Harnessing the Tension

Libby Byrne and Patricia Fenner

Recent research suggests that there is a tension that exists between the practices of making art and teaching art and yet there can be great benefit in managing to sustain both practices concurrently over time (Bennett et al. 2010; Hall 2010; Imms and Ruanglertbutr 2013a, 2013b). Drawing on personal experience, we note that a similar tension exists in making art whilst maintaining a practice as an art therapist or a university lecturer within an Art Therapy training programme. A dedication to combining a solitary art-making practice with regularly working in social contexts can result in a confluence of conflicting energies and demands. We argue that the drive to undertake research practice can, in fact, be stimulated by harnessing the creative tension generated by these conflicting demands.

In order to explore this idea we have utilized a case study method, analysing a series of figurative artworks produced over time by Libby Byrne, the first author here. She has balanced the practice of art-making with working as a teacher, university lecturer, an art therapist and a researcher. The works selected for analysis become the data for an inquiry into the nature of tension experienced, combining an art-making practice with teaching in institutional settings and working clinically as a therapist. An ontological exploration of questions of identity that emerge leads us to address issues of professional identity and how integrating the two activities concurrently leads to the development of a third professional identity, of being a researcher.

The experience of turning attention – Libby Byrne

When I am painting, I am aware that there is a job I need to be doing elsewhere and when I am doing that job I am aware that I need to be painting. This split attention requires a continuous turning from one task to the other. As attention is focused in one direction, the other direction is seemingly ignored. Whilst the agency we exercise in making the choice is, however, an expression of desire, making the choice to attend to one activity over the other creates an experience of tension.

Tension

Before going any further, it is important to consider what we mean when we speak of an experience of 'tension'. If we try to imagine 'tension' the first thing that comes to mind is something that is pulled tight, a rope or cable suspended in mid-air. There may be something precarious or threatening about this image, though it could equally be stimulating and exciting. Poised in a heightened state of alertness, we are waiting for something that is still unresolved to happen. High levels of stimulation, expectation and anticipation can lead to tension, with the potential to create anxiety, and we may describe this feeling as 'tense'. Working with uncomfortable experiences of tension can, however, release a reserve of creative energy that can resolve the experience, expanding our thinking and creative capacities.

Recent research by James Hall into the experiences of artists involved in the Artist Teacher Scheme (ATS) in the United Kingdom found that when the teacher of art is reframed as an artist-teacher there are some very particular 'tensions between the professional territories and cultures inhabited by artists and teachers' (Hall 2010: 105). Hall surveyed the growing body of literature concerned with the implementation of the ATS and other articles relating to aspects of artists in education and concludes that there are five distinct but interrelated sources of tension for these professionals. These themes relate to Professional Identities, Curriculum Development, Teacher Development, Theoretical Perspectives and Reflective Practice (Hall 2010). These tensions seem to eventually stem back to the question, '*What are we doing and why are we doing it?*' – a question that must be renegotiated on a routine basis when turning attention between the practices of making art ourselves and working clinically or educationally for example, across various institutional settings with people who are making their own art.

Can these tensions be productive?

Many different tensions can surface when artists and teachers work in an interdisciplinary way, but does this need to be simply a difficult experience or can it also be productive? Within this turning of attention, there is a cognitive dissonance experienced between what I want and what I have. '*I want more time in the studio, but I have a class to teach*' or '*I want my students to understand how to risk making their own mistakes, but I have students who are looking to me for answers*'. This cognitive dissonance between our visions for what we want and the reality of what we have can be the source of what Peter Senge (1990) describes as creative tension. Rather than wallowing in the ideal vision, or being stuck in a less than ideal reality, Senge proposes that when we engage the creative tension that this dissonance provokes, our minds can work to release and direct our energies and resources into resolving the dissonance with a creative solution. In choosing to place ourselves in the position whereby our attention is perpetually drawn away, we are choosing to live with creative tension that has the capacity to enrich both our art-making and teaching practice.

The fear of failure

Creative tension can, however, feel uncomfortable and it is easy to mistake this experience as one of anxiety or even fear. Inherent in the creative experience of making art lurks the fear of failure. 'Making art can feel dangerous and revealing [...] [it] precipitates self-doubt, stirring deep waters that lay between what you know you should be, and what you fear you might be' (Bayles and Orland 1993: 13). The fears that artists are prone to experiencing, are described by Bayles and Orland, as falling into two categories, those being 'fears about yourself and fears about your reception by others' (1993: 23). For some, fear is a constant companion in the work of making art. Cam Gilmour offers us a glimpse into the pervasive nature of this fear when he says:

> I'm not entirely sure about other people, but I usually spend most of my working hours in quiet alarm, feeling less like the captain of some great steam train traversing a continent (or at least a few prickly suburbs) and more like a nervous fare evader unsure of everything except for the heavy sense that I'm doing something wrong and will likely be found out.
> (Gilmour 2014: 11)

Although this may be so for Gilmour, others may find that fear surfaces in peaks and troughs at different stages of the creative process. Whilst the fear of failure may be familiar to the practising artist, teaching art can also provoke such anxieties: fear about oneself and the reception by others. Increasingly, teaching success is measured via Student Feedback Surveys. Accordingly, successful teachers must be able to engage and challenge students in face-to-face interactions in the classroom and across a range of multi-media platforms, providing them with the resources they need to work independently and ultimately achieve their learning goals. Paul Pedota (2015) argues that student success or lack of success has such a strong impact upon teacher self-efficacy that it can affect a teacher's decision as to whether to remain in the profession. This strong link between student success and teacher self-efficacy suggests that the success of a teacher's work is in some way being measured against the achievements of their students. The implication of this thinking for an art teacher is that the success of their teaching work can be evaluated by the creative output of their students. For the artist who teaches and exhibits concurrently, the risk of failure in their own creative output may be the source of an additional pressure in both their teaching and artistic practice. The perceived failure of an exhibition may affect the teacher's reputation and professional standing, thereby impacting on their capacity to be successful in the work of teaching art. Likewise, the artist who seeks work as a teacher or lecturer needs to feel capable of producing routinely successful exhibitions. Having said this, artists who teach are well positioned to address this as creative tension within their own reflexive practice by harnessing the intersubjective communication that occurs as images are created within the classroom and the studio.

Gilmour acknowledged the ever-present fear of failure that accompanies him in his artistic practice and proposes that the artist must learn to trust the experience of failure itself: 'I trust failure in a strange way because I recognise it as the struggle' (Gilmour 2014: 28). As a practising artist, this statement resonates powerfully, but the lived experience of taking the risk to trust failure in our practice can be strained and constrained by a range of mitigating factors, including the need to earn a living and the expectations associated with working for and within an institution (Addison 2010). When these concerns are weighted heavily in our practice, it can be tempting to think that *failure is not an option* (Kranz 2000). Such an attitude towards failure is, however, likely to extinguish the capacity for innovation. Harnessing a fear of failure and nourishing it as 'trust in the creative struggle' is essential if we are to sustain working as artist researchers across disciplines.

The fear of 'being found out', which Gilmour describes, raises the question of identity. The question of identity may present as a dilemma about filling in a tax return: Am I an artist or a teacher? It may however be, as Addison suggests, a deeper question about what it means to choose to work in a way that is meaningful personally, socially and even culturally (Addison 2010). In this case the discussion about identity may become an ontological question, a consideration explored and expressed in Gadamer's question, 'Who am I and who are you?' (Gadamer 1997: 67). The question of identity for both the artist and the teacher engages the other, who may see the work through multiple lenses as viewer, colleague and/or student.

Mikel Dufrenne proposes that in apprehending the work, the viewer confers particular significance and meaning upon the work itself. The viewer's experience of the work is therefore considered to be an important contribution to the development of a work of art. In a similar way, the work of a teaching is given significance when meaning is conferred upon the experience by the students themselves. The experience of the other is always a consideration within our understanding of identity as artist and teacher and the significance of the work therefore takes on the qualities of an 'I-Thou' relationship (Buber 1971).

An analysis of figurative forms

Over the past twenty years I have been professionally engaged with teaching art in primary schools and higher education, working as an art therapist in the Public Health sector and now lecturing in a Post-Graduate Art Therapy programme at La Trobe University. As a researcher my commitment to my own art-making practice began with a minor Heuristic Thesis in the Master of Art Therapy programme and led me to undertake a Practice-led Theological Inquiry as a Ph.D. with the University of Divinity. I now lecture about the use of art as a methodology for engaging with theological inquiry in Post-Graduate programmes at the University of Divinity. Throughout that time I have worked consistently as a practising and exhibiting artist, offering 14 solo exhibitions in the years between 1998 and 2016. My career has been a rich and varied opportunity to work creatively with art and with people.

The figurative works chosen for this study (Figure 1) have featured prominently in exhibitions and have been chosen to represent times when I was transitioning into different professional roles. In choosing works that were exhibited concurrently with the beginning of a new way of working with people, I am wondering if these works contain some visual and thematic clues to help explore the experience under investigation in this chapter.

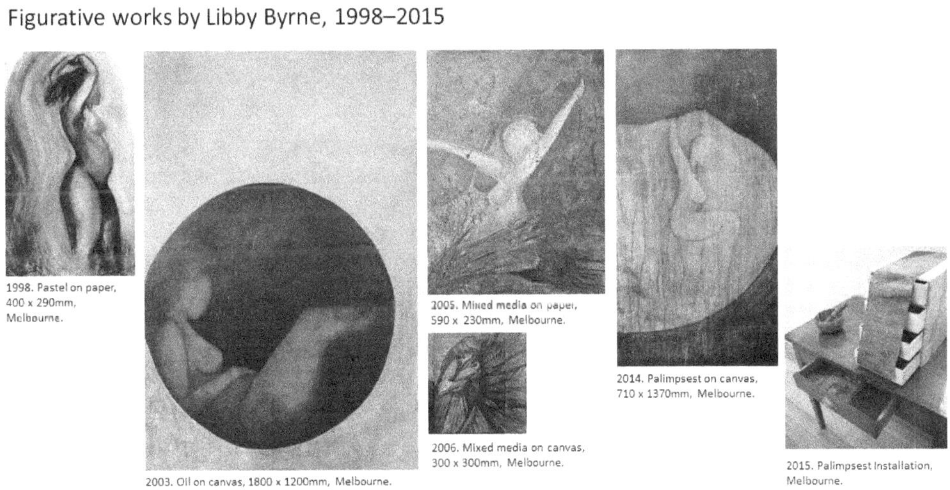

Figure 1: Libby Byrne, *Selected Figurative Works* (1998–2015).

We began by undertaking a Compositional Interpretation of each of the images (Rose and Tolia-Kelly 2012). Following Gillian Rose's method of analysis, we examined the images to consider the Content, Colour, Spatial Organization, Light and Expressive Content or mood of the paintings. We worked separately with coloured reproductions to consider these elements of the composition of the images, recording all of our responses to each image before moving onto the next. We did not discuss our individual processes until after the two data sets had been combined. I collated the data and undertook a qualitative thematic analysis to discern some basic, organizing and global themes (Attride-Stirling 2001; Marshall 2010). The emergent themes enabled us to identify the nature of the tension contained within these images, which in turn led us to identify the ontological significance of living with the challenge of sustaining an art-making practice whilst working with people as a therapist, teacher or researcher.

The themes

The first thing to note is that none of the figures fit completely within the frame. Hands and feet are missing; faces are obscured or just missing. In each of the works there are elements of the body that are either unfinished or simply existing beyond the frame of our vision. How does what is missing define what is being seen? 'What falls beyond one's immediate attention visibly defines, shapes and empowers or limits what is being seen or not seen' (Tapsell 2003: 244). Perhaps working as an artist enables me to pay attention to what may be falling beyond my immediate attention in the work I am doing, but defining and shaping my professional identity.

The missing elements of the human form lead us to consider what lies beyond the frame. The unfinished or unseen aspects of the form are a visual reminder that there is a world beyond what is present and visible, to consider what else may be still be possible. In most cases the body has a life that is unseen beyond the frame. Hands and feet that exist beyond the frame suggest work and movement that falls beyond the immediate attention.

The question of empathy

What is unseen and unfinished draws our attention to the question, 'What is it like to be like this?' (Van Lith 2014: 26). It is interesting to note that all the figures, except one, are naked. The skin, that is the edge of the body, the boundary between the body and the world, can be seen by the viewer. In the example where the figure is clothed, there are many layers protecting the skin – so many in fact that the skin is not visible. The fact that the figures are human is implied in the pose, as the female form cradles an infant. This figure reminds us not only of boundaries that are continually negotiated but also of our vulnerability and interdependence in the world. The figures are also faceless. Does this mean that they lack an identity or are they in fact more relatable without a distinct face? Are they figures who do not see? Without eyes, do they rely on bodily ways of knowing and being to *see* what is beyond the frame?

The material knowing that emerges from art-making practice relies heavily on tacit and embodied knowing, which emerges through the movement of the body and the materials. Our human experience is necessarily embodied and we initially perceive the world through our physical senses. These senses inform the development of our tacit knowing, which Michael Polanyi considered to be foundational in our human experience of the world (Polanyi 1966). According to Gendlin we do not experience our bodies as objects, rather we experience the world to which we are attending from our body (Gendlin 1997). These figurative works, therefore, represent the way that the artist experiences the world.

When we encounter an artwork, we are attending towards the object from the position of our body. We can be aware of a full range of physical and perceptual experiences that may be provoked in the aesthetic encounter. Seeing these works displayed in this way together is, therefore, an opportunity for the viewer to bring his/her own lived experience of the world and into relationship with the artist's experience. The tacit knowing that emerges in seeing these works displayed in this way can assist both the artist and viewer in the work of making sense of the world around us, which is a creative process. 'Viewing art is not only a receptive process, but a creative one as well' (Csikszentmihalyi and Robinson 1990: 153). In seeing what it is like to be like this, I grow in empathy for myself and for other people.

These figurative works made at seminal points of time in my professional development were also an opportunity to see my experience beyond the frame of what was most immediate in my attention. Spending time before the canvas to paint and then exhibit the works was a receptive process – a giving and receiving, seeking and finding. These works were a way to integrate the practice wisdom that was growing beyond the frame, whilst attending to what was immediately present. Making and then exhibiting these works was an empathic response to a growing and changing professional self. The images are the result of engaging with the lived experience of creative tension.

One narrative that has run parallel to the making of the images is the exchanges about these art works between the two of us writing this chapter. Our relationship has run parallel to the making of these paintings, transforming and developing initially from teacher and student, to academic colleagues. A back and forth communication evolved whereby, at a pause in the painting process, Libby, using iPhone created images, texted Patricia up-to-date visual accounts of her painting in its emergence. Patricia, in response, sent back key word intersubjective responses. These exchanges were simple and unselfconscious; parts of the usual kinds of communication, which takes place between like-minded and attuned people. However, the intentional nature of the act demonstrated evolving empathic sensibilities, and provided impetus to the further development of the images.

A professional identity: Reimagined and re-formed

Returning to the paintings themselves, it is also important to note that the figures take different positions within each frame and in doing so reflect the changes in personal and professional boundaries. Sometimes the figure is central as in 1998 and 2005 (Figure 2). At other times the composition of the work suggests that the figure is in relationship with a surrounding space that has agency of its own. This is particularly notable in 2003 and 2015 (Figure 3).

The positions that these figures take up reflect experiences of significant professional growth. These years were times when my professional identity was reshaped: firstly in 2003 by integrating my work as an artist with that of a therapist, and in 2015 with the emergence of an artist researcher. The growth and development of these professional identities has happened in a way that is akin to the development of a body of artwork, in that it has required me to be immersed in a cycle of making and reflecting over time. The reflexive practice of making art whilst working with people has facilitated phases of contemplation, analysis and interpretation, enabling me to consider what is happening within the artwork and how this may relate to questions in my teaching and therapeutic practice. By noting new ideas, questions, social, political and cultural references in the work that is emerging, the artist develops what Gadamer describes as, 'a receptivity to the *otherness* of a work of art' (1975: 16). It is the otherness of a work of art that alerts our attention towards a phenomenology of experience that may otherwise have been missed. Becoming aware of a relational experience of what is present in the work of art and in the creative process enables the artist to undertake the hermeneutical work of interpreting and making sense of what has been revealed in the research.

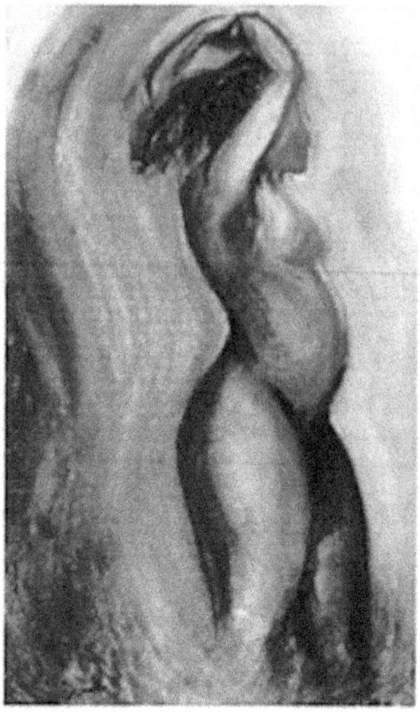

1998. Pastel on paper, 400 x 290mm.

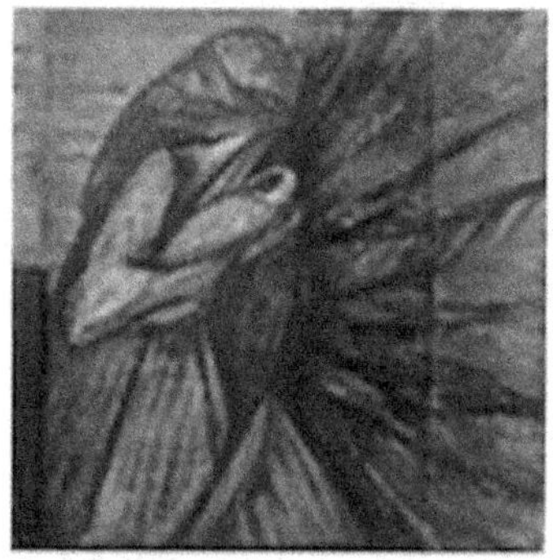

2005. Mixed media on canvas, 300 x 300mm.

Figure 2: Libby Byrne, *Figurative Works* (1998 and 2005).

Whilst Gadamer argues that hermeneutic work needs to be framed with the structure of dialogue, question and answer, he refers to the 'horizon of the question' as the means for thinking beyond what has already been said and known (1975: 378). Developing a hermeneutical understanding of the actions and reactions that take place within a reflexive studio practice engages the artist with an ongoing and complex phenomenological inquiry whereby the whole is only ever known by understanding the parts, and the parts can only be known in relation to the whole (Heidegger 1960). Continuing to bracket assumptions about the nature of the practice and the possible outcomes for the work means that I remain open to fresh and unexpected encounters in the phenomenology of my aesthetic experience. The creative tension experienced in working in this way provides the energy and capacity to work across perceived interdisciplinary boundaries.

Seeking and finding

The nature of this creative tension can be characterized as a rhythm of 'Seeking and Finding' (Quash 2013). The agency required to turn one's attention to the different facets of the work

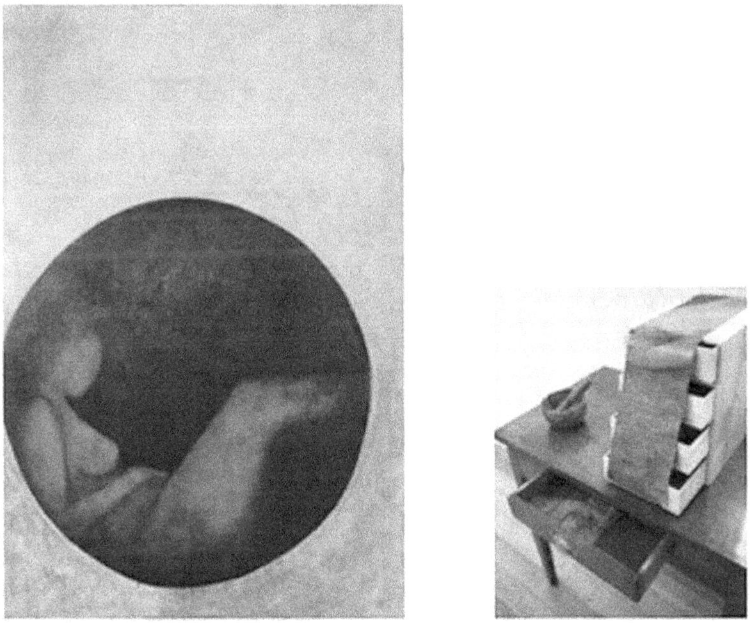

2003. Oil on canvas, 1800 x 1200mm.

2015. Palimpsest Installation.

Figure 3: Libby Byrne, *Figurative Works* (2003 and 2015).

is a response to the desire to seek and find that which may be missing or even lost. The images in this case study reveal a constant and dynamic movement of questioning and creating, stretching and breaking free. The figures challenge and ultimately redefine boundaries as I have been seeking and finding new professional identities, new ways of being with art and people.

Between 1998 and 2015, the female forms in this study shifted through different experiences of containing and being contained (Figure 4). Ultimately the figure in the final image has been 'decreated' (Weil 2002). She continues to exist, but no longer in the same way. She has entered into the realm of the uncreated and from this place she may be re-created or re-formed. This suggests an ontological significance to the questions of identity addressed in these images.

Choosing to work across disciplines has enabled the formation of an identity that allows for personal and professional growth and transformation. Being present to the embodied experience of de-creation and re-creation in the studio whilst continuing to arrive for class on time is, to say the least, challenging. It does, however, enhance and grow my capacity for empathy. Anthony Bond reminds us that:

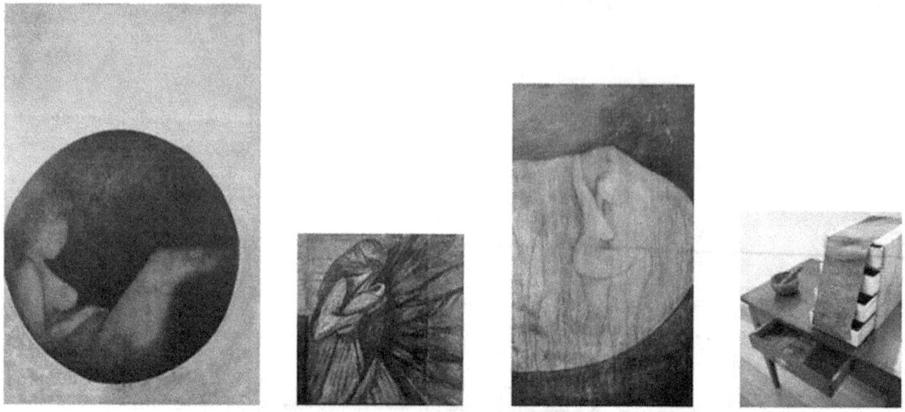

2003, *"Contained"*. Oil on canvas, 1800 x 1200mm.

2006, *"Containing"*. Mixed media on canvas, 300 x 300mm.

2014, *"Contained"*. Palimpsest on canvas, 710 x 1370mm.

2015, *"Decreated"*. Palimpsest Installation.

Figure 4: Libby Byrne, *Contained, Containing, Contained* and *Decreated* (2003, 2005, 2014 and 2015).

> [...] it is art [that] has the best chance of making something of the creative tension these questions produce. We are most fully alive when we balance third-person consciousness of the objective world with our first-person experience of being with it and the body.
>
> (Bond 2015: 26–27)

In shifting between making, being with and seeing art I have been able to find the balance between my consciousness of the roles that I have juggled and my lived experience of being with this tension in my body.

Building a capacity for empathy

In his seminal work, *I and Thou*, Martin Buber contends that we become conscious of ourselves as people only in relationship with others (Buber 1971; Morrison 1988). It is the integrity and equality of this relationship that grows empathy. This experience of mutuality seems also to exist within the relationship I have with art. Michael Franklin helps me to understand this when he speaks of a self-referential mutuality between object and artist and accords the quality of an I–thou relationship to his relationship with the art object (Franklin 2013). The practice of making art is an opportunity to become increasingly aware of our own identity as we grow in empathy for the other.

Matthew Fox proposes that there is an interrelationship between creativity and compassion, going as far as to suggest creativity is what compassion does – the realization of the interconnectedness of all things (Fox 1999). Fox submits that we are creative when we are able to see relationships between matter and form that have not been imagined before. Further, he proposes that creativity happens when we see the relations or connections that we deeply want and need to see. Creativity and compassion are, therefore, interdependent upon one another, to the extent that they may even be considered the same energy. When we are working with the creative tension of sustaining the practice and identity as an artist researcher, we draw on reserves of compassion to build our capacity for empathy.

The emerging artist researcher

I recently spoke with an artist who had just completed his Master's degree. He was concerned to take on a Ph.D., having been warned that he would spend several years making 'crap' before the good stuff emerged. This would mean a break in his exhibiting capacity and thus income from his art-making. Without such a period in his artistic production he would not find a way through to that good stuff, but would continue to produce work in response to the market and his current practice. Post-graduate study scares people as they see it as time out from their chosen career path.

Being a student whilst simultaneously working can create tension – financial tension as well as emotional, but in this same study it appears to have been a resource to stretch and challenge ideas. To be persistently in 'study mode' across the disciplines of art, art therapy and theology has meant that I have been consistently open to new ideas and paradigms. Undertaking a minor heuristic thesis embedded the value of the researcher within an art-making practice. Working in the studio and exhibiting as an art researcher:

- builds capacity to think critically;
- builds reflexive capacities rather than reflective thinking;
- offers structure to the art-making process, which in turn creates the environment for disciplined and critical work;
- creates new pathways to possible employment.

Rather than being a break in the career trajectory of an artist, study has been a resource that strengthens and refines my reflexive art-making practice – creating space and time for necessary periods of incubation for new ideas.

Making, being with and seeing art

Managing the creative tension between making and teaching art requires making time for these stages of the process – particularly the 'being with' and 'seeing'. It is tempting when time is short to think that you must get into the studio and get making, but even when you are not 'in the studio' it is possible to be with and see art. These experiences nourish the creative energy – and do not necessarily require extended and separate scheduling. Rather, they are all different rhythms of attention that are part of a reflexive approach to the practices of living and working with art and people.

To be reflexive involves thinking from within experiences. It requires a willingness to make aspects of the self, strange in order to stand back from assumptions and habitual thinking and notice what may have been previously missed (Bolton 2005). Cora Marshall (2010) draws our attention to a long history of reflexivity as an aspect of research in the arts, citing Locke (1689), Dewey (1910), Eisner (1972), Gardner (1982) and Sullivan (2005). Marshall describes reflexive studio practice as being characterized by the gathering of thoughtful and critical reflections and actions for the purpose of bringing to light the underpinnings of our practice, our assumptions, biases and perspectives (Marshall 2010). It is a method of working that seeks to stand back and see what is happening whilst wondering – why is this so? The thoughtful questioning that wonder inspires is capable of sustaining what Heidegger calls a creative tolerance for the unconditioned (Rubenstein 2008). It is this tolerance that enables us to see the difference between what must necessarily be sustained and what is open to the possibility of transformation.

Hall (2010) argues that teachers of art need to build reflexive capacities rather than rely on familiar reflective practice techniques. I would argue that the Art Therapy component of my study and working life has equipped me with this capacity for reflexivity. Not only does this mode of analysis benefit my art and teaching practice, it builds my capacity for empathy and compassion. My reflexive practice skills developed as a therapist and art therapy supervisor were transferable within my Ph.D. inquiry as I researched in the studio and gallery about the question of healing in the absence of cure.

Taking time and making sense

Reflexive studio practice involves the habit of taking time to think with materials in order to make sense of what can be known about the question being researched. Making sense, however, is not necessarily the same as knowing. Reflexive practice does not necessarily assure answers to our questions, rather true reflexivity can result in the discovery of what cannot be known. A sustained rhythm of double attention to the practice of *taking time and making sense* enables the artist researcher to make new discoveries whilst at the same time remaining aware of what was just beyond the limits of possibility, and therefore cannot be known (Volpe 2013).

To work in this way requires an intentional commitment to un-mastery, to work that will always be in some way unfinished. 'To say that art-making is a practice indicates from the outset that the task of art is unfinished' (Stewart 2005: 17). In the practice of making art, the artist thinks with materials to make things visible in specific and particular ways. The practice is not, however, an inexhaustible and uninterrupted flow of doing. Within a sustained reflexive art-making practice, one can expect to encounter periods of stillness that are sometimes marked by not knowing what to do next. This time can be a time for the artist to spending time looking and then seeing the work as it emerges in all its strangeness. In these moments, there is a shift from the action of making into the creative contemplation that is embodied seeing.

Working with the then Archbishop of Canterbury, Rowan Williams, to describe an essential rhythm within the life of a contemplative person, Lawrence Freeman directs our attention towards the Desert Mothers and Fathers, who were Christian ascetics living in Egypt, Palestine and Syria in the fourth and fifth centuries AD. Freeman reminds us that whilst they loved and sought the silence of a monastic community, these people lived within the tension of a network of relationships and community (Freeman 2003; Williams 2003). They relied on the movement between action and contemplation to enable them to thrive in solitude and flourish in community. In the same way, a contemplative practice of working alone in a studio can enable the artist to navigate experiences of tension between the need for silence and the commitment to living and working alongside other people. One experience equips and resources them for the other. The rhythm of attention that moves between action and contemplation can be equally employed in the movement between the different roles of making, teaching and researching with art.

Conclusion

Managing the creative tension that is part of working as an artist researcher across different disciplines requires a willingness to seek and find balance. The images in this analysis were produced because Libby found the need to balance solitary time making art in the studio with time spent interacting and being with people. Whilst it can deplete us, the time spent interacting with people also feeds us with ideas and questions to be explored in the studio and then released back into the world around us as the works are publicly exhibited. When we strike this balance well, we experience a sense of unity in the work that we do with art and people, and this sustains us when we are next pulled in different directions by competing professional demands.

Our engagements with fellow artist researchers or simply compassionate others provides opportunity for empathy-fuelled exchanges that further enrich this dynamic. Whilst this process is not without personal and professional risk, this case study demonstrates that forming a professional identity as an artist researcher offers artist teachers and art therapists an epistemological framework to gather the creative threads and harness the tension required to sustain the challenges of working across these different disciplines.

References

Addison, Nicholas (2010), 'Artist teachers/teaching artists: Negotiating pedagogic identities', *Journal of Research in Art and Education*, 11:1, pp. 51–67.

Attride-Stirling, Jennifer (2001), 'Thematic networks: An analytic tool for qualitative research', *Qualitative Research*, 1:3, pp. 385–405.

Bayles, David and Orland, Ted (1993), *Art & Fear: Observations On the Perils (and Rewards) of Artmaking*, Santa Cruz: The Image Continuum.

Bennett, Dawn, Wright, David and Blom, Diana M. (2010), 'The artistic practice-research-teaching (ART) nexus: Translating the information flow', *Journal of University Teaching & Learning Practice*, 7:2, http://ro.uow.edu.au/jutlp/vol7/iss2/3. Accessed 1 May 2017.

Bolton, Gillian (2005), *Reflective Practice*, London: Sage.

Bond, Anthony (2015), *The Idea of Art: Building a Contemporary International Art Collection*, Sydney: New South Publishing.

Buber, Martin (1971), *I and Thou*, Edinburgh: T. & T. Clark.

Csikszentmihalyi, Mihaly and Robinson, Rick E. (1990), *The Art of Seeing: An Interpretation of the Asethetic Encounter*, Malibu: J.Paul Getty Museum and the Getty Center for Education in the Arts.

Dewey, John (1910), *How We Think*, Boston: D.C. Health.

Eisner, Elliot (1972), *Educating Artistic Vision*, Oxford: Macmillan.

Fox, Matthew (1999), *A Spirituality Named Compassion*, Rochester: Inner Traditions International.

Franklin, Michael (2013), 'Know thyself: Awakening self-referential awareness through art-based research', in S. McNiff (ed.), *Art as Research: Opportunities and Challenges*, Chicago: The University of Chicago Press.

Freeman, Laurence (2003), 'Introduction', in R. Williams (ed.), *Silence and Honey Cakes: The Wisdom of the Desert*, Oxford: Lion Hudson.

Gadamer, Hans Georg (1975), *Truth and Method*, London: Sheed & Ward.

——— (1997), *Gadamer on Celan: 'Who am I and Who are You?' and Other Essays*, Albany: SUNY Press.

Gardner, Howard (1982), *Art, Mind, and Brain: A Cognitive Approach to Creativity*, New York: Basic Books.

Gendlin, Eugene (1997), *A Process Model*, New York: The Focusing Institue.

Gilmour, Cam (2014), *As Dire as Its Title: Writings on the Daily Struggles of the Working Artist*, Melbourne: Camgilmour.wordpress.com.

Hall, James (2010), 'Making art, teaching art, learning art: Exploring the concept of the artist teacher', *The International Journal of Art & Design Education*, 29:2, pp. 103–10.

Heidegger, Martin (1960), *The Origin of a Work of Art*, Berlin: Reclam-Ausgabe.

Imms, Wesley and Ruanglertbutr, Purnima (2013a), 'Can early career teachers be artists as well?', *Canadian Review of Art Education*, 39:1, pp. 7–23.

——— (2013b), 'The teacher as an art maker: What do new teachers identify as "the issues"', *Australian Art Education*, 35:1&2, pp. 81–92.

Kranz, Gene (2000), *Failure is Not an Option: Mission Control from Mercury to Apollo 13 and Beyond*, New York: Simon & Schuster Inc.

Locke, John (1689), *An Essay Concerning Human Understanding, Book 1*, London: St Paul's Church Yard, M DC XC.

Marshall, Cora (2010), 'A research design for studio-based research in art', *Teaching Artist Journal*, 8:2, pp. 77–87.

Morrison, Karl F. (1988), *'I Am You' The Hermeneutics of Empathy in Western Literature, Theology, and Art*, Princeton: Princeton University Press.

Pedota, Paul J. (2015), 'How can student success support teacher self-efficacy and retention?', *The Clearing House: A Journal of Educational Strategies, Issues and Ideas*, 88:2, pp. 54–61.

Polanyi, Michael (1966), *The Tacit Dimension*, Chicago: The University of Chicago Press.

Quash, Ben (2013), *Found Theology: History, Imagination and the Holy Spirit*, London: Bloomsbury T&T Clark.

Rose, Gillian C. and Tolia-Kelly, Divya P. (2012), *Visuality/Materiality; Images, Object and Practices*, Farnham: Ashgate Publishing.

Rubenstein, Mary-Jane (2008), *Strange Wonder: The Closure of Metaphysics and the Opening of Awe*, New York: Columbia University Press.

Senge, Peter (1990), *The Fifth Discipline: The Art & Practice of the Learning Organization*, New York: Doubleday.

Stewart, Susan (2005), *The Open Studio: Essays on Art and Aesthetics*, Chicago: The University of Chicago Press.

Sullivan, Graeme (2005), *Art Practice as Research: Inquiry in the Visual Arts*, Thousand Oaks, CA: Sage.

Tapsell, Paul (2003), 'Beyond the frame', in L. Peers and A. K. Brown (eds), *Museums and Source Communities: A Routledge Reader*, London: Routledge, pp. 242–51.

Van Lith, Theresa (2014), 'Painting to find my spirit: Art making as the vehicle to find meaning and connection in the mental health recovery process', *Journal of Spirituality in Mental Health*, 16:1, pp. 19–36.

Volpe, Medi Ann (2013), '"Taking time" and "making sense": Rowan Williams on the habits of theological imagination', *International Journal of Systematic Theology*, 15:3, pp. 345–60.

Weil, Simone (2002), *Gravity and Grace*, New York: Routledge Classics.

Williams, Rowan (2003), *Slience and Honey Cakes: The Wisdom of the Desert*, Oxford: Lion Hudson.

Chapter 15

Future Approaches in Using Artistic Research from Human Experience

Petar Jandrić and Sarah Hayes

In discussing future approaches towards using art as research, we firstly raise the issue of a trend towards an academization of the arts that prioritizes expanding scientific authority over more traditional artistic expertise and autonomy. We argue that these days, art in the context of higher education is less and less about the mastery of material and the production of physical artefacts. Increasingly, art and artists are under pressure to adapt to fit within academic and economic models that replace independence and authenticity with a more institutionalized approach. For example, during the past decade or so, many art academies throughout the world have started research Ph.D. degrees in arts, leading to an academization of artistic practice that slowly but surely transforms the whole field. We highlight the following issues: *Funding*, because dominant ways of financing artists (through projects and exhibitions) slowly shifts to a more academic approach consisting of research proposals and grants; *Employment*, because more and more art academies do not want to employ teaching staff without Ph.D. degrees; *The social position of artists*, because independent arts projects get institutionalized in higher education; *The evaluation of artwork*, because standards of artistic excellence (the number and prestige of exhibitions, the price of an artwork, etc.) give way to standards characteristic for science and research (citations, numbers of publications, etc.). However, many of these changes can be understood as inappropriate for the arts as they reduce the unique forms of authority inherent to artistic works. Therefore, we bring to light the following questions, before proceeding to suggest ways forward: *Why would we institutionalize independent art projects, if we know that some of the best artwork has arrived from the independent sphere? Why would the academy want to employ someone with a Ph.D., instead of someone who staged 100 well-appraised exhibitions? What is the relationship between the quality of artwork and the number of citations?*

It is important to consider what conditions may generate authentic artworks and from here to begin to imagine future approaches in using artistic research. So far we have used the term 'artistic research' to be broadly inclusive of social aspects that move beyond a personal mental and physical contact with the art medium. Later we will explain this distinction in relation to other terms such as art-based or arts-based research. Having raised the concerns above about the factors at play in and around artists and their works, we now propose that it is worth stepping back a little to consider just how we understand the 'art' in artistic research anyway. Shaun McNiff (1993) argues there is really no such thing as art, only artists. With such a concept in mind, we develop our position of focus, not to be on artefacts alone, but rather on the powerful expressions of human experience that emerge through the artistic process. In this chapter we raise the proposition that new and intensely personal research methods and pedagogies emerge from the hybrid spaces linking, for example, human artistic creativity, digital technologies and visual culture, physical activities, discourse, learning and research. We consider artistic research as autoethnography, with the human experience of the artistic process as the narrative and expression that provides a lens on these developments.

Secondly, given our 'process' rather than 'product' based approach towards art-based research, we proceed to expand on two forms of demarcation: *boundary work* and *human experience.* In terms of boundaries, the transformations we have mentioned above have strongly divided the arts community. Some people may praise transparency and the apparent fairness of academic practices, but in other arguments, their inappropriateness and damaging effects to existing practices may be of concern. Such turmoil is characteristic for all emerging disciplines. For instance, after the Middle Ages, the sciences underwent a long process of detachment from religion before scientists could claim professional integrity. More recently, computer science took several decades to emerge from its mother disciplines such as electrical engineering and become a discipline in its own right. Such detachment has profound practical consequences. In the context of science, Thomas Gieryn writes:

> Construction of a boundary between science and varieties of non-science is useful for scientists' pursuit of professional goals: acquisition of intellectual authority and career opportunities; denial of these resources to 'pseudoscientists'; and protection of the autonomy of scientific research from political interference.
>
> (Gieryn 1983: 781)

Certainly, neither art nor science is a new discipline. However, disciplinary boundaries are continually constructed and reconstructed, and the disciplines are never complete. In the age of information, which has brought about significant changes in many disciplines from journalism to education, existing disciplines require a renewed focus towards boundary work. For instance, processes we may regard as routine within daily life now also present photo, video and publishing opportunities. The visual results of these encounters produce artefacts that may be posted on blogs and social media spaces. Therefore, in terms of human experience, self-publication can mean anything from a tweet to a novel and these 'productions' are linked to longer personal narratives over time. Due to a proliferation of more 'packaged adventure experiences', people are now engaged in practices of self-branding, though perhaps often unconsciously. Gerald Argenton (2015: 924) argues that there is no such thing as an 'adventure' out there waiting to be lived. However, due to multiple media and marketing techniques mingling with other more traditional communicative practices, such impressions about human experience can be swiftly shared. Therefore, do new digital techniques, which cut across subject areas, suggest a need to review what we believe we 'know' via existing (educational) theories about learning, experience and expression?

In the sections to come, we suggest that taking an approach towards artistic research through human experience enables connections across mind, body and soul that integrate rather than divide our research which enables us to cross boundaries. Human experience gives us opportunities to cut across the objective and subjective positions of research to span the disciplines. We show that human experience is shaped both by the 'external' aspects of contemporary artistic research (e.g. structures of education and funding) and the 'internal' aspects of artistic research (e.g. human experience). Therefore, we engage in boundary work using an autoethnographic approach and we develop our inquiry in two interrelated steps. In the first step, we use the works of Gieryn (1983) and Marcell Mars and Tomislav Medak (in Jandrić 2017: 243–69) to consider 'external' aspects of demarcation via boundary work. In the second step, we consider 'internal' opportunities based on living artistic research through human experience (Hayes 2015: 147, Hayes 2018, forthcoming). Through the dialectics between the external and the internal, we suggest a bottom-up approach through an autoethnography of human experience, as a central tenet of future development in artistic research.

Autoethnography of human experience

The growing field of artistic research exhibits a wide diversity of approaches and perspectives. Tom Barone and Elliot Eisner (1997) suggest that arts-based educational research (ABER) is intended to enhance perspectives pertaining to certain human activities. They add the important epistemological point, though, that this is not aimed towards a quest for certainty, reliability or validity. Rather the arts offering new ways of viewing educational phenomena to which we may now, twenty years on, absorb digital encounters too. ABER therefore does not, like many educational theories, offer instructions on how to proceed within the confines of a particular educational scenario or policy-related episode. Instead, it crosses pre-supposed boundaries to enable us to confront what is taken for granted. At its best ABER 'is capable of persuading the percipient to see educational phenomena in new ways, and to entertain questions about them that might have otherwise been left unasked' (Barone and Eisner 1997: 96).

Tobin Hart suggests '*how* we know is as important as *what we know*' (2004: 28, emphasis added). This suggests a process of 'knowing', rather than something static and 'known'. The element of 'movement' in knowing as a process, therefore, seems to us to be important in considering future approaches. It is at this point that ontology and epistemology are brought into dialogue together, through fluid art-informed interventions. Here we establish the role of the human body, and a sense of being, as well as the mind and a process of knowing, in any discussion about the future of any form of artistic research. Long before encountering the digital, humans were able to inhabit the virtual. Readers of a novel or viewers of a film were able to move away from the 'real' world and enter one with which they are less familiar (Barone and Eisner 1997: 98). So there is a certain continuity in relation to human encounters with virtual or storied worlds, paintings or digital applications, sculptures, dance or other art forms that might unlock within us states of empathy and responses of creativity. As characters or ideas are encountered in forms of art and popular culture, the construction of personal narratives or artefacts can offer powerful individual or collective educational responses. Thus, deeply personal and contemplative routes, where the arts challenge us to examine our own experiences and question our assumptions, can move us beyond simple disciplinary disagreements.

We develop the idea that new, hybrid and intensely personal research methods and pedagogies exist in the 'spaces' between human artistic creativity, digital technologies and visual culture, physical activities, discourse, learning and research. One way to explore such a proposition is to take the human experience of artistic process as the narrative and expression that provides a lens on these developments. In the first two lines of Ernst Gombrich's book *The Story of Art* the point is made that 'There is really no such thing as art. There are only artists' (1972: 6). In his article 'The authority of experience', McNiff (1993: 3) reflects on why imaginative expression is considered fundamental to the making of art, yet such principles have not guided our treatment of artworks, and those who created them, once they arrive. Rather than creatively acknowledging the role of human experience, a scientific approach or methodology is imposed in subsequent research processes. Whilst we might believe creative artefacts to be powerful constructions, they are also really powerful expressions of human experience, through artistic process. They are also experienced by those who encounter them, question them or, in the case of ABER, apply them in another practice or artistic process to question what might indeed be 'known'. Our focus on expressions drawn from human experience as artistic process is deliberate, because this cuts across the disciplines of both art and science, and re-makes these in the form of personal learning that pushes boundaries. Fragments of artefacts, voices, recollections, re-imaginings and theory, when drawn together through a creative autoethnographical approach, explore human experience that cannot be disputed, because the boundaries have been personally, intimately and authentically re-drawn. We therefore understand ABER as deeply experiential and drawn from art, but also *of* art. New artistic processes, as expressions of human educational experiences of art, are released to yield new art forms.

McNiff makes an important distinction in defining art-based research that supports our discussion on artistic research:

> Art-based research can be defined as the systematic use of the artistic process, the actual making of artistic expressions in all of the different forms of the arts, as a primary way of understanding and examining experience by both researchers and the people that they involve in their studies. These inquiries are distinguished from research activities where the arts may play a significant role but are essentially used as data for investigations that take place within academic disciplines that utilise more traditional scientific, verbal, and mathematic descriptions and analyses of phenomena.
>
> (McNiff 2008: 29)

The key point here rests on 'examining experience'. Rather than confining inquiry within one academic discipline, where the artistic process has yielded some data for analytic interest, we might instead systematically explore our own experience as researchers by freely crossing any boundaries that appear to limit our explorations. Systematically using the artistic process as a primary way of understanding and examining personal experience requires critical self-reflexivity, not simply as a characteristic, but where 'the artist is evident through the work' (Savin-Baden and Wimpenny 2014: 2) as discussed below:

> Heightened reflexivity is not just a characteristic of this form of inquiry, but is central to it, since art-based research takes a critical stance towards itself and the world around. Therefore for most art-based researchers, the moral stance and sense of interruption through art is central to the research.

Art as 'interruption' triggers an experiential encounter, but critical reflexivity as a central tenet of artistic research enables personal exploration across boundaries. There are endless combinations of contemplative techniques that might aid us in making such transformative discoveries. Once these channels are crossed, the possibilities for research and learning are then without boundaries. This conclusion does not diminish the importance of boundary work – in order to freely cross boundaries, we need to understand what they are made of and how they operate. It seems that any inquiry that starts from existing disciplinary practices seems to inevitably end up in the dichotomy of 'us' vs. 'them'. Therefore, we suggest expressions of personal human experience, captured through autoethnography, as a possible place to start our inquiry. Such work should not follow the path of current practices of academization of artistic practice, and/or impose standards from other disciplines to the arts. However, such work should recognize social, technological and other transformations that affect our modernity – consequently, artistic research cannot remain locked within the confines of traditional practices.

Embarking on a route of human experience does not marginalize what has been written in the field of art-based or arts-based research. Instead, it offers a unique and a shared position from which contributions across disciplinary boundaries might be viewed. Human experience, as a narrative or as an art form, encompasses these boundaries. Human experience cuts across both the objective and subjective positions of research. Through experience, we can notice and interpret personal observations that span the paradigms. The proposed approach might seem controversial. Yet, similar forms of inquiry are already well established in autoethnographic work in many disciplines. In autoethnographic studies, individuals re-draw boundaries through personal lived experience, boldly adopting techniques from multiple disciplines. Experience gives us an overview and how we structure an account (whether through mastery of material and production of artefacts, or through the written word, or both) needs to be legitimate and authentic. Perhaps it also needs to challenge or displace existing power relationships.

Argenton (2015: 918) argues that experience is one of the 'major paths to growth and autonomy, and as such, of outstanding educational value'. Within this he defines the process of 'learning that which cannot be taught', learning to think and cope with encounters with the unknown and uncertainty. However, what we do not give this process is time (2015: 918). If art can interrupt, perhaps in a digital era and competitive global society, we have become less willing or able to allow interruptions to intervene and challenge what we 'know'. Instead we *accept* that much of our experience is now provided for us and delivered to us across many forms of media. Argenton raises the issue of 'packaged' experiences in contemporary, consumer-focused society. In educational programmes a 'readiness' for an experience can be emphasized, but this predicted route is not the same as authentic, human, lived experience (2015: 929). This is something incomplete that we 'produce' rather than passively 'receive' and Argenton suggests it offers a shared product of our journey outside of our boundaries (2015: 931). Linking these considerations with autoethnography provides a channel to examine some future approaches towards using artistic research from the point of view of human experience. It enables us to resist limitations imposed by disciplinary boundaries and institutionalized research:

> Autoethnography […] often explicitly challenges the exclusivity of supposedly value-neutral, rationally-based categorical thinking and abstracted theory in explicitly celebrating emotionality, political standpoint position and social activism. Many autoethnographers, explicitly and implicitly, do this in pursuit of a social justice agenda, aiming for the reduction of the oppression of individuals and groups within broader socio-political structures.
>
> (Short et al. 2013: 5)

Autoethnography does not merely consist of re-shifting the focus of ethnography from one subject to another. Instead, autoethnography entails a radically different approach: it abandons the ethnographer's attempts to limit their own subjectivity within research, and embraces a researcher's subjectivity as an inherent part of research. In this sense, autoethnography radically shifts the traditional 'scientific' relationships between the object and the subject of research. This shift has significance for all aspects of research. For instance, autoethnography also radically changes the concept of 'fieldwork'. While the traditional 'field' of research is always external to the researcher, the 'field' of autoethnography often lies with(in) the researcher. Analysing current trends in the world of academia, it seems that autoethnography aligns quite well with artistic research. Dmitry Vilensky, the Russian artist and the founder of The School of Engaged Arts in St Petersburg, Russia, asserts that such research is:

> More flexible, less explicable, and generally has less defined criteria than traditional degrees in the social sciences and the humanities. Obviously, this brings us to the meaning of art.

> What does it mean to learn art? You learn something which is unclassified, impossible to evaluate, impossible to calculate, impossible to predict.
>
> (Jandrić 2017: 341)

However, such epistemic correspondences cannot be understood without reference to political economy. Based on her vast experience in exhibition boards and committees, the US curator Kathy Rae Huffman reminds us, in the context of art-based research, that artists have always researched through their practice, but this is ultimately linked to money:

> I think that 'art-based research' is a concept predominantly linked to funding and academe. Haven't artists always been researching through their practice? And, always seeking new ways of expressing ideas or principles? Is it art practice, described as research, in order to get more money? Some artists have become very influenced by their surroundings and by their support structures [...].
>
> (Huffman cited in Jandrić 2017: 324)

We therefore focus on how what has emerged from artistic process (whether to earn money or not) might be re-applied to interrupt or extend processes of research and learning, to change their direction unexpectedly, and even to arouse and excite in us what might even be reclaimed as 'erotic' forms of pedagogy via affective ties (Carrillo Rowe 2012). Here a communal (as opposed to an isolated) practice reclaims the erotic – not as pornographic or individuation – but as a necessarily communal project, which works against the competitive drive of neoliberalism and a heavy investment in the individual, to embrace the erotic in mindful and embodied ways (Carrillo Rowe 2012: 1034). The described forces powerfully shape the human experience of (doing) arts and artistic research. In order to embark on the experiential, autoethnographic route to exploring the future of artistic research, we therefore need to explore its political economy.

Demarcation, take one: Gieryn's boundary work

We discussed in our introduction our position that human experience is shaped both by the 'external' aspects of contemporary artistic research, such as structures of education and funding, and the 'internal', experiential aspects. We now proceed to consider the works of Thomas Gieryn to examine the 'external' aspects of demarcation via boundary work. In 1983, Gieryn analysed boundary work required for demarcation between science and religion during the Renaissance. In 2017, Marcell Mars and Tomislav Medak successfully applied Gieryn's approach to analyse the recent birth of the (academic) field of computing (Jandrić 2017: 243–69). Based on Gieryn's original work, and recent work of Mars and

Medak, we apply Gieryn's three main characteristics of the boundary work of demarcation to the context of art-based research. Gieryn (1983: 791–92) writes:

(a) when the goal is expansion of authority or expertise into domains claimed by other professions or occupations, boundary work heightens the contrast between rivals in ways flattering to the ideologists' side;
(b) when the goal is monopolization of professional authority and resources, boundary work excludes rivals from within by defining them as outsiders with labels such as 'pseudo', 'deviant' or 'amateur';
(c) when the goal is protection of autonomy over professional activities, boundary work exempts members from responsibility for consequences of their work by putting the blame on scapegoats from outside.

The current trend towards an academization of the arts is clearly aimed at expanding scientific authority over traditional artistic expertise. New art lecturers are increasingly required to obtain Ph.D. degrees, and the very notion of 'bending' artistic research to conform to scientific standards (abovementioned by Huffman) is an obvious reflection of that disciplinary expansion. Similar trends have been documented in various contemporary disciplines. For instance, worldwide scholars in the humanities report that their field is being 'hijacked' by standards and principles originating in the natural sciences (Bonnell 2014). The expansive body of literature shows that these general trends go in hand with the increasing commodification and bureaucratization of education and research (Ginsberg 2010). As worldwide, universities and research centres become increasingly oriented towards essentially positivist funding structures, even the so-called 'fundamental' sciences such as physics or chemistry experience a strong shift from the so-called blue-skies research towards applied, marketable research (Braben 2002). Using George Ritzer's (1993) metaphor of fast-food restaurants: in its quest towards McDonaldization of research and education, this scientific 'hijack' does not discriminate much between the disciplines.

The second type of boundary work is creating divisions between 'insiders' and 'outsiders' using criteria such as 'proper' degrees and credentials. In many experimental sciences, arguably, these divisions are cut clearly – for instance, research in nuclear physics or organic chemistry cannot be done outside expensive laboratories, so these fields generally have a very small number of 'outsiders'. However, in fields that do not require access to expensive equipment (such as the humanities and computer science), and in fields that may sometimes not require access to much equipment at all (such as the arts), the division between 'insiders' and 'outsiders' is much more blurred. Similar developments can be found across contemporary fields and disciplines. The most exciting developments in the emerging artistic fields such as video art and net art have been first developed outside of mainstream institutions such as arts galleries and museums (see Jandrić 2017 for details). In the field of computing, Mars and Medak report:

> The computer world remains a weird hybrid where knowledge is produced in both academic and non-academic settings, through academic curricula – but also through fairs, informal gatherings, homebrew computer clubs, hacker communities and the like. Without the enthusiasm and the experiments with ways knowledge can be transferred and circulated between peers, we would have probably never arrived to the Personal Computer Revolution in the beginning of the 1980s. Without the amount of personal computers already in use, we would have probably never experienced the Internet revolution in the beginning of the 1990s. It is through such historical development that computer science became the academic centre of the larger computer universe which spread its tentacles into almost all other known disciplines and professions.
>
> (cited in Jandrić 2017: 266)

Disciplines such as the arts or computing develop through complex dynamics between 'insiders' and 'outsiders'. For these disciplines, boundary work consisting of creating divisions between 'insiders' and 'outsiders' is not only artificial – instead, it is downright detrimental. It places barriers at many levels (not all of them visible) to new, exciting, creative partnerships between artists and educators.

The last type of boundary work, blaming scapegoats from outside for individual's own mistakes, seems quite common in all disciplines. In the field of arts: decreased funding is blamed on inadequate funding bodies; precaritization of professions is blamed on ruthless markets and inadequate support systems; the increasing divide between a few 'superstar' artists and the anonymous majority is blamed on (the political economy of) social networking (Jandrić and Taylor 2016). This kind of boundary work may indeed be important for demarcation of the field. Unfortunately, however, it effectively transfers responsibility for problems outside the realm of disciplinary influence.

This brief analysis arrives at some grim conclusions. Global forces such as commodification and bureaucratization of research and education push the arts to pursue their own line of boundary work. However, the expected type of boundary work simply does not correspond to the nature of the arts for three main reasons: (1) In order to successfully compete within academia, the arts need to 'bend' their own epistemologies and research methods – and this effectively takes them beyond their own field of expertise; (2) the arts cannot make clear-cut divisions between 'insiders' and 'outsiders', because such divisions are fundamentally contradicted by the nature of the discipline; and (3) the arts can (and do) blame others outside of their field of work for their own mistakes, but such blaming can be detrimental to their own position of authority. Following these conclusions, the broad area of artistic research is in dire need of seeking a radically different type of boundary work.

Demarcation, take two: The human experience

Therefore re-imagining art as research, through the lens of human experience, offers a route that enables us to shed some of the baggage from our conclusions above, based on Gieryn's work. If a consumer culture takes us towards a 'McDonaldization' (Ritzer 1993) of research and education, and scientific approaches 'hijack' the arts and humanities by imposing scientific authority, standards and principles over traditional fields of art, starting from human experience offers us another 'way in'. From here we can begin to reply to the conditions described in (1) and instead of bending our epistemologies and research approaches, we can re-assert these via autoethnography. This enables us to respond also to concerns about divisions in (2) by demonstrating how, through an experiential and personal narrative, insiders and outsiders are in constant dialogue with each other. This, in turn, avoids a need to blame outsiders for issues as discussed in (3) because instead, they are drawn in, and a conversation is maintained under the broad and powerful methods and authority of the humanities.

If 'science' is about understanding how the natural world works, via observable physical evidence and experimentation under controlled conditions, in the 'humanities', which are often placed alongside and interlinked with the arts, we study how people themselves process and document human experience. Human experience is thus the environment that both surrounds and connects us with contemporary practices, including the cultural and scientific, and those that took place before we were born. When the arts (such as literature, music and visual art) are valued as modes of expression for understanding and recording our world through experience, the potential for collective, as well as individual transformative growth and autonomy, reaches beyond any imposed standards or boundaries. The adoption of autoethnography is one way to notice what new possibilities are presented. This still requires rigour, but it is applied through multiple layers of researcher critical reflexivity. Autoethnographic pieces open up our reflexive worlds, enabling dialogues with ourselves and those we research, but this requires time too. Time is of the essence in a consumer culture, but as expressed below, autoethnography requires us to think of time in a different, less linear, way and to be prepared to be interrupted by art: 'This iterative process of reflection and reflexivity within the autoethnographic process does not lend itself to linear chronological progression, specificity and concreteness' (Short et al. 2013: 2).

Thus reviewing how we approach time in art-based research is important. The focus needs to shift towards ways of living art-based research through the flow of human experience (Hayes 2015: 147). This involves looking ahead and back, taking into account historical time and prior experience from life, as well as real and anticipated time (Hayes 2015: 132). We can draw on the idea of maintaining a Sociological Imagination throughout life, in the form of intellectual craftsmanship (Mills 1959). This though requires a conscious choice to shift our individual and collective focus from art, education or research as 'product' to an ongoing and deeply affective process (Hayes 2015: 132). The movement that is implied here is significant, in that we are shifting our focus from a position where we may discuss what is known to one where we ask how we know. The answer is often found through embodied experience that is both epistemological and ontological. We can interrogate it and in doing so learn much more. Interrogating our own human experience constantly crosses boundaries:

> It might jump from one thought/feeling/memory or experience up or down or backwards, forwards or sideways to another. Fractions of an experience link to other fractions of another experience becoming 'felted', with 'no separation of threads, no intertwining, only an entanglement of fibres [...] it is in principle infinite, open, and unlimited in every direction.
>
> (Deleuze and Guattari 1987: 525)

Thinking about this in the context of art, popular culture and digital media, we are constantly entangled with these and other phenomena, but for these to be 'felt' in the form of art as research, perhaps they also have to be 'felt' through human experience. We can critically and reflexively 'live' artistic research via construction of personal narratives and artefacts drawn from experience. These offer powerful individual or collective educational responses that, if authentic, are not easily refuted. Thus, deeply personal and contemplative routes, where the arts challenge us to examine our own experiences and question our assumptions, can move us beyond simple disciplinary disagreements. We need to allow room for the story of art as research to change, develop and grow through human imagination that is multi-dimensional and not confined within only disciplinary experience.

Conclusion

We regard disciplinary boundaries as forever changing and an autoethnographic approach as one way to marry or 'felt' the struggle between the 'external' educational and research-funding structures and the 'internal' aspects of art-based research, through human experience. Through the dialectics between the external and the internal, we have suggested that human experience is a central tenet of future development in art as research. It is then important to consider the conditions that generate authentic artworks, and to move from here to begin to imagine what the future might hold. If we start from a view where the focus is not so much on art, as on the people who make art, then we have a position of human experience to work with. From here we can begin to freely imagine art as research without boundaries. We can ask, amongst other questions: When does an artist move closer towards being an educator? Or, when does an academic, who is an educator or researcher and perhaps also a scientist begin to also be an artist? There are, of course, questions about formal experience, in terms of knowledge traditions and routes of training and expertise in fields of art and academia. In order to apply art as research however, we do not have to cross boundaries permanently to drastically change our occupations. For instance, as an academic, I might move across boundaries for periods of time where I am challenged to absorb elements of a new artistic or scientific culture. As a practising artist, I might challenge myself to cross certain boundaries for a while, yet still know I can return to what is my art, in my experience.

However, when it comes to support and research grants, there are pitfalls for artists to navigate. There are linguistic barriers and the bureaucracy of forms, declarations of intent and an insistence that the knowledge generated be practical and usable. The ranking and assessment measures are additional barriers put in place simply to support a dominant, if unspoken ideology (Jagodzinski and Wallin 2013). It is for these reasons, as well as others we have discussed, that the humanities need to preserve and grow their core strength. Art-based research offers a way to do this in studying how people themselves process and document their own human experience.

If art as research manages to distinguish its unique form of inquiry, if it manages to give a unique contribution to humankind, and if it articulates a clear and unparalleled social role – then the discipline of art-based research will flourish. We suggest human experience as a central tenet because it inscribes our human bodies, as mind, body and soul – integrated and not divided – into our research to cross boundaries. Our passions, which are culturally produced and therefore sometimes restrained, might also be redirected through powerful, even erotic explorations (Carrillo Rowe 2012: 1034). These can help to displace conditions of knowing that set up boundaries. As we mentioned earlier, human experience cuts across the objective and subjective positions of research to span the disciplines. Art-based research in the future could be very powerful if it breaks from the confines of disciplinarity and becomes a lived experience.

If, however, those enacting art as research fail to be bold in claiming such possibilities, then artistic research risks being eaten up by more powerful academic disciplines – working outside of its own field of expertise, artistic research is doomed to become meaningless. As various academic departments in artistic research are opening throughout the world, boundary work will become essential for their survival. This chapter suggests that traditional forms of boundary work, described by Gieryn (1986) and Mars and Medak (Jandrić 2017: 243–69) are inappropriate for art as research, and that pursuing that type of boundary work will inevitably end up in its marginalization. Our conclusions about autoethnography and boundary work do not diminish the importance of traditional disciplines. Instead, they support the argument that as artistic research is not a traditional discipline, there is a possible route for demarcation to be found through the vehicle of individual human experience.

References

Argenton, Gerald (2015), 'Time for experience: Growing up under the experience economy', *Educational Philosophy and Theory*, 47:9, pp. 918–34.

Barone, Tom and Eisner, Elliot (1997), 'Arts-based educational research', *Complementary Methods for Research in Education*, 2, pp. 75–116.

Bonnell, Andrew (2014), 'Humanities and social science under attack', *Advocate: Newsletter of the National Tertiary Education Union*, 21:1.

Braben, Donald W. (2002), 'Blue skies research and the global economy', *Physica A: Statistical Mechanics and Its Applications*, 314, pp. 768–73.

Cahnmann-Taylor, Melisa and Siegesmund, Richard (eds) (2013), *Art-Based Research in Education: Foundations for Practice*, New York: Routledge.

Carrillo Rowe, Aimee (2012), 'Erotic pedagogies', *Journal of Homosexuality*, 59:7, pp. 1031–56.

Deleuze, Gilles and Guattari, Felix (1987), *A Thousand Plateaus: Capitalism and Schizophrenia* (trans. B. Massumi), Minneapolis: University of Minnesota Press.

Ellis, Carolyn and Bochner, Arthur (2000), 'Autoethnography, personal narrative, reflexivity', in N. Denzin and Y. Lincoln (eds), *Handbook of Qualitative Research*, 2nd ed., Thousand Oaks: Sage.

Gieryn, Thomas F. (1983), 'Boundary-work and the demarcation of science from non-science: Strains and interests in professional ideologies of scientists', *American Sociological Review*, 48:6, pp. 781–95.

Ginsberg, Benjamin (2010), *The Fall of the Faculty: The Rise of the All-Administrative University and Why It Matters*, Oxford: Oxford University Press.

Gombrich, Ernst H. (1972), *The Story of Art*, London: Phaidon.

Hart, Tobin (2004), 'Opening the contemplative mind in the classroom', *Journal of Transformative Education*, 2:1, pp. 28–46.

Hayes, Sarah (2015), 'Encouraging the intellectual craft of living research: Tattoos, theory and time', in P. Bartholomew, C. Guerin and C. Nygaard (eds), *Learning to Research – Researching to Learn*, London: Libri Publishing.

——— (forthcoming 2018), 'Invisible labour: Do we need to re-occupy student engagement policy?', *LATISS: Learning & Teaching in the Social Sciences*, special issue, 'Contextualising student engagement: The case of recent reform in English Higher Education'.

Jagodzinski, Jan and Wallin, Jason (2013), *Arts-Based Research: A Critique and a Proposal*, Rotterdam: Springer Science & Business Media.

Jandrić, Petar (2017), *Learning in the Age of the Digital Reason*, Rotterdam: Sense.

Jandrić, Petar and Taylor, Astra (2016), 'Unschoolers of the world, unwork! Grassroots lessons and strategies against 21st century capitalism', *Journal of Critical Education Policy Studies*, 14:3, pp. 131–53.

McNiff, Shaun (1993), 'The authority of experience', *The Arts in Psychotherapy*, 20:1, pp. 3–9.

——— (1998), *Art-Based Research*, London: Jessica Kingsley Publishers.

——— (2008), 'Art-based research', in J. Gary Knowles and Ardra L. Cole (eds), *Handbook of the Arts in Qualitative Research: Perspectives, Methodologies, Examples, and Issues*, Los Angeles: Sage, pp. 29–40.

Mills, C. Wright (1959), *The Social Imagination*, New York: Oxford University Press.

Ritzer, George (1993), *The McDonaldization of Society: An Investigation into the Changing Character of Contemporary Social Life*, Thousand Oaks: Pine Forge Press.

Savin-Baden, Maggie and Wimpenny, Katherine (2014), *A Practical Guide to Art-Based Research*, Rotterdam: Sense Publishers.

Short, Nigel P., Turner, Lydia and Grant, Alec (eds) (2013), *Contemporary British Autoethnography*, Rotterdam: Springer Science & Business Media.

Notes on Contributors

Dr Maxine Bristow is an artist, associate professor and MA programme leader in Fine Art, University of Chester, United Kingdom. She has exhibited nationally and internationally, was selected for the Jerwood Textiles Prize (2002) and nominated for the Northern Arts Prize (2008). A member of the Art and Design sub-panel for RAE 2008, she currently serves on the AHRC's Peer Review College. She completed a practice-based Ph.D. at Norwich University of the Arts in 2016.

Dr Kevin Burrows has enjoyed a lifetime of commitment to the arts as a practising artist, musician, teacher/educationalist, special education arts coordinator, counsellor and expressive arts therapist. He is a British Association of Counsellors and Psychotherapists (BACP) accredited counsellor and a Registered Expressive Arts Consultant Educator (REACE). He has a counselling and expressive arts therapy private practice in the United Kingdom, where he also works with eco-therapy and Jungian sandplay.

Dr Libby Byrne is an art therapist who has worked in trauma recovery and palliative care. She is currently involved in the work of academic teaching in the Master of Art Therapy programme at La Trobe University, Australia, and works as an honorary post-doctoral researcher with the University of Divinity. Her art-making practice is a means to explore questions of meaning and existence that capture her attention. Within the studio she is seeking to discover ideas, images and experiences that will extend the way she thinks, perceives and responds to these questions. In this way her studio practice is theology in the making.

Dr Patricia Fenner is a senior lecturer and course coordinator of the Master of Art Therapy programme at La Trobe University, Melbourne, Australia. She is a researcher with diverse interests in art-based research, art-making and mental health recovery, and in particular, how the everyday material settings of our work play a role in what occurs in practice. Prior to working in the university sector, she worked in diverse contexts, including public mental health and school education, as well as working as a community artist in both Melbourne and Berlin.

Professor Carole Gray is an artist, independent researcher and higher education consultant in the United Kingdom. A contributor to research development internationally, she has also served on various AHRC panels and the UK RAE 2008 sub-panel for Art and Design. She has a longstanding interest in experiential learning in Art and Design education, especially at postgraduate levels. The core of this pedagogic work has been concerned with creative and visual approaches to inquiry and its intimate relationship to practice.

Professor Fiona Hackney is a professor of Fashion Textiles Theories at the University of Wolverhampton, United Kingdom. Her research interests are in arts research and design history, specifically dress and fashion culture, interwar print media, crafting, co-creation and social design. Recent publications include: 'The power of quiet: Re-making amateur and professional textiles agencies', *Journal of Textile Design, Research and Practice* (2016). A monograph and an edited collection were published in 2017: *Women's Magazines and the Feminine Imagination: Opening Up a New World for Women in Interwar Britain* and *The Edinburgh Companion to British Women's Print Culture between the Wars.*

Dr Sarah Hayes is a senior lecturer and programme director for the PG Diploma and Masters in Education in the Centre for Learning Innovation and Professional Practice, at Aston University, Birmingham, United Kingdom. She previously taught Sociology. Her research includes critical analysis of educational policies for digital technology and student engagement, focused on ways that human academic labour is frequently diminished. She is a principal fellow of the Higher Education Academy, co-edited a special issue for *Knowledge Cultures* and has published in *European Political Science, Open Review of Educational Research, Libri* and *Springer.*

Petar Jandrić is an educator and academic researcher at Zagreb University of Applied Sciences, Croatia. He publishes books, scholarly articles, chapters and popular texts. His background is in physics, education and information science, and his research interests are situated at the post-disciplinary intersections between technologies, pedagogies and the society. He worked at Croatian Academic and Research Network, University of Edinburgh, Glasgow School of Art and University of East London. At present he works as professor and director of BSc (Informatics) at the Zagreb University of Applied Sciences, and visiting associate professor at the University of Zagreb.

Dr Mitchell Kossak is an associate professor in the Expressive Therapies department at Lesley University, USA. He was the division director for the Expressive Therapies programme 2006–2013. He was the president and executive co-chair for the International Expressive Arts Therapy Association (IEATA) 2010–2016. He has been a licensed mental health counsellor, since 1994, and is a Registered Expressive Arts Therapist (REAT). He is the associate editor of the *Journal of Applied Arts and Health* and co-chair of the Institute for Arts and Health at Lesley University. He is the author of *Attunement in Expressive Arts Therapy: Toward an Understanding of Embodied Empathy.*

Dr Megan Lawton is a senior adviser in Academic Practice in the College of Learning and Teaching (CoLT) at the University of Wolverhampton, United Kingdom. She has an eclectic background, qualifications and experiences. She identifies the following key drivers: enabling people to reach their potential, innovation and creativity and playing with technology to support learning. Her Doctorate in Professional Studies (Learning and Teaching) thesis titled 'Of sea anemones and clownfish: Exploring a mutually beneficial approach to educational development through Soft Systems Methodology' features in her chapter. She has published research on flipped learning, ePortfolio-based learning, patchwork text assessment, developmental mentoring and international and transnational education (TNE). In 2017, she was awarded a National Teaching Fellowship.

Professor Julian Malins is a designer, independent researcher, entrepreneur in the United Kingdom. His early career was spent making studio ceramics. He returned to full-time education in 1985. After completing his Ph.D. at the Robert Gordon University in Aberdeen in 1990, he worked as a research fellow and academic. He was awarded a professorship at RGU in 2007. In 2014 he became director of research at Norwich University of the Arts. Now retired from full-time academia, he is currently working as a design consultant, based in Aberdeen, Scotland.

Professor Shaun McNiff has a significant international following. He is author of *Imagination in Action*; *Art as Research*; *Trust the Process*; *Art as Medicine*; *Art Heals*; *Depth Psychology of Art*; and numerous other books. His works have been translated into many languages and he has lectured and taught throughout the world. In 1998 he wrote *Art-Based Research*, documenting his work with artistic knowing beginning in the early 1970s, and the book helped spur fast growth of the discipline. The recipient of numerous prestigious honours and awards, he was appointed as the first University Professor at Lesley University, USA, in 2002.

Professor Ross W. Prior is best known for his book *Teaching Actors: Knowledge Transfer in Actor Training* (Intellect and University of Chicago Press) and his work in applied arts and health as founding principal editor of the *Journal of Applied Arts and Health*, established in 2009. In 2015 he was appointed Professor of Learning and Teaching in the Arts in Higher Education at the University of Wolverhampton, United Kingdom. He has a record of research surrounding learning and teaching within a range of educational and training settings. At the time of publication he is a member of the Arts & Humanities Research Council (AHRC) Peer Review College. He is a Fellow of the Royal Society for Public Health and Principal Fellow of the Higher Education Academy.

Mah Rana is an artist, researcher and academic based in London. Projects include: *Meanings and Attachments* (2002 ongoing), a worldwide series of public-participation events archiving 'jewellery' stories through text, portrait photography and film; and *It's Nice to*

Make (2011) that draws upon the model of the quilt-making circle as an exemplar of organized communal activity to investigate 'making' as a mode of being, experiential learning and teaching, and the intersubjective embodied experience.

Professor Malcolm Ross, an internationally recognized figure in arts education, read English at Cambridge (1953–1956) and then taught the subject in schools and colleges until 1967, when he joined the staff at Exeter University's School of Education. Together with Robert Witkin, he led the School Council's Arts and the Adolescent national research (1968–1972), a project jointly sponsored by the University and Dartington College of Arts. Witkin published his *The Intelligence of Feeling* in 1974, and Malcolm his *The Creative Arts* in 1978. Malcolm went on to develop separate part-time MEd degrees in Arts Education and the Arts Therapies, together with the University's annual summer schools for arts teachers and therapists. Routledge published his most recent book, *Cultivating the Arts in Education and Therapy*, in 2011. In 2017 he became a visiting professor of Aesthetic Education at the University of Wolverhampton.

Professor Peter Sinapius is a painter and art therapist. He is Professor for Intermedial Art Therapy at MSH Medical School Hamburg, Germany, and runs the Expressive Arts in Social Transformation (EAST) programme. He is active in national and international research projects about applied arts and health and is director of the Institute for Subjective Experience and Research (ISER). He has a Ph.D. from EGS with his dissertation 'Aesthetics of therapeutic relationships'. He is editor of the series *Scientific Foundations of Art Therapy* and is a Board member of the *Journal of Applied Arts and Health*. He has published numerous books on theory and practice of art therapy.

Dr Jacqueline Taylor is an artist-researcher and lecturer in Research Practice at Birmingham City University, United Kingdom, where she coordinates Ph.D. training at the Faculty of Arts, Design and Media. Her research interests include developing alternative pedagogies to support Arts and Design doctoral researchers, the ontological and epistemological dimensions of practice-led research and the interrelations between painting, signification and poetics. She has taught and lectured on Research Practice and Researcher Development globally, including the University of Worcester and Victoria University, Australia. She has also presented and published widely on artistic research practice, creative identity and para-academia and exhibited her work internationally.

Dr Daniel Vuillermin is a lecturer and researcher at the Institute for Medical Humanities at Peking University, China. He is an editor of the *Chinese Medical Humanities Review* and Reviews Editor of the *Journal of Applied Arts and Health* and has written for the *a/b: Auto/Biography Studies*, *Life Writing*, the *Journal of Modern Life Writing Studies*, *The Conversation* and the *Australian Book Review* (ABR), among others. Currently he is developing Yimovi, a website dedicated to Euro-American medical humanities approaches to teaching with

Chinese cinema and researching photography and representations of health, illness and disability in China.

Dr Petronilla Whitfield is an associate professor in Voice and Acting on the acting degree course at the Arts University Bournemouth, United Kingdom. She has a Ph.D. in Arts Pedagogy (focusing on the support of acting students with dyslexia) from Warwick University and a Master's degree in Voice Studies from the Royal Central School of Speech and Drama. Trained originally as an actor at Arts Educational Schools, she was a professional actor for twenty years appearing with theatre companies nationally and internationally, such as the Royal Shakespeare Company, The Peter Hall Company and The Space Theatre (the first multi-racial theatre in South Africa). She has also worked in television, film and radio. Her work has been published in several journals and she is currently writing a book about actor training and dyslexia.

www.ingramcontent.com/pod-product-compliance
Lightning Source LLC
LaVergne TN
LVHW080831240826
846232LV00015B/54